The PM PrepCast™

PMP® Exam Formula Study Guide

Know the formulas, pass your exam.

CORNELIUS FICHTNER

Get in touch:
OSP International LLC
8502 E Chapman Ave, Suite 349
Orange, CA 92869 USA
Email: support@pm-prepcast.com
Internet: www.osp-international.com

A book by Cornelius Fichtner
Published by: OSP International LLC

ISBN: 978-0-9964060-8-6

For the PrepCast Formulas visit https://www.project-management-formulas.com
For the PrepCast Training visit https://www.project-management-prepcast.com
For the PrepCast Simulator visit https://www.pm-exam-simulator.com/pmp

CONTENTS

INTRODUCTION

Three major shifts have occurred on the PMP exam in recent years.

First, lessons learned from our students who passed their PMP exam have shown that the main focus of formula-based questions has shifted from calculation to interpretation. This means that you are now less likely to be required to calculate the planned value (PV) on the exam. Instead, exam candidates now have to understand how PV is used and what actions they would take if, for example, the PV is negative. "What do you do now?" PMI will ask.

Second, PMI added four more question types to the exam. In addition to the familiar multiple-choice questions, the new question types of multiple response, drag-and-drop, hotspot, and fill-in-the-blank have been added.

And finally, about 50% of the questions on the exam cover predictive project management approaches, while the other 50% center around agile and hybrid approaches. Yet, when it comes to formula-based questions, the predictive project management approach still dominates.

With the above in mind, we have developed *The PMP® Exam Formula Study Guide* that you hold in your hands and organized it into four parts for optimal exam relevance. Here is what each of the four parts contains and how you should divide your study time for the formulas:

What each part contains	How much time to spend on it
Part One introduces you to all the formulas that are traditionally needed on the PMP exam. Even with the shift from calculation to interpretation, you need to first and foremost understand the concepts behind the formulas and how they are used.	**35%**
Part Two contains interpretational questions. After learning the formulas in Part One you can now apply your knowledge to questions that are very similar to what you get on the actual exam. About half of them cover the agile and hybrid project management approaches and a good number use the new question types introduced by PMI.	**35%**
Part Three is all about applying the formulas and calculating. Being able to correctly answer these questions means you have gained a deep conceptual understanding of each formula, which is the first step in being able to interpret the result.	**15%**
Part Four closes the guide with the Formula Pocket Guide as well as a number of reference articles.	**15%**

Lastly, formulas are not affected by the *PMBOK® Guide*. For example, the communications channels formula was developed decades ago and has not changed once. Therefore, no matter which version of the *PMBOK® Guide* you use, the formulas in this guide apply.

Good luck on your exam!

PART ONE

The Formula Guide

Let's begin by laying the foundation and introducing you to all the formulas you may need for the exam, with a particular emphasis on how to interpret the results.

Answering formula-based questions correctly is not just about finding an average, solving for the median, or calculating earned value. Instead, understanding each element of a formula provides you with critical decision-making criteria. When you know what each element represents, you understand which figures or information mentioned in the question scenario should be used in the calculation. Also, a good grasp of the formulas will speed up your time to answer the questions, as you can quickly eliminate any answer choices that are clearly incorrect. And understanding the elements of each formula makes it easier to interpret the result and what it means for your project.

But there is really only one way to fully internalize the formulas and prepare yourself for the math on the exam: you have to study and practice using them.

Here's what that study and practice looks like: you must first review around 50 formulas, 20 important values, and close to 30 formula-related acronyms. Armed with that knowledge you can then move on to apply the formulas to a project scenario, or given the result of a formula, you must be able to interpret what that figure means for your project.

Here is a tip: If you struggle with a formula concept, then take a look at the "Complete Guide" in Part Four, where we explain in more detail many of the concepts that students traditionally struggle with.

Important to Know

The Formula Table Explained

The next section contains a table with the essential formulas that you need to know and apply in order to pass the PMP Exam. The formulas are listed in a table with three columns. For each entry, we explain the concept, list the formula(s), and – most importantly – explain how to interpret the result of the calculation.

For example:

Concept	Formula	Result Interpretation
The first column contains the "concept" behind the formula. Instead of just giving you the formula "CV = EV – AC" we want to make sure that you understand what the formula is trying to achieve. The best way to do that is by explaining its concept.	We list the actual formula in the second column. For some concepts, multiple formulas are needed so we list them all. When helpful, we also add examples for better understanding.	The formula won't do you much good if you cannot explain what the result is or means. That is why we include an interpretation in the third column. Many PMP questions require interpretation.
Example: **Cost Variance (CV)** Provides cost performance of the project. Helps determine if the project is proceeding as planned.	Example: **CV = EV – AC**	Example: Negative = over budget = over planned cost Zero = on budget = on planned cost Positive = under budget = under planned cost

Result Interpretation is the most important column for you to focus on!

While it is important to understand the formula as well as the concept behind the formula, the PMP exam more and more tests your ability to interpret results. Expect questions like "What action will you take, if you calculated TCPI = 1.1?". Studying and understanding this column is a must.

Exponentiation

While it is unlikely that you will need to calculate exponentiation on your PMP exam, we need to help you understand this concept (just in case, since you never know what PMI will throw at you).

The exponent is usually shown as a superscript to the right of the base. For instance: 3^4. This exponentiation can be read as *3 raised to the 4th power or as 3 raised to the power of 4.* And 3^4 would be calculated as 3 * 3 * 3 * 3 = 81. The superscript notation 3^4 is convenient in handwriting but can lead to errors when you are in a hurry like on the PMP exam. For instance, it is very easy to forget to "raise" the exponent in a formula when you are hurriedly typing or writing it out during the exam. So, it could easily happen that the formula $PV = FV / (1 + r)^n$ gets written down as PV = FV / (1 + r)n. The difference may seem trivial, but the result is disastrous. Therefore, we chose to use an accepted, alternative way of expressing the exponentiation by using the ^ character.

When using this character, 3^4 is now expressed as 3^4 and $PV = FV / (1+ r)^n$ is expressed as PV = FV / (1 + r)^n. This removes any margin for visual errors.

The Question Types Covered in this Guide

Part Two and Part Three of this guide include the following question types that you may encounter on your PMP exam:

- Applying a formula. These are straightforward questions where you are given values and are expected to calculate a result by applying the correct formula.
- Applying two formulas. In these questions, you will be given a set of values and asked to calculate a result. At first, these will look as if you can simply apply one formula; however, as you apply this formula, you realize that one value is missing. This missing value must then first be calculated via a second formula.
- Inverting a formula. These questions test your ability to take a basic formula and invert it. For instance, instead of asking "4 + 6 = ?" the question would be "4 + ? = 10" and it is your job to invert the formula and calculate "10 – 4 = 6".
- Find the correct formula. In these questions, you are given a scenario and then offered various formulas. Your task is to read and understand the scenario and define which of the given formulas are correct based on the circumstances described.
- Use a formula based on keywords. There is more than one way to calculate the EAC and the ETC. Which formula to use depends on the project's progression (or health) as described in the question. These are

scenario-based questions that will contain certain keywords. You must recognize these keywords and apply the correct formula.

- Result interpretation. In these questions, you are given a result of a calculation that has already been made for you (based on a formula provided in the scenario or implied by it) or you are given a project status and asked, "What does this mean for the project?"
- Selecting the best course of action. You are given a scenario describing a project status (either explicitly or implicitly) and are requested to suggest a course of action. If the question is a standard multiple-choice, you would need to select one answer choice. If the question requires multiple responses, you must select more than one.
- Matching items. These questions require you to drag-and-drop the answers. They cover a wide variety of skills and knowledge, such as matching a formula with an assumption, selecting the best course(s) of action based on the scenario described, aligning various metrics with project selection methods, etc.
- Visual interpretation. You are given a chart, such as a burndown or a burnup chart, and are requested to interpret the status of the project or suggest the best course(s) of action to move ahead with the project, to meet its original goal, to meet the new goal described in the scenario, etc.

Essential PMP Exam Formulas

Concept	Formula	Result Interpretation
Cost Variance (CV) Provides cost performance of the project. Helps determine the amount of budget deficit or surplus at a given point in time.	**CV = EV – AC**	Negative = over budget = over planned cost Zero = on budget = on planned cost Positive = under budget = under planned cost
Cost Performance Index (CPI) The measure of cost efficiency on a project. The ratio of earned value to actual cost.	**CPI = EV / AC**	<1 = over budget = over planned cost. The project is getting <$1 for every $1 spent. 1 = on budget = on planned cost. The project is getting $1 for every $1 spent. >1 = under budget = under planned cost. The project is getting >$1 for every $1 spent.
Schedule Variance (SV) Provides schedule performance of the project. Helps determine if the project work is proceeding as planned.	**SV = EV – PV**	Negative = behind schedule Zero = on schedule Positive = ahead of schedule
Schedule Performance Index (SPI) The measure of schedule efficiency on a project. The ratio of earned value to planned value. Used to determine if a project is behind, on or ahead of schedule. Can be used to help predict when a project will be completed.	**SPI = EV / PV**	<1 = behind schedule. The project is progressing at a slower rate than originally planned. 1 = on schedule. The project is progressing at the originally planned rate. >1 = ahead of schedule. The project is progressing at a faster rate than originally planned.
Schedule Variance (SV), an alternative method Provides schedule performance of the project in terms of Earned Schedule (ES) and Actual Time (AT).	**SV = ES – AT**	Negative = behind schedule. The project earned less than planned Zero = on schedule. The project earned as planned. Positive = ahead of schedule. The project earned more than planned.

Concept	Formula	Result Interpretation
Schedule Performance Index (SPI) (Alternative Method) Measure of schedule efficiency on a project in terms of Earned Schedule (ES) and Actual Time (AT).	**SPI = ES / AT**	<1 = behind schedule. The project is progressing at a slower rate than originally planned. 1 = on schedule. The project is progressing at the originally planned rate. >1 = ahead of schedule. The project is progressing at a faster rate than originally planned.
Estimate at Completion (EAC) Expected final and total cost of a project based on project performance. Helps determine an estimate of the total costs of a project based on actual costs to date. There are several ways to calculate EAC depending on the current project situation and how the actual work is progressing as compared to the budget. Look for *keywords* in the exam questions to determine what assumptions were made.	**EAC = BAC / CPI** Assumption: use this formula if the current cost performance is expected to remain the *same* for the remainder of the project.	Original budget modified by the cost performance. The result is a monetary value.
	EAC = AC + Bottom-up ETC Assumption: use this formula if the original estimate was *fundamentally flawed* or conditions have changed and invalidated original estimating assumptions.	Actual cost plus a new bottom-up estimate for the remaining work. The result is a monetary value.
	EAC = AC + (BAC - EV) Assumption: use this formula if the current cost variance is *not* expected to occur again for the remainder of the project, which means the original budget is still reliable.	Actual cost to date (AC) plus unearned budget (BAC - EV). The result is a monetary value.
	EAC = AC + [(BAC - EV) / (CPI * SPI)] Assumption: use this formula if *both* the CPI and SPI influence the remaining project work.	Actual cost to date (AC) plus unearned budget (BAC - EV) modified by both cost performance and schedule performance. The result is a monetary value.

Concept	Formula	Result Interpretation
Estimate to Complete (ETC) The expected cost needed to complete all the remaining project work. Helps predict what the final cost of the project will be upon completion. There are many ways to calculate ETC depending on the assumptions made. Look for keywords in the exam questions to determine what assumptions were made.	**ETC = EAC - AC** Use this formula if *no keywords* could be found.	Expected total cost minus actual cost to date. The result is a monetary value that tells how much more the project will cost.
	ETC A new estimate is developed when it is thought that the original estimate was *flawed*.	This is neither a formula nor the result of a calculation. It is simply a new bottom-up cost estimate (re-estimate) of the remaining project work.
	ETC = BAC - EV Assumption: use this formula if current variances are not expected to occur again for the remainder of the project, which means the original budget is still reliable.	The value of the unearned project work. The result is a monetary value.
	ETC = (BAC - EV) / (CPI * SPI) Assumption: use this formula if both the CPI and SPI influence the remaining project work.	The value of the unearned project work modified by both cost performance and schedule performance. The result is a monetary value.
	ETC = (BAC / CPI) - AC Assumption: use this formula if current cost performance is expected to remain the same for the remainder of the project.	Original budget modified by the cost performance minus the actual cost. The result is a monetary value.
Percent Complete How much of the planned budget has been completed?	**Percent Complete = (EV / BAC) * 100%**	What is currently completed divided by the original budget times 100. The result is a percentage value.
To-Complete Performance Index (TCPI) A measure of cost performance that must be achieved on the remaining work to meet a specific management goal (e.g., BAC or EAC). It is the work remaining divided by the funds remaining.	Based on BAC: **TCPI = (BAC - EV) / (BAC - AC)** Based on EAC: **TCPI = (BAC - EV) / (EAC - AC)**	>1 = harder to complete. The project needs to improve its cost performance to be completed on target. 1 = same to complete. Same cost efficiency can be maintained to complete the project. <1 = easier to complete. The project is expected to achieve its cost targets.

Concept	Formula	Result Interpretation
Variance at Completion (VAC) Anticipates the difference between the originally estimated BAC and a newly calculated EAC. In other words, the cost that was originally planned minus the cost that is now expected.	**VAC = BAC - EAC**	The result is a monetary value that estimates how much over or under budget (the variance) the project will have by its completion. <0 = over planned budget =0 = on planned budget >0 = under planned budget
Earned Value (EV) A measure of completed work expressed in terms of the budget authorized for that work.	**EV = Sum of PV of completed work** Assumption: use this formula if PV for all completed work is given. **EV = % complete * BAC** Assumption: use this formula if PV for all completed work is not given.	The result is the EV, a monetary value.
Earned Schedule (ES) A measure of completed work expressed in terms of the authorized schedule for that work.	The formula for the ES is relatively complex. Therefore, it is unlikely that you will be required to make any ES calculations on the exam.	The ES is a numeric value expressed in the same units as these of the project duration.
Three-Point Estimating (Beta Distribution) Three-point estimate for the expected duration (or cost) of a schedule activity using pessimistic, optimistic, and most likely values. This is a probabilistic approach, using statistical estimates of durations (or cost) to get a weighted average. Also known as the PERT estimate.	**Estimate = [Pessimistic + (4 * Most Likely) + Optimistic] / 6** This is the **preferred** formula for the PMP Exam unless the use of triangular distribution is explicitly called for.	The result is the estimated duration/ cost of a schedule activity expressed as a **weighted** average.
Three-Point Estimating (Triangular Distribution) Three-point estimate for the expected duration (or cost) of a schedule activity using pessimistic, optimistic, and most likely values. A probabilistic approach, using statistical estimates of durations (or costs) to get a simple average.	**Estimate = (Pessimistic + Most Likely + Optimistic) / 3**	The result is the estimated duration/ cost of a schedule activity expressed as a simple average.

Concept	Formula	Result Interpretation
Program Evaluation and Review Technique (PERT) Estimate/Average	Please see Three-Point Estimating (Beta Distribution)	
PERT Activity Standard Deviation The standard deviation (σ) is a reflection of the uncertainty in the estimates. It is a measure of the statistical variability of an activity. If an activity has different estimates: optimistic, most likely, and pessimistic, the standard deviation will determine the variation in the same units of the measurements.	**σ = (Pessimistic – Optimistic) / 6**	A large standard deviation indicates that the data points are far from the mean; a small standard deviation indicates that the data points are clustered closely around the mean. Hence, the larger the standard deviation, the greater the risk.
PERT Activity Variance The variance is a reflection of the uncertainty in the estimates expressed in squared units of the measurements. It is also a measure of the statistical variability of an activity. The difference between variance and the standard deviation is that the variance is in the squared units of the measurements while the standard deviation is in the same units as the measurements. The standard deviation is not additive and hence cannot be used in mathematical formulas for studying variations among different populations; only variance can be used in such cases.	**Variance = [(Pessimistic – Optimistic) / 6]^2**	Unlike expected absolute deviation, the variance of a variable has units that are the square of the units of the variable itself. For example, a variable measured in inches will have a variance measured in square inches. For this reason, describing data sets via their standard deviation or root mean square deviation is often preferred over using the variance.
Activity Duration Determines how long an activity lasts. There are two formulas; both will give the same result.	**Duration = EF – ES + 1** **Duration = LF – LS + 1**	Number of days an activity lasts.
Free Float The amount of time a schedule activity can be delayed without delaying the early start date of any successor activity or violating a schedule constraint.	**Free Float = ES of Successor Activity – EF of Present Activity – 1**	A number of time units (typically days) an activity can be delayed without delaying the early start of the successor activity. Note: If the present activity has more than one successor activity, then use the *earliest* ES of any of the successor activities.

Concept	Formula	Result Interpretation
Total Float The amount of time a schedule activity can be delayed or extended from its early start date without delaying the project finish date or violating a schedule constraint. There are two formulas, both will give the same result.	**Total Float = LS - ES** **Total Float = LF - EF**	A number of time units (typically days) an activity can be delayed without delaying the finish date of the project.
Early Finish (EF)[1] Determine when an activity can finish at the earliest.	**EF = (ES + duration) - 1**	The earliest day on which an activity can finish.
Early Start (ES)[1] Determine when an activity can start at the earliest.	**ES = (EF of predecessor) + 1**	The earliest day on which an activity can start.
Late Finish (LF)[1] Determine when an activity can finish at the latest.	**LF = (LS of successor) - 1**	The latest day on which an activity can finish.
Late Start (LS)[1] Determine when an activity can start at the latest.	**LS = (LF - duration) + 1**	The latest day on which an activity can start.
Present Value (PV) Receiving an amount of money today is more valuable than receiving the same amount of money in the future (e.g., in three years). This formula calculates how much the future cash flow is valued today. Note: PV in this case should not be confused with the Planned Value (PV).	**PV = FV / (1 + r)^n**	The result is the amount of money that should be invested today (PV) for **n** years at **r**% interest rate in order to achieve the desired future value (FV). The higher the PV the better.
Future Value (FV) Receiving an amount of money in the future (e.g., in three years) is less valuable than receiving the same amount of money today. This formula calculates the future value of an amount invested today.	**FV = PV * (1 + r)^n**	The result is the amount of money (FV) that will be received if a sum of money (PV) is invested today for **n** years at **r**% interest rate.

[1] See Formula Elaboration section

Concept	Formula	Result Interpretation
Net Present Value (NPV) Method for the financial evaluation of projects. Also described as present value (PV) of all cash inflows minus the present value of all cash outflows.	The formula for the NPV is relatively complex. Therefore, it is unlikely that you will be required to make any NPV calculations on the exam.	Positive NPV is good. Negative NPV is bad. The project with the **higher** NPV is the "better" project.
Discounted Cash Flow (DCF) A valuation method for potential investment that uses future free cash flow projections and discounts them (most often using the or weighted average cost of capital (WACC)).	The formula for the DCF is relatively complex. Therefore, it is unlikely that you will be required to make any DCF calculations on the exam.	The project with the **higher** DCF of net cash flows is the "better" project.
Return on Investment (ROI) The ratio of money gained or lost on an investment relative to the amount of money invested. The amount of money gained or lost is often referred to as interest, profit/loss, gain/loss, or net income/loss.	Even though the formula for the ROI is relatively simple, it is unlikely that you will be required to make any ROI calculations on the exam.	The project with the **higher** ROI is better.
Internal Rate of Return (IRR) The interest rate at which the present value of all future cash flows equals the initial investment.	The calculation for the IRR is relatively complex. Therefore, it is unlikely that you will be required to make any IRR calculations on the exam.	The project with the **higher** IRR is better.
Payback period The time it takes to recover the initial investment by adding up the future cash inflows until they are equal to the initial investment. In plain English: the time it takes until you are break-even.	**Add up the projected cash inflow minus expenses until the result of the calculation is equal to the initial investment.**	A project with a shorter payback period is better.
Benefit-Cost Ratio (BCR) A ratio that describes the cost versus benefits of a project.	**Benefit / Cost**	BCR < 1 is bad. BCR > 1 is good. The project with the higher BCR is the "better" one.
Cost-Benefit Ratio (CBR) A ratio that describes the benefits versus cost of a project. This is simply the reverse of the Benefit-Cost Ratio.	**Cost / Benefit**	CBR < 1 is good. CBR > 1 is bad. The project with the lower CBR is the "better" one.

Concept	Formula	Result Interpretation
Opportunity Cost Opportunity cost is the benefit foregone by choosing one option over an alternative one. Thus, opportunity cost is the cost of pursuing one choice instead of another.	**Opportunity Cost = The profit/gain of the project not chosen**	For the PMP exam, the opportunity cost is usually a monetary value: Project B was selected over project A, therefore the opportunity cost is the unrealized profit of project A. Note that NO calculation is required.
Communication Channels The number of all possible communication channels on a project.	**n * (n – 1) / 2**	A total number of communication channels among **n** people of a group.
	n – 1	A number of communication channels that one member of the team has with everyone else on the team. For example, you have to make this many phone calls to call everyone else.
Expected Monetary Value (EMV) An estimate that tells how much money (gained or lost) can reasonably be expected by taking the probability of the event into account. For instance: if it rains, we will lose $200. There is a 25% chance that it will rain. Therefore, the EMV is: 0.25 * $200 = $50.	**EMV = Probability * Impact**	A monetary value that represents the expected gain or loss of an event.
Straight-line Depreciation A method that depreciates the same amount (or percent) each year by dividing the asset's cost by the number of years it is expected to be in service. The simplest of the depreciation methods.	**Depreciation Expense = Asset Cost / Useful Life** **Depreciation Expense = (Asset Cost – Scrap Value) / Useful Life** **Depreciation Rate = 100% / Useful Life**	The result is either the depreciation expense (the yearly depreciation amount, for example, $200) or the depreciation rate (the yearly depreciation percentage, for example, 5%). If a scrap value is given, then it can also be factored in by subtracting it.
Double Declining Balance A depreciation method that provides for a higher depreciation charge in the first year of an asset's life and gradually decreasing charges in subsequent years. The method does this by depreciating twice the straight-line depreciation rate from an asset's book value at the beginning of the year.	**Depreciation Rate = 2 * (100% / Useful Life)** **Depreciation Expense = Depreciation Rate * Book Value at Beginning of Year** **Book Value = Book Value at beginning of the year – Depreciation Expense**	The depreciation rate stays the same over the years, but the depreciation expense gets smaller each year because it is calculated from a smaller book value each year.

Concept	Formula	Result Interpretation
Average In mathematics, an average refers to a measure of the "middle" of a data set. The most common method is the arithmetic mean. That is why the "Average" is sometimes also and simply called the "Mean".	**The sum of all the members of the list divided by the number of the members** Average of 2, 3, 7 = (2 + 3 + 7) / 3 = 4	A result is a number representing the arithmetic mean of a data set.
Mean	See Average	
Median The middle value that separates the higher half from the lower half of the data set.	**Arrange the values from lowest value to highest value and pick the middle one** Example: 5 is the median in 1, 5, 6 **If there is an even number of values in the data set, calculate the mean of the two middle values** Example: 3 is the median in 1, 2, 4, 9 because (2 + 4) / 2 = 3	A result is a number representing the median of a data set.
Mode The most frequent value in a given data set.	**Find the value in a data set that occurs most often** Example: 2 is the mode of 1, 2, 2, 3	A result is a number representing the mode of a data set.

Values You May Need to Know

Description	Value	Comment
1 sigma	68.27% (68.2689492...)	Also: 1 standard deviation
2 sigma	95.45% (95.4499736...)	Also: 2 standard deviations
3 sigma	99.73% (99.7300204...)	Also: 3 standard deviations
6 sigma	99.99% (99.9999998027...)	Also: 6 standard deviations Note: 99.9999998027... is the so-called "true" 6 sigma value for normal distribution. The "practical" 6 sigma is 99.999666666..., but 99.99 is sufficient for the PMP Exam and you do not need to know these differences.
Control Limits	Usually 3 standard deviations above and below the mean	Control limits reflect the expected variation in the data.
Control Specifications	Not fixed but defined by the customer	Must be looser than the control limits. Represents the customer's requirements.
Rough Order of Magnitude estimate	-25% to +75%	The estimate ranges are not 100% agreed upon. Some books set the ROM at -25% to +75% others at -50% to +100%. For more details, see the explanation below this table.
Preliminary estimate	-15% to + 50%	
Budget estimate	-10% to +25%	
Definitive estimate	-5% to +10%	
Final estimate	0%	
Float on the critical path	0 days	
Pareto's Law	80/20	For instance: 80% of your problems are due to 20% of the causes.
Time a PM spends communicating	90%	According to Harold Kerzner.
Crashing a project	Crash the tasks with the least expensive crash cost first	Only crash activities that are on the critical path.
Value of the inventory in a Just in Time (JIT) environment	0% (or very close to 0%)	
Sunk Cost	A cost that has been incurred and cannot be reversed	Sunk cost is never a factor when making project decisions.
Negative Numbers	(100) -100	In the USA the number -100 is the same as (100). Both indicate "minus one hundred".

There is no agreement on estimate ranges.

We often receive questions from students about the fact that they see different numbers for the estimate ranges when they compare various training materials. That is true because there is, unfortunately, no final authority that defines these ranges.

There is a disagreement both on the names as well as on the actual ranges. Some books set the ROM at -25% to +75% and others do so at -50% to +100%. In the real world, estimate ranges are both application area and industry dependent. Everyone does it slightly differently in their industry and on their projects. Therefore, it really isn't surprising that you will see different numbers in different books.

The numbers that we provide in the table above have been successfully used by our students on the exam, so we believe applying them on the exam leads to success.

Formula Acronyms

Acronym	Term	Description
AC	Actual Cost	Total cost expended and reported during the accomplishment of a project task or project. This can be labor hours alone; direct costs alone; or all costs, including indirect costs.
AT	Actual Time	The time in calendar units between the actual start date of the project till the project status date.
BAC	Budget at Completion	The sum of all budgets allocated to a project.
BCR	Benefit-Cost Ratio	A ratio that compares benefits to cost.
CBR	Cost-Benefit Ratio	A ratio that compares cost to benefit (inversion of BCR).
CPI	Cost Performance Index	Cost efficiency rating on a project, expressed as a ratio of EV to AC.
CV	Cost Variance	A measure of cost performance on the project, expressed as the difference between earned value and actual cost.
EAC	Estimate at Completion	The expected total cost for a scheduled activity, a group of activities, or the project when the work will be completed.
EF	Early Finish	Early finish of an activity.
EMV	Expected Monetary Value	This is a statistical technique that calculates the probable financial results of events.
ES	Early Start	Early start of an activity.
ES	Earned Schedule	A method of deriving time-based performance measure.

Acronym	Term	Description
ETC	Estimate to Complete	ETC is the expected cost needed to complete all the remaining work for a scheduled activity, a group of activities, or the project. ETC helps project managers predict what the final cost of the project will be upon completion.
EV	Earned Value	EV is the value of completed work expressed in terms of the approved budget assigned to that work for a scheduled activity or a work breakdown structure component.
FV	Future Value	Value of money on a given date in the future.
IRR	Internal Rate of Return	A capital budgeting metric used to decide whether an investment should be made. It is an indicator of the efficiency of an investment.
JIT	Just-in-Time	An inventory strategy that strives to improve a business's return on investment by reducing in-process inventory and associated carrying costs.
LF	Late Finish	Late finish of an activity.
LS	Late Start	Late start of an activity.
NPV	Net Present Value	A standard method for the financial appraisal of long-term projects. Measures the excess or shortfall of cash flows, in present value (PV) terms, once financing charges are met.
PERT	Program Evaluation and Review Technique	A method that allows the estimation of the weighted average duration of tasks.
PV	Planned Value	The authorized budget assigned to the scheduled work to be accomplished for a scheduled activity or a work breakdown structure component.
PV	Present Value	Value of money received today instead of in the future.
ROI	Return on Investment	A ratio of money gained or lost on an investment relative to the amount of money invested.
SPI	Schedule Performance Index	A ratio of work accomplished versus work planned, for a specified time period. The SPI is an efficiency rating for work accomplishment, comparing work accomplished to what should have been accomplished. It is a ratio of earned value and planned value. Alternatively, it is also expressed as a ratio of earned schedule to actual time.
SV	Schedule Variance	A measure of schedule performance on the project, expressed as the difference between earned value and planned value. Alternatively, it is also expressed as the difference between earned schedule and actual time.
TCPI	To-Complete Performance Index	The calculated project cost performance that must be achieved on the remaining work to meet a specific project goal (e.g., BAC or EAC). It is the work remaining divided by the funds remaining.
VAC	Variance at Completion	VAC forecasts the difference between the Budget-at-Completion and the expected total costs to be accrued over the life of the project based on current trends.

PART TWO

Interpretational Questions

The PMP exam has changed with regards to formula-based questions: You are now more likely to be asked to interpret numbers and figures in an exam question scenario and to identify the proper action to take.

That is why here, in Part Two, we focus almost exclusively on interpretational questions. Go through these first and test yourself on interpreting the situations. And if you select the wrong answer, we strongly recommend that you invest the time to understand why you got it wrong.

To help you with this review, the answers for many (but not all) of our interpretational questions include the following:

- **General explanation:** This is a high-level overview of the question background.
- **Per-choice explanation (PCE):** For each answer option we tell you why it is either correct or incorrect. Many of our PMP Exam Simulator students, tell us that PCEs were one of the most essential features of the simulator that contributed to their success in passing the exam with Above Target in all domains.
- **References:** Knowing where the explanation came from and how the correct answer is supported can be very helpful, especially if you want to look up additional information while preparing for the exam.

Interpretational Questions

iQ1

Question 1

You are leading a hybrid project, and you have just updated the daily burndown chart for the current sprint. A key stakeholder has expressed concern that the project team may not meet their objectives for the iteration.

Based on the burndown chart, what is your best course of action to keep the project on track?

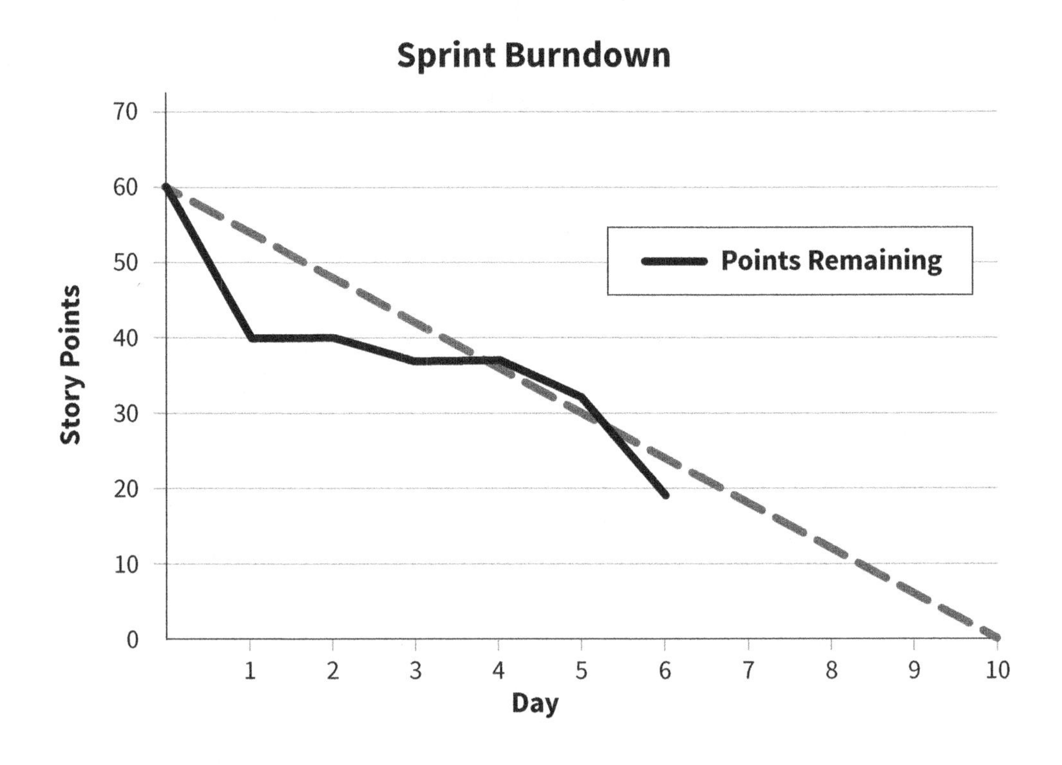

- ☐ A) Crash the schedule
- ☐ B) Fast track some of the user stories
- ☐ C) Allow the team to continue working as planned
- ☐ D) Hold a retrospective before the end of the day

Question 2

A project manager meets with company executives to apprise them of value gain progress on the project. To make it easier for the executives to understand the various earned value metrics without complex formulas and calculations, the project manager draws a chart, as shown below. The date of the meeting is indicated by "Today" on the X-axis.

What is the schedule variance (SV) of the project?

(On the real PMP exam you may be asked to provide your answer by clicking the correct area in the image. But here in the book, we are asking you to select the answer below.)

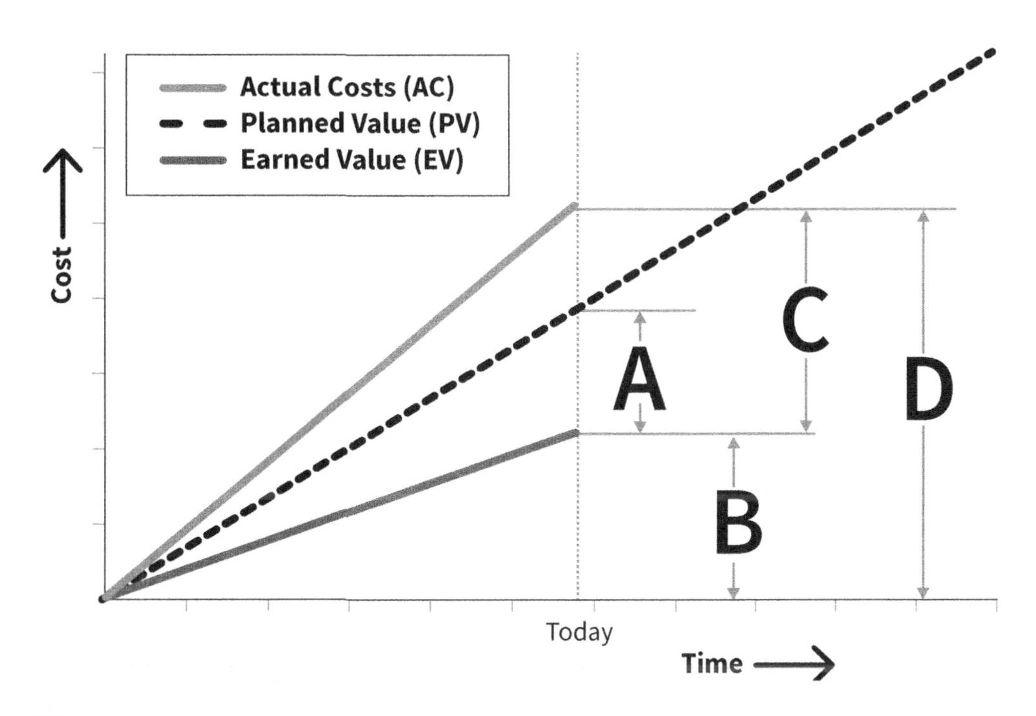

- [ ] A) A
- [ ] B) B
- [ ] C) C
- [ ] D) D

Question 3

iQ3

Your project has a CV of -200.

This means:

- [ ] A) Your project is under budget
- [ ] B) Your SPI is also negative
- [ ] C) Your project is above budget
- [ ] D) CV cannot be negative and there must be an error in the calculation

Question 4

iQ4

An agile team uses Scrumban as the development approach and, after completing four out of eight planned sprints, has established a stable velocity of 30 story points per sprint. The team is confident in maintaining this velocity for the remainder of the project. The current schedule performance index (SPI) is 0.91, and the project has a fixed deadline.

Which of the following actions would be most appropriate for the project leader to take? (Choose three.)

- ☐ A) Ask the project sponsor if an additional developer can be added to the team
- ☐ B) Ask the product owner if they would be willing to cut scope to complete the project on time
- ☐ C) Release one of the developers early to reduce cost since the project is ahead of schedule
- ☐ D) Review the Kanban board and look for opportunities to reduce work in progress (WIP)
- ☐ E) Ask the product owner for additional features to take advantage of the excess capacity

iQ5

Question 5

You are the project manager of the Sterling project. The goal is to explore two possible new products for your company. Over €150,000 has been spent on this exploratory project. Market studies with focus groups show that there is a need for both products. Your sponsor is worried that only 60% of the project work has been completed so far. The current ETC tells you that another €175,000 is required to complete the project.

What should you do?

- ☐ A) Stop the project because you are over budget
- ☐ B) Ignore the sunk cost in the decision-making process
- ☐ C) The SPI is positive; therefore, the project can continue
- ☐ D) Defer the decision to the project control board

iQ6

Question 6

A project team has completed four out of eight planned sprints. The initial project backlog consisted of 22 user stories of the same size and complexity, of which the team has completed 10. Each user story has a budgeted value of $1,000. $11,000 has been spent on the project thus far. A bottom-up estimate to complete the remaining work yields $15,000 for an estimated $26,000 at completion. The agile coach has been asked to provide an estimate at completion (EAC).

What options might the agile coach consider in deriving the estimate at completion (EAC)? (In your exam, on a question like this, you would be asked to drag and drop the items to create matching pairs. In this book, please arrange the answers in the correct order.)

Answer choices	Answers
Future work will be accomplished at the planned rate	
The original plan is no longer valid	
Both SPI and CPI influence the remaining work	
The current CPI is expected to remain the same	

- EAC = AC + BAC – EV
- EAC = AC + bottom-up ETC
- EAC = AC + [(BAC – EV) / (CPI * SPI)]
- EAC = BAC / CPI

Question 7

iQ7

Using the payback period as a means of project selection, which of the following projects would you select?

Project Name	Project Team	Investment	Yearly Income	Overall Risk
Gold	10 Resources	1,500,000	450,000	1.0
Silver	8 Resources	1,700,000	400,000	0.9
Platinum	15 Resources	2,000,000	640,000	1.3
Diamond	26 Resources	3,500,000	850,000	1.2

- ☐ A) Gold
- ☐ B) Silver
- ☐ C) Platinum
- ☐ D) Diamond

Question 8

A project team has established a stable velocity of 30 story points per sprint and has completed 15 of 30 planned sprints. The team is confident they can maintain this velocity for the remainder of the project. The project has an SPI of 0.8 and a CPI of 1.2. The sponsor asks the scrum master for recommendations to get the project back on track.

Which of the following actions would be most appropriate for the scrum master to take? (Choose two.)

- ☐ A) Seek approval to add another developer to the project team
- ☐ B) Fast track some project activities that are off the critical path
- ☐ C) Outsource some of the project deliverables to a vendor
- ☐ D) Release one of the project team members to reduce costs
- ☐ E) No action is needed since SPI and CPI even out one another

Question 9

An agile coach is leading a project using Scrumban and has updated the Kanban board below. He is currently exploring options for reporting metrics that can be provided to key stakeholders.

How would the agile coach derive each of the metrics? (In your exam, on a question like this, you would be asked to drag and drop the items to create matching pairs. In this book, please arrange the answers in the correct order.)

Ready (WIP Limit = 8)	**Development (WIP Limit = 4)**	**Unit Testing (WIP Limit = 2)**	**Integration Testing (WIP Limit = 3)**	**Final Approval (WIP Limit = 3)**	**Done**
User story 21	User story 19	User story 17	User story 14	User story 11	User story 1
User story 22	User story 20	User story 18	User story 15	User story 12	User story 2
User story 23			User story 16	User story 13	User story 3
User story 24					User story 4
User story 25					User story 5
User story 26					User story 6
User story 27					User story 7
User story 28					User story 8
User story 29					User story 9
User story 30					User story 10

Answer choices	Answers
Track the number of days a user story spends in the "Ready" column	
Track the time from when a user story is placed in the "Ready" column until it has been delivered to the customer	
Measure the number of days from when a user story is pulled into the "Development" column until it arrives in the "Done" column	
Calculate the average number of user stories completed per iteration	
Divide the number of story points completed by the number of story points planned	

- Response time
- Lead time
- Cycle time
- Velocity
- Schedule performance index (SPI)

Question 10

iQ10

Using the internal rate of return as a means of project selection, which of the following projects would you select?

Project Name	Project Team	IRR	Investment	Bank loan needed?	Overall Risk
Gold	10 Members	6.0%	4,500,000	Yes	1.0
Silver	8 Members	5.8%	1,700,000	No	0.9
Platinum	15 Members	5.9%	2,000,000	No	1.3
Diamond	26 Members	3.0%	3,500,000	Yes	1.2

☐ A) Gold
☐ B) Silver
☐ C) Platinum
☐ D) Diamond

iQ11

Question 11

A scrum master creates the burnup chart below for the sprint that was just completed.

During the sprint retrospective, what might be said of the sprint?

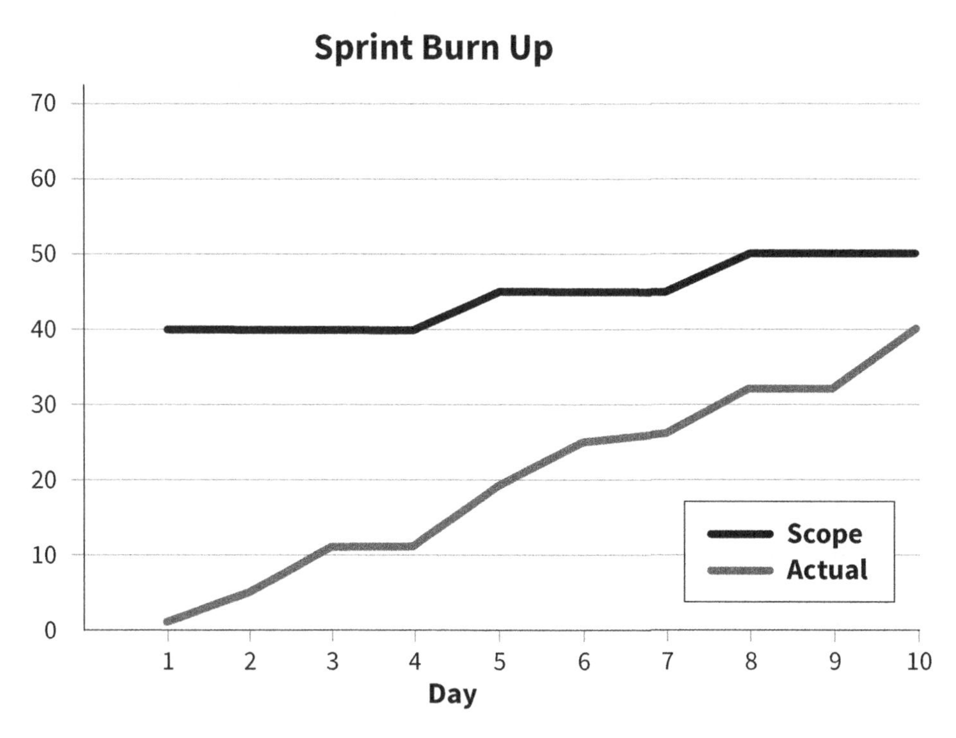

- [ ] A) The project team achieved the sprint goal with a velocity of four story points per day.
- [ ] B) The sprint failed with a velocity of four story points per day because the team did not do any project work on Days 4 and 9.
- [ ] C) The sprint succeeded by attaining a velocity of five story points per day versus a target of four.
- [ ] D) The team achieved a velocity of four story points per day, but the sprint failed because the scope was increased.

iQ12

Question 12

Inspection shows that roughly 72% of your products are produced defect-free.

What sigma level does this finding represent?

- [ ] A) 1 sigma
- [ ] B) 2 sigma
- [ ] C) 3 sigma
- [ ] D) 4 sigma

Question 13

iQ13

A project manager meets with company executives to apprise them of value gain progress on the project. To make it easier for the executives to understand the various earned value metrics without complex formulas and calculations, the project manager draws a chart, as shown below. The date of the meeting is indicated by "Today" on the X-axis.

What is the cost variance (CV) of the project?

(On the real PMP exam you may be asked to provide your answer by clicking the correct area in the image. But here in the book, we are asking you to select the answer below.)

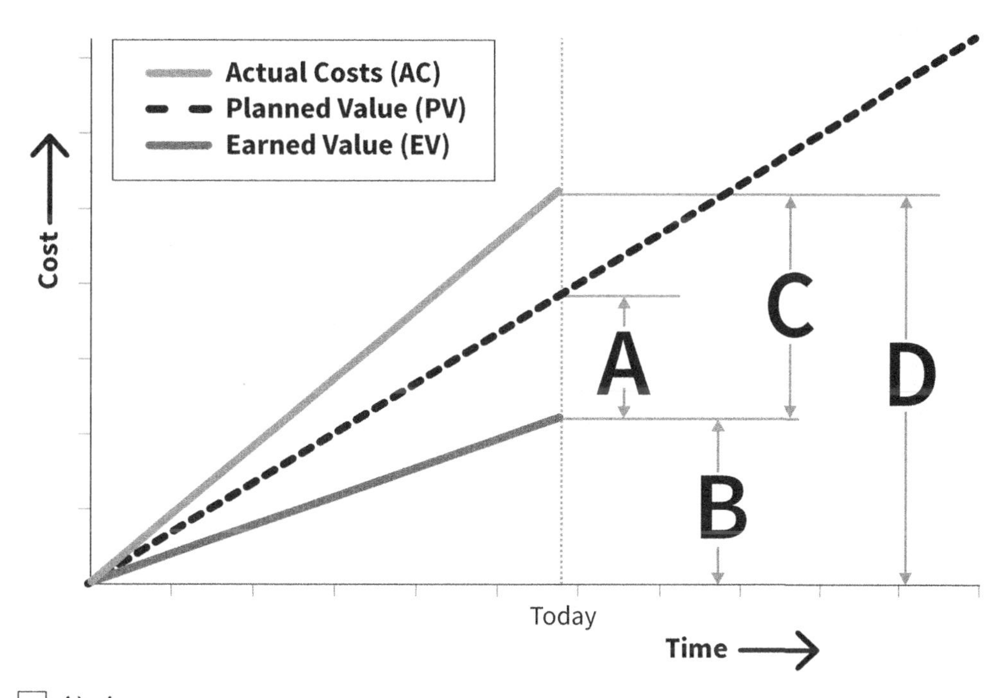

- ☐ A) A
- ☐ B) B
- ☐ C) C
- ☐ D) D

Question 14

iQ14

An agile coach facilitates a project retrospective and reviews the project performance metrics attained at various points throughout the project life cycle.

How can the agile coach describe each of the metrics? (In your exam, on a question like this, you would be asked to drag and drop the items to create matching pairs. In this book, please arrange the answers in the correct order.)

Answer choices	Answers
The cost performance index (CPI)	
A schedule performance index (SPI)	
The schedule variance (SV)	
The cost variance (CV)	
The project team's velocity	

- The ratio of earned value to the actual cost
- The ratio of earned value to planned value
- The amount by which the project is ahead or behind schedule
- The amount of budget surplus or deficit at a given point in time
- The sum of story points completed for a particular iteration

iQ15

Question 15

Every sprint planning meeting, the team commits to 40 story points. However, after completing the first five sprints, the team's velocity is only 35 story points per sprint. An agile coach determines that the earned schedule exceeds the actual time.

What is the best course of action for the agile coach? (Choose two.)

- ☐ A) Ask the project sponsor for approval to add another developer to the project team
- ☐ B) Allow the testers to begin testing partially completed user stories and not to wait until they are finished
- ☐ C) Discuss the topic during the next retrospective and suggest being less aggressive during sprint planning
- ☐ D) Stress the importance of achieving the sprint goal and suggest committing to fewer story points during sprint planning
- ☐ E) Inform the stakeholders that the project is running behind schedule and request that the product owner reduce the scope

Question 16

iQ16

Your project has an SPI of 1.1 and a CPI of 0.9.

What does this mean?

- ☐ A) The project is over budget and ahead of schedule
- ☐ B) The project is ahead of schedule but under budget
- ☐ C) The project is over budget and behind schedule
- ☐ D) The project is behind schedule and under budget

Question 17

iQ17

The following burnup chart shows the team's progress for the project. At Sprint 9 review, the product owner rejects the deliverables.

What can be said of the project's velocity per sprint between Sprints 8 and 9?

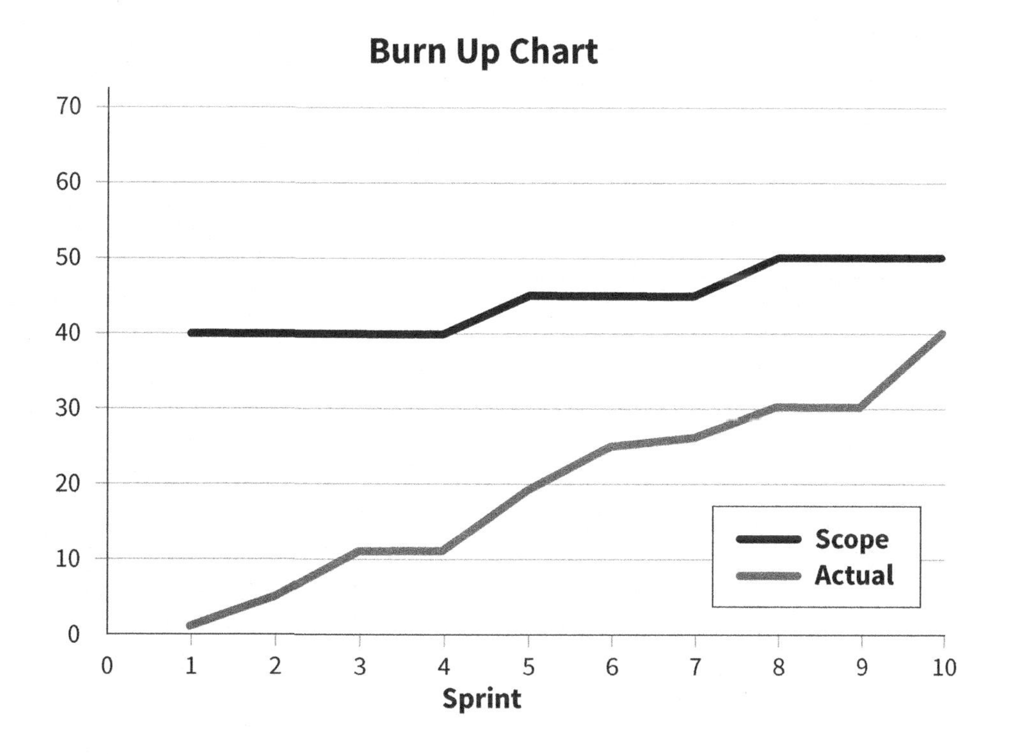

- ☐ A) Decreased from 3.75 to 3.33
- ☐ B) Remained the same at 30 story points
- ☐ C) Decreased from 6.25 to 5.56
- ☐ D) Remained stable at 50 story points

iQ18

Question 18

Using the benefit-cost ratio (BCR), which of the following projects do you select?

- ☐ A) Project Gold with a BCR of 0.9
- ☐ B) Project Silver with a CBR of 0.9 and cost of $100,000
- ☐ C) Project Diamond with a cost of $100,000 and benefits of $110,000
- ☐ D) Project Platinum with a BCR of 1.2

iQ19

Question 19

After four sprints, an agile project has completed five features worth 80 story points. Each story point has a budgeted value of $900 for a BAC of $144,000. The agile coach believes the current cost performance will continue for the remainder of the project and, based on this assumption, calculates a variance at completion (VAC) of -$5,000.

Of the following, which actions should the agile coach consider taking? (Choose two.)

- ☐ A) Take no action as the project is trending to complete all planned features under budget
- ☐ B) Apply value stream mapping to eliminate waste and reduce actual cost (AC)
- ☐ C) Maintain the current cost performance index (CPI) for the remainder of the project
- ☐ D) Submit a change request to increase the budget at completion (BAC)
- ☐ E) At the sprint retrospective, ask the team for suggestions to increase the earned value (EV)

iQ20

Question 20

In preparation for the meeting with the company executives, a program manager reviews the cost and schedule performance metrics for the projects in the program she is overseeing.

What shall the program manager report to the company executives? (In your exam, on a question like this, you would be asked to drag and drop the items to create matching pairs. In this book, please arrange the answers in the correct order.)

Answer choices	Answers
Project Alpha has a CPI of 0.8	
Project Bravo has an SPI of 0.9	
Project Charlie has a CV of $2,000	
Project Delta has an SPI of 1.0	
Project Echo has an SV of 25 story points	

- The project is running over budget
- The project is at risk of jeopardizing its deadline
- The project currently has a budget surplus
- The project is on track to complete on time
- The project will likely be completed early

Question 21

iQ21

Which of the following two projects should be selected if the goal of the company is to maximize the return on investment?

Project	NPV	IRR
A	2,581	29%
B	4,313	25%

☐ A) Project A because the IRR is 29%
☐ B) Project A because the NPV is 2,581
☐ C) Project B because the IRR is 25%
☐ D) Project B because the NPV 4,313

Question 22

iQ22

An agile coach needs to provide a revised estimate at completion (EAC) to the sponsor. The project backlog consists of user stories totaling 300 story points. The budget at completion (BAC) was initially established at $300,000. The development team has completed 100 story points with expenditures totaling $100,000 and a cost performance index (CPI) of 1.0.

What options for determining the EAC should the agile coach consider? (Choose three.)

- [ ] A) Assuming that the cost performance will remain the same for the remainder of the project, divide the BAC by the CPI
- [ ] B) Assuming the remaining work will be completed at the planned rate, subtract the earned value from the BAC and add the actual cost
- [ ] C) Assuming the work is proceeding according to the original plan, subtract the actual cost from the estimate at completion
- [ ] D) If the original budget is no longer valid, re-estimate the cost for the remaining backlog items and add the actual costs
- [ ] E) Re-estimate the cost associated with the work items remaining in the project backlog and report this estimate as the EAC

iQ23

Question 23

Your company has a very elaborate project selection method. You use multiple factors to determine if a project will be undertaken.

Which of the following factors is unlikely to be a part of this system?

- [ ] A) Internal Rate of Return
- [ ] B) Present Value
- [ ] C) Pareto Analysis
- [ ] D) Benefit-Cost Ratio

iQ24

Question 24

A senior leader reviews the business cases for three different software development projects (Alpha, Beta, and Gamma). Project Alpha has an NPV of $100,000 and will take 10 sprints to complete. Project Beta has an NPV of $25,000 and will take 9 sprints to complete. Project Gamma has an NPV of -$125,000 and will take eight sprints to complete.

Assuming resources are available, what is the best course of action?

- [ ] A) Approve project Alpha
- [ ] B) Approve projects Alpha and Beta but reject Gamma
- [ ] C) Approve project Gamma
- [ ] D) Approve all three projects

iQ25

Question 25

An organization considers two projects but only has the resources to support one of them. Project Alpha will provide $100,000 in revenue annually for 10 years with an investment of $500,000. Project Beta will produce $75,000 in annual revenue for 10 years and will cost $500,000. Based on this information, the organization approves project Alpha and rejects Beta.

How did the organization most likely derive the metrics used in its decision-making process? (In your exam, on a question like this, you would be asked to drag and drop the items to create matching pairs. In this book, please arrange the answers in the correct order.)

Answer choices	**Answers**
$500,000 / ($100,000 * 10) = 0.5	
$750,000 – $500,000 = $250,000	
$500,000 / $100,000 = 5 years	
($100,000 * 10) / $500,000 = 2	
$500,000 / ($75,000 * 10) = 0.67	
($75,000 * 10) / $500,000 = 1.5	
$500,000 / $75,000 = 6.67 years	

- Cost-benefit ratio (CBR) of project Alpha
- Opportunity cost
- Payback period for project Alpha
- Benefit-cost ratio (BCR) of project Alpha
- Cost-benefit ratio (CBR) of project Beta
- Benefit-cost ratio (BCR) of project Beta
- Payback period for project Beta

Question 26

iQ26

A project manager meets with company executives to apprise them of value gain progress on the project. To make it easier for the executives to understand the various earned value metrics without complex formulas and calculations, the project manager draws a chart, as shown below. The date of the meeting is indicated by "Today" on the X-axis.

What is the earned value (EV) of the project?

(On the real PMP exam you may be asked to provide your answer by clicking the correct area in the image. But here in the book, we are asking you to select the answer below.)

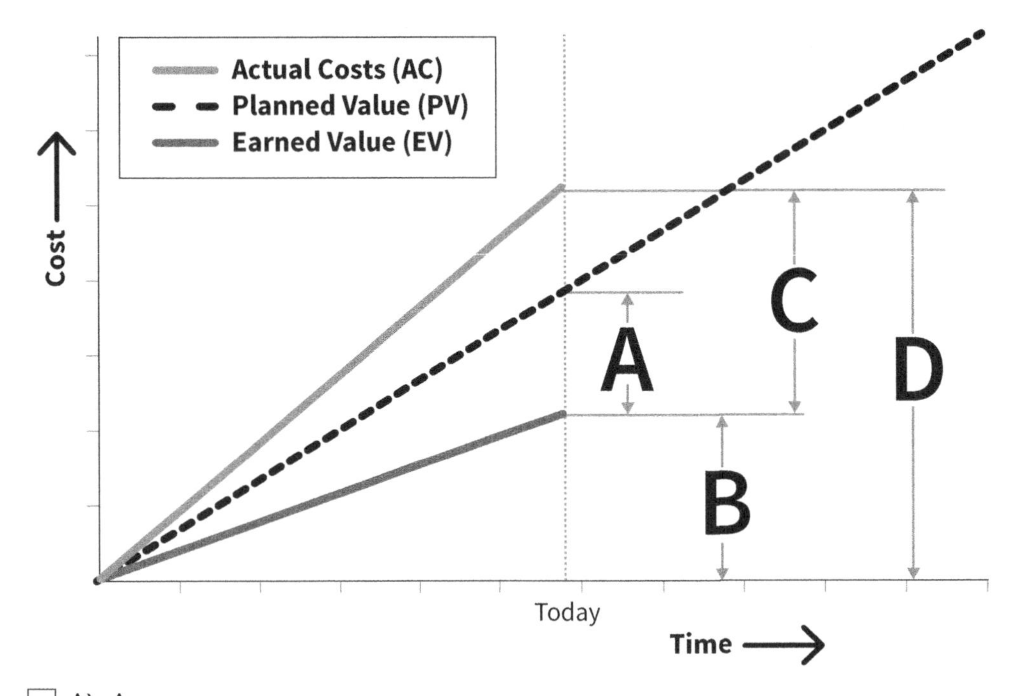

- [ ] A) A
- [ ] B) B
- [ ] C) C
- [ ] D) D

iQ27

Question 27

You are in the procurement process for a high-tech product that is needed for your current project. You have sent out an RFP to several vendors and you expect a target price of about £10,000. The first estimate has arrived this morning. You open the envelope and you see that the vendor is offering the product to you at a cost of £9,500 – £11,000.

What type of estimate have you received from this vendor?

- [ ] A) Preliminary estimate
- [ ] B) Definitive estimate
- [ ] C) Rough order of magnitude estimate
- [ ] D) Final estimate

iQ28

Question 28

An agile project is being performed by a virtual team. The project manager calculates the schedule and cost efficiency and finds that the schedule performance index (SPI) is 0.85 and the cost performance index (CPI) is 1.35.

What actions should the project manager consider to meet the project goals? (Choose two.)

- [ ] A) Do nothing because the project is behind schedule but well under budget
- [ ] B) Colocate the development team for a limited time in order to increase velocity
- [ ] C) Add another developer to the team to expedite the completion of project work
- [ ] D) Ask the product owner to add scope to take advantage of the team's excess capacity
- [ ] E) Reduce cost by releasing one of the project team members early

Question 29

iQ29

A company reviews the various projects that are currently underway as well as potential projects under consideration. Projects A, B, and C are all roughly halfway complete. Projects D and E are both at the pre-project stage.

Based only on the metrics provided, what is the best course of action for the company? (In your exam, on a question like this, you would be asked to drag and drop the items to create matching pairs. In this book, please arrange the answers in the correct order.)

Answer choices	Answers
Project A has a CPI of 1.2 and an SPI of 0.8	
Project B has a CPI of 0.8 and an SPI of 1.2	
Project C has a CPI of 1.0 and an SPI of 1.0	
Project D has a cost-benefit ratio (CBR) of 0.8	
Project E has a benefit-cost ratio (BCR) of 0.8	

- Approve the use of overtime
- Release a member of the project team early
- No action is needed at this time
- Approve the project
- Reject the project

iQ30

Question 30

What information does the EAC contain?

- ☐ A) The cost of the work to be performed to finish the project
- ☐ B) The value of the work that has already been performed
- ☐ C) The cost of the work that was completed
- ☐ D) The expected total cost of our project once it is finished

iQ31

Question 31

A project has completed six sprints. The entire project backlog has been estimated at 250 story points, and each point is worth $1,200 of budgeted value. The project leader has calculated a cost performance index (CPI) of 0.92.

Based on this information, what else can be said of the project's performance? (Choose three.)

- ☐ A) The CV must be a negative value
- ☐ B) The TCPI is most likely greater than 1.0
- ☐ C) The SPI must be less than 1.0
- ☐ D) The VAC should be a negative value
- ☐ E) The project is trending to complete under budget

iQ32

Question 32

You are behind schedule when...

- ☐ A) SPI = 1
- ☐ B) SPI = -1
- ☐ C) SPI > 1
- ☐ D) SPI < 1

iQ33

Question 33

A manufacturing company is considering two potential projects. Project A will streamline production based on a recent Kaizen event and provide an estimated ROI of $15,000. Project B will reduce downtime by replacing equipment on the production line and yield an estimated ROI of -$20,000. Project A has a backlog of 300 story points, and project B has a backlog of 250 story points. The company has sufficient resources to support both of the projects.

What is the company's best course of action?

- [ ] A) Approve both projects
- [ ] B) Approve project A and reject project B
- [ ] C) Reject both projects
- [ ] D) Approve project B and reject project A

Question 34

iQ34

At the project retrospective, the project manager reviews each of the monthly status reports produced over the course of the project. Included in the reports are the various performance metrics.

What could be said of the project's past performance at those points?
(In your exam, on a question like this, you would be asked to drag and drop the items to create matching pairs. In this book, please arrange the answers in the correct order.)

Answer choices	Answers
Month 1: SPI = 1.1	
Month 2: CV = $0.00	
Month 3: TCPI = 1.1	
Month 4: TCPI = 0.9	
Month 5: SV = -$1,000	

- The project was running ahead of schedule
- The project was progressing on budget
- The project was trending over budget
- The project was running under budget
- The project was behind schedule

Question 35

iQ35

How do you calculate the estimate to complete (ETC)?

- [ ] A) You subtract the actual cost from the estimate at completion
- [ ] B) You subtract the budget at completion from the actual cost
- [ ] C) You divide the budget at completion by the schedule performance index
- [ ] D) You subtract the actual cost from the budget at completion

iQ36

Question 36

A project team has completed eight sprints. The project backlog consists of 350 story points, and each point is worth $800 of budgeted value. The team has calculated a schedule performance index (SPI) of 0.87.

Based on this information, what else can be said of the project's performance? (Choose two.)

- ☐ A) The CV must be a positive value
- ☐ B) The CPI is greater than 1.0
- ☐ C) The VAC must be a negative value
- ☐ D) The SV must be a negative value
- ☐ E) The project is running behind schedule

iQ37

Question 37

Your project is to manufacture screws. Your production control limits are set from 2.51 grams to 2.58 grams. Your customer informs you that they would like to have the control limits set from 2.54 grams to 2.57 grams.

What do you tell your customer?

- ☐ A) Thank you, we will change the control limits as required
- ☐ B) I am sorry, but your specifications have to be =2.51 and =2.58
- ☐ C) Please change your specifications to be less than 2.51 and less than 2.58
- ☐ D) Please provide your specifications and we will statistically determine the appropriate control limits

iQ38

Question 38:

During a sprint retrospective, the agile coach presents the burndown chart as shown below. The team discusses what went well during the sprint and what improvements might be applied to the following sprint.

What did the team members most likely find about their performance while analyzing the chart? (Choose three.)

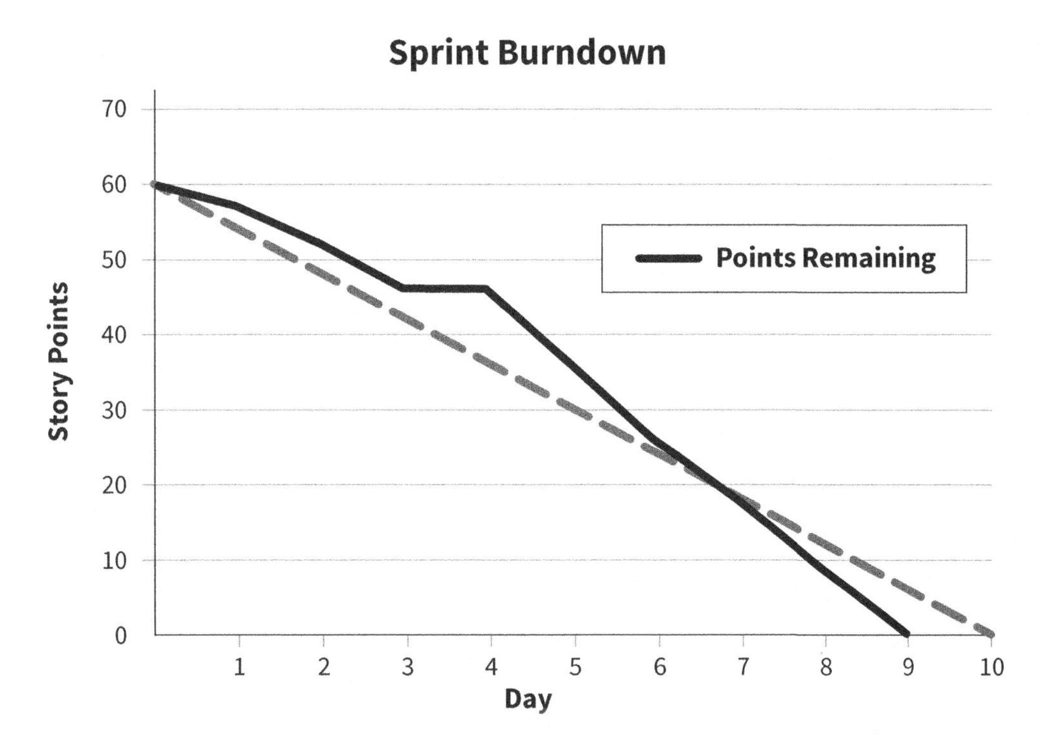

- [ ] A) The team's velocity slowed, and they failed to achieve the sprint goal
- [ ] B) To meet the sprint goal, the team's velocity had to be at least six story points per day
- [ ] C) Scope was added to the sprint on day four which caused the sprint to fail
- [ ] D) The team had finished all of the deliverables for the sprint by day nine
- [ ] E) The SPI on day seven of the sprint would have been 1.0

Question 39

iQ39

A project manager meets with company executives to apprise them of value gain progress on the project. To make it easier for the executives to understand the various earned value metrics without complex formulas and calculations, the project manager draws a chart, as shown below. The date of the meeting is indicated by "Today" on the X-axis.

What is the actual cost (AC) of the project?

(On the real PMP exam you may be asked to provide your answer by clicking the correct area in the image. But here in the book, we are asking you to select the answer below.)

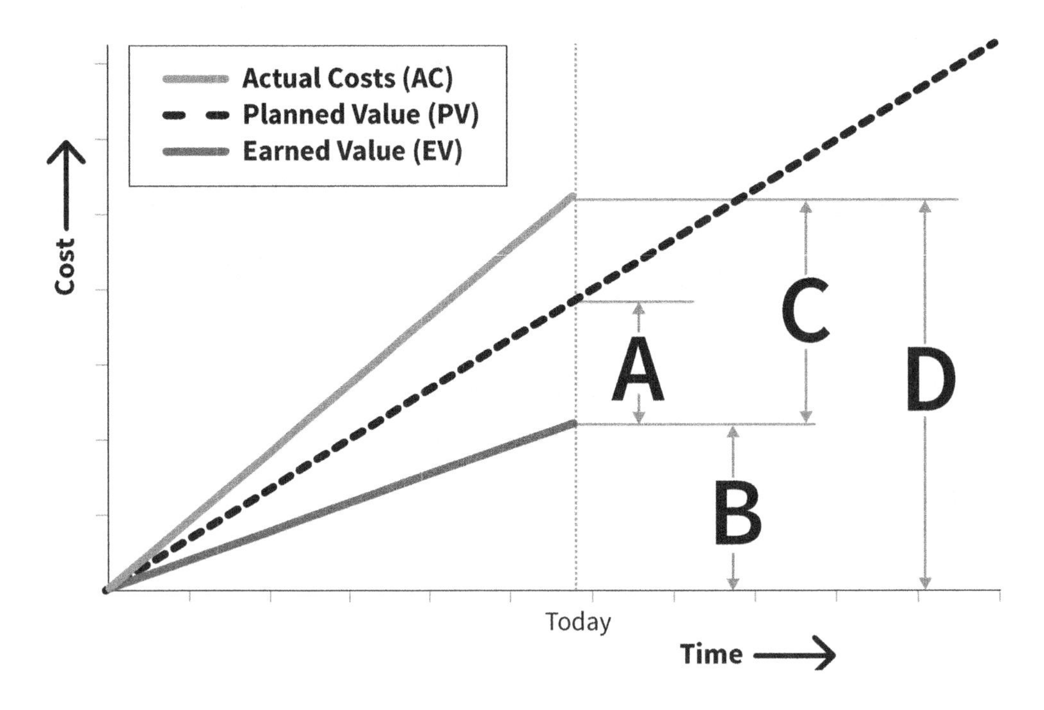

- [ ] A) A
- [ ] B) B
- [ ] C) C
- [ ] D) D

iQ40

Question 40

You have just received an email from your customer that contains the specification limits that they expect from your production process. You add these specification limits to your chart. The chart also contains the control limits.

What do the control limits represent?

- [ ] A) 1 standard deviation above and below the mean
- [ ] B) 2 standard deviations above and below the mean
- [ ] C) 3 standard deviations above and below the mean
- [ ] D) 6 standard deviations above and below the mean

Question 41

A project has completed 11 of 22 planned sprints. The team has finished 200 of 500 story points, with each point having a budgeted value of $1,000. The EV is $200,000, the BAC is $500,000, and the CPI is 0.8. $250,000 has been spent on the project thus far. The steering committee has asked the project manager to provide an estimate for the final and total project cost at completion.

Which options might you consider in preparing the estimate for the steering committee? (Choose three.)

- ☐ A) Assuming that the original plan is still valid, take the earned value of $200,000 and subtract the actual cost of $250,000
- ☐ B) Assuming that plan is fundamentally flawed, re-estimate the remaining work from the bottom up
- ☐ C) Assuming the cost performance will remain the same for the remainder of the project, use the formula EAC = BAC / CPI
- ☐ D) Assuming that conditions have changed and the original plan is no longer valid, develop a new cost estimate for the work remaining and add $250,000
- ☐ E) Assuming that the remaining work will be completed at the planned rate, use the formula EAC = AC + BAC – EV

Question 42

iQ42

As the project progresses, the project manager collects work performance data and calculates the various earned value metrics, such as the variance at completion (VAC) and to-complete performance index (TCPI). The results of the calculations along with their interpretations are published for the stakeholders on the company's internal website.

How should the stakeholders read the results? (In your exam, on a question like this, you would be asked to drag and drop the items to create matching pairs. In this book, please arrange the answers in the correct order.)

Answer choices	Answers
Variance at completion (VAC) is positive	
Variance at completion (VAC) is equal to zero	
Variance at completion (VAC) is negative	
To-complete performance index (TCPI) is greater than 1.0	
To-complete performance index (TCPI) is equal 1.0	
To-complete performance index (TCPI) is less than 1.0	

- The project is under budget
- The project is on budget
- The project is over budget
- Completing the project will be harder
- Completing the project will be neither harder nor easier
- Completing the project will be easier

iQ43

Question 43

Which of the following represent the work that has been completed on the project so far?

☐ A) PV
☐ B) SV
☐ C) EV
☐ D) CPI

Question 44

An organization is conducting a meeting to determine the budget for the next fiscal year. Under discussion are several proposed software development projects. Since the organization only has one scrum team available, just the most profitable project can move forward.

Which project should the organization select?

☐ A) The project with the highest cost-benefit ratio
☐ B) The project with the lowest benefit-cost ratio
☐ C) The project with the highest discounted cash flow
☐ D) The project with the lowest internal rate of return

Question 45

At a meeting to communicate the project status to stakeholders, the project manager uses the various earned value metrics. Some stakeholders are unfamiliar with the various terms and their meanings and request clarification.

How should the project manager respond? (In your exam, on a question like this, you would be asked to drag and drop the items to create matching pairs. In this book, please arrange the answers in the correct order.)

Answer choices	Answers
Schedule variance (SV) is positive	
Schedule variance (SV) is equal to 0	
Schedule variance (SV) is negative	
Cost variance (CV) is positive	
Cost variance (CV) is equal to 0	
Cost variance (CV) is negative	

- The project is ahead of schedule
- The project is on schedule
- The project is behind schedule
- The project is under budget
- The project is on budget
- The project is over budget

Question 46

iQ46

You are on the phone with your project sponsor discussing the most recent project figures. There are slight variances to the original budget. Your project sponsor says: "If I look at the budget at completion and the cost performance index, then our estimate to complete should still be around 200,000. So, we are OK."

Based on this information, what do you know?

- ☐ A) The sponsor doesn't know how to calculate the ETC
- ☐ B) The sponsor thinks that the variances will remain
- ☐ C) The sponsor thinks that the variances will not happen again
- ☐ D) The sponsor thinks that our budget is flawed

Question 47

iQ47

A project has been carried out using 10 two-week sprints. The project is now complete, and, as part of its closure, the project manager uses the following feature chart to analyze the project's performance that will be included in the final report.

What will most likely be included in the report? (Choose three.)

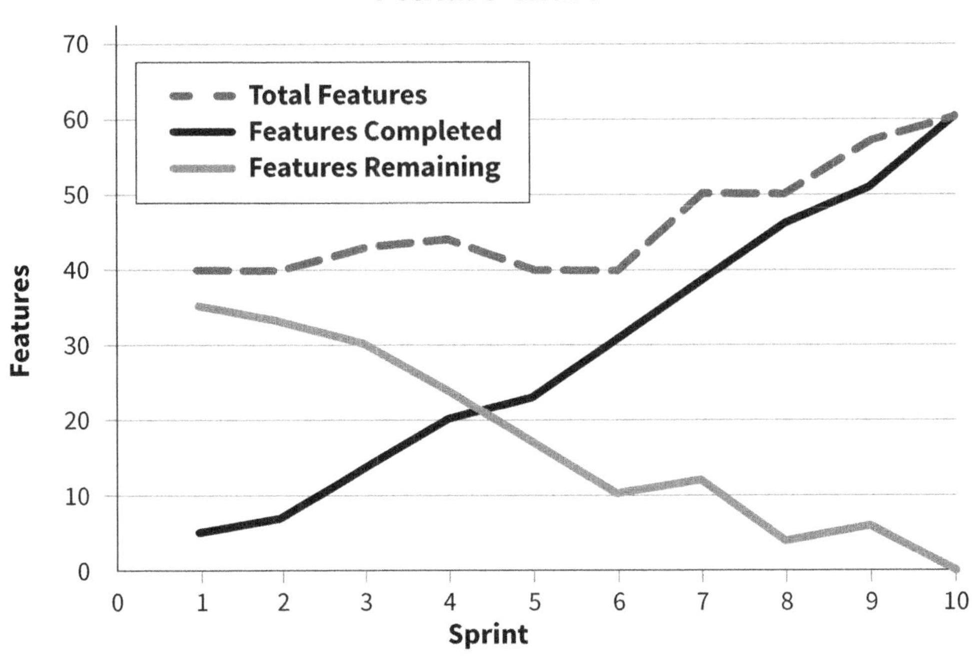

- [ ] A) The project team completed the project with a velocity of six features per sprint
- [ ] B) The project team met the project's objectives and ended with a CPI of 1.0
- [ ] C) The project scope increased over the course of the project
- [ ] D) The project team failed to complete all of the features due to added scope
- [ ] E) At the end of the project, the project team attained an SPI of 1.0

Question 48

To communicate project progress to stakeholders, the project manager assigns a team member to prepare a weekly presentation. The team member is supposed to calculate the various earned value metrics and provide their interpretation in the presentation.

How should the team member interpret the following metrics? (In your exam, on a question like this, you would be asked to drag and drop the items to create matching pairs. In this book, please arrange the answers in the correct order.)

Answer choices	Answers
Cost performance index (CPI) is greater than 1.0	
Cost performance index (CPI) is equal to 1.0	
Cost performance index (CPI) is less than 1.0	
Schedule performance index (SPI) is greater than 1.0	
Schedule performance index (SPI) is equal to 1.0	
Schedule performance index (SPI) is less than 1.0	

- The project is under budget
- The project is on budget
- The project is over budget
- The project is ahead of schedule
- The project is on schedule
- The project is behind schedule

Question 49

iQ49

You are a consultant specializing in the recovery of troubled projects. Your latest assignment is on a project where the CPI = 0.78 and the SPI = 0.65.

Without knowing anything else about this project, which of the following could be the root cause of the situation?

☐ A) The project manager did not create a resource loaded schedule
☐ B) 35% of the tasks were not finished on time
☐ C) The construction machines used were too expensive
☐ D) This project has been staffed with a team that was not sufficiently experienced

Question 50

To track project performance, a project manager creates a feature chart. Each feature is of the same size and value. The project has a budget of $600,000 and is carried out using two-week sprints. The project was planned to be completed in 16 weeks but ended up taking 20. The project manager facilitates the project retrospective.

What can the project manager tell about the project? (Choose three.)

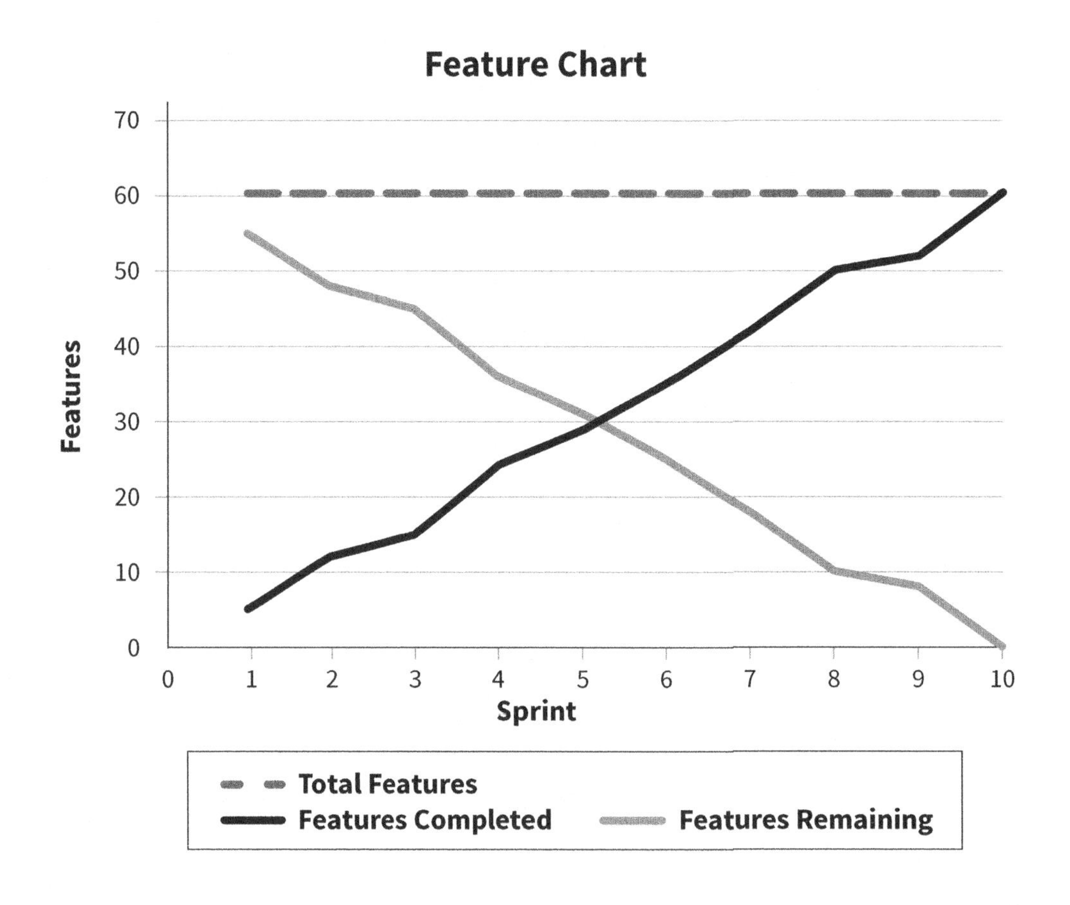

- [ ] A) After eight sprints, the project's schedule performance index (SPI) was less than 1.0
- [ ] B) The project scope remained at 60 features throughout the project
- [ ] C) To complete on time, the team had to achieve a velocity of 7.5 features per sprint
- [ ] D) After eight sprints, the schedule variance (SV) was a positive value
- [ ] E) The project ran over budget with a cost performance index (CPI) of less than 1.0

Question 51

iQ51

If the cost variance is negative and the SPI is less than one, what does this indicate?

- [ ] A) Your project is under budget but behind schedule
- [ ] B) Your project is under budget but on schedule
- [ ] C) Your project is over budget and ahead of schedule
- [ ] D) Your project is over budget and behind schedule

Question 52

iQ52

As the project progresses, the product owner reviews the various earned value metrics. The data indicates that the schedule variance (SV) is -15 story points and the cost variance (CV) is $1,200. The team members believe that their velocity of 20 story points per sprint has stabilized.

What actions might the product owner consider taking? (Choose two.)

- [ ] A) Ask the team for suggestions on increasing earned value (EV)
- [ ] B) Reprioritize the product backlog to lower planned value (PV)
- [ ] C) No action is needed as the current team's velocity is sufficient
- [ ] D) Search for strategies to reduce actual cost (AC)
- [ ] E) Look for opportunities to reduce the earned value (EV)

Question 53

iQ53

What rule is the Pareto diagram based on?

- [ ] A) The 50/50 rule
- [ ] B) The 80/20 rule
- [ ] C) The rule of diminishing returns
- [ ] D) The 90/10 rule

Question 54

iQ54

Your company is considering three potential agile projects. The first project will cost $25,000 and has an NPV of $35,000. The second project will cost $30,000 and has an NPV of $37,000. The third project will cost $40,000 and has an NPV of $20,000. The company only has the resources to approve two of the projects.

What is the opportunity cost of only selecting two of the projects?

- [ ] A) $72,000
- [ ] B) $35,000
- [ ] C) $20,000
- [ ] D) $40,000

iQ55

Question 55

The project is over budget when...

- ☐ A) CPI = 1
- ☐ B) CPI = 0
- ☐ C) CPI > 1
- ☐ D) CPI < 1

iQ56

Question 56

After 10 sprints, 100 of the planned 200 story points have been completed. Based on the current velocity, the project scope can be completed after 15 of the originally planned 20 sprints. The project was budgeted at $1,000 per story point but only consumed $750 per story point. A stakeholder requests three new features to be included in the final product and wants to know if the project can be delivered within the original budget.

What should the project manager do?

- ☐ A) Develop a revised ETC based on a bottom-up estimate and add the actual cost
- ☐ B) Calculate a new EAC by applying the formula EAC = AC + BAC – EV
- ☐ C) Reject the new features since new features can only be requested by the product owner
- ☐ D) Determine a new EAC by dividing the BAC by the current CPI

iQ57

Question 57

Which of the following projects would you select?

- ☐ A) Project A with an internal rate of return of 13%
- ☐ B) Project B with a future value of $300,000
- ☐ C) Project C with benefit-cost ratio of 1:1.1
- ☐ D) Project D with an estimated income of $310,000

iQ58

Question 58

A project team has established a stable velocity of 50 story points per two-week iteration, and there are 500 story points remaining in the project backlog. As the team is about to begin the next sprint, the project sponsor informs the project manager that due to market conditions the remaining scope must be completed in 18 weeks.

What is the best course of action for the project manager?

- [ ] A) Recommend project termination so that the team can fail fast
- [ ] B) Ask the product owner which user stories can be eliminated
- [ ] C) Change development cadence from two-week iterations to weekly
- [ ] D) Request that the project sponsor reprioritize the backlog

Question 59

iQ59

Project A has an IRR of 15% and an NPV of $26,000 for a 2-year duration.
Project B has an IRR of 14% and an NPV of $28,000 for a 4-year duration.

What is the opportunity cost, if you select project A over project B?

- [ ] A) -2,000
- [ ] B) 2,000
- [ ] C) 26,000
- [ ] D) 28,000

Question 60

iQ60

Halfway through the project, the project manager is informed by the program manager that all projects in the program will have an immediate 10% cut in their budgets. Based on the revised budget at completion (BAC), the project manager calculates a to-complete performance index (TCPI) of 0.96.

What is the best course of action for the project manager to comply with the revised budget?

- [ ] A) Cut costs by reducing the size of the project team
- [ ] B) Add resources to the project team in order to shorten the schedule duration
- [ ] C) Submit a change request to reduce the project scope
- [ ] D) Work with the project team to maintain their cost performance for the remainder of the project

Question 61

iQ61

Your project engineer has just been fired. It turned out that he had lied about his professional experience. He had claimed to have worked on several similar projects such as yours, but it turned out that this was not the case. Your project sponsor is now understandably nervous and would like to know how much more the project will cost. You promise that you will get back to him in two days with a new estimate to complete. You set up a meeting with the two junior engineers on the project to work your way through the original estimates. You know already that the current project figures are as follows: EAC = 2,100,000; AC = 230,000; BAC = 2,140,000; EV = 233,000; CPI = 1.01 and SPI = 1.03.

How will you calculate the new ETC for your sponsor?

- [ ] A) ETC = BAC – EV
- [ ] B) We will create a new bottom-up ETC
- [ ] C) ETC = EAC – AC
- [ ] D) ETC = (BAC – EV) / CPI

iQ62

Question 62

An agile team is working within a comprehensive overarching project management plan. The team has completed 140 story points of the planned 150. The project budget is $150,000, and each story point is worth $1,000. Based on the money spent to date, the agile coach calculates a cost variance (CV) of -$2,000.

What is the best course of action to ensure the project achieves its goals?

- [ ] A) Crash the schedule
- [ ] B) Return the cost savings to the organization
- [ ] C) No action is necessary
- [ ] D) Check the risk register for reserves

iQ63

Question 63

Which of the following is correct?

- [ ] A) EAC = AC + [(BAC – EV) / (CPI * SPI)], when project schedule and budget is a factor
- [ ] B) EAC = AC + BAC – EV, when variances will remain
- [ ] C) EAC = BAC / CPI, when what the project has experienced to date will not continue
- [ ] D) ETC = EAC – AC, when the original estimate was flawed

iQ64

Question 64

During project execution, the sponsor is concerned whether the project will be completed on time and requests the project manager to provide an update on the schedule performance metrics.

What data should the project manager collect to perform the calculations? (Choose two.)

- [ ] A) The sum of all project expenditures to date
- [ ] B) The expected cost to finish all of the remaining work
- [ ] C) The authorized budget assigned to the scheduled work

- [ ] D) The planned value of all the work completed to date
- [ ] E) A bottom-up estimate for the work remaining plus the actual cost

Question 65

iQ65

You work for the PMO of a Fortune 1000 company. Every month you are a member of a panel that grills project teams about their proposed projects. You ask them to provide more background on their data and calculations for the NPV. You want to know why they chose the double-declining balance depreciation method. You point out errors in the cost-benefit ratio formulas and watch their reactions. You also ask them to explain the PTA calculations for government contracts.

What is this type of project selection called?

- [ ] A) Constrained optimization methods
- [ ] B) Mathematical model
- [ ] C) Murder board
- [ ] D) Economic model

Question 66

iQ66

A project has a budget of $300,000. After four iterations, 200 story points have been completed versus 220 planned. By this point, the project has spent $25,000 and earned $30,000. To bring the project back on track, a developer has been added to the project team. Based on a new bottom-up estimate, it's expected that the project will meet its original goals.

What can be said of the current project performance? (Choose three.)

- [ ] A) The schedule variance (SV) is zero
- [ ] B) The schedule performance index (SPI) is less than 1.0
- [ ] C) The cost variance (CV) is a positive value
- [ ] D) The cost performance index (CPI) is equal to 1.0
- [ ] E) The estimate at completion (EAC) is $300,000

Question 67

iQ67

What is the required level of accuracy for a budget estimate?

- [ ] A) -10% – +10%
- [ ] B) -10% – +25%
- [ ] C) -15% – +10%
- [ ] D) -15% – +25%

iQ68

Question 68

Your company's accountant informs you that she will be using a 40% depreciation rate for one of your project assets. You know that the asset costs $24,650, has been used on the project for less than three months and that it has an expected life of five years.

Which of the following depreciation methods is the accountant most likely using?

- ☐ A) Double-declining balance
- ☐ B) Straight-line depreciation
- ☐ C) Sum-of-the year's digits
- ☐ D) Units of time depreciation

iQ69

Question 69

The to-complete performance index (TCPI) is calculated by:

- ☐ A) Multiplying the estimate at completion by the cumulative cost performance index
- ☐ B) Adding the estimate at completion to the actual costs to date and multiplying by the cumulative cost performance index
- ☐ C) Dividing the budgeted cost of the remaining work by the difference between the estimate at completion and actual costs to date
- ☐ D) Subtracting the actual costs to date from the estimate at complete

iQ70

Question 70

As the project progresses, the project manager and the team determine that the estimate at completion (EAC) is higher than the initial budget at completion (BAC).

What can be concluded about this project?

- ☐ A) The initial cost estimate for the project was wrong
- ☐ B) The project is running behind schedule
- ☐ C) Due to unforeseen issues, EAC is always higher than BAC
- ☐ D) No definitive conclusion can be made

Answers to Interpretational Questions

Question 1: Answer

iA1

You are leading a hybrid project, and you have just updated the daily burndown chart for the current sprint. A key stakeholder has expressed concern that the project team may not meet their objectives for the iteration.

Based on the burndown chart, what is your best course of action to keep the project on track?

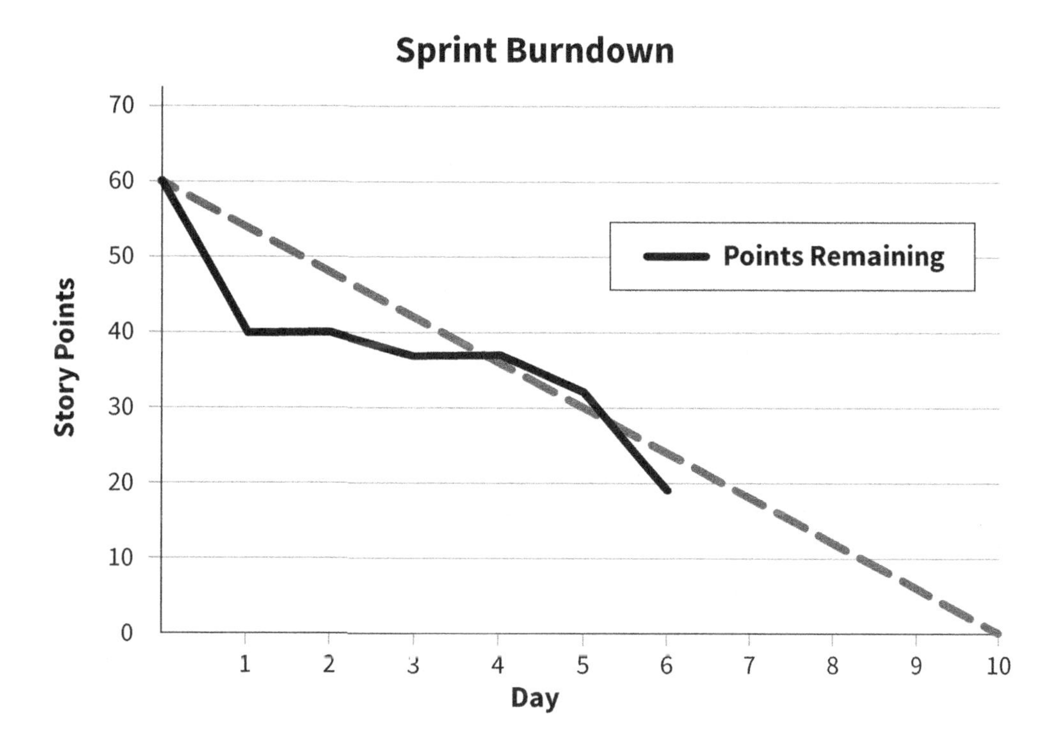

A) Crash the schedule
Incorrect. Hybrid projects, like the one described by the scenario, can include elements of both predictive and agile methodologies. Crashing is a schedule compression technique typically used in predictive projects where resources are added to expedite delivery at greater expense. However, the burndown chart indicates that the project team is on track to meet the sprint goal. Therefore, crashing the schedule is not warranted.

B) Fast track some of the user stories
Incorrect. Fast tracking is a schedule compression technique in which tasks that were originally scheduled to run sequentially are performed concurrently, thus expediting delivery. However, the sprint burndown

chart suggests that the team is on track to meet the sprint goal. Therefore, there is no compelling reason to fast track user stories.

☑ **C) Allow the team to continue working as planned**
Correct. The scenario indicates that a stakeholder is concerned about the team completing the work on time; however, the sprint burndown chart indicates that the team is trending to complete the sprint goal successfully. Since there is no compelling reason to believe the sprint goal is in jeopardy, the team should be allowed to continue working as planned.

D) Hold a retrospective before the end of the day
Incorrect. A retrospective is an agile ceremony in which the project team takes time to review their performance and look for opportunities for improvement. Retrospectives are typically held at the end of each sprint but can be held at any time it would be beneficial to do so. In this case, the burndown chart indicates that the team is making good progress, and there is no reason to believe the sprint goal is at risk. Pulling the team away from their development work for a retrospective would not likely be beneficial at this point.

Explanation:
A burndown chart is a graphical representation of the work remaining versus the time left in a timebox. When the curve representing completed work (story points) is trending below the curve representing the planned work, the project earns more than planned and/or is ahead of schedule. The burndown chart in the scenario described indicates that the project team is slightly ahead of the plan. Thus, there is no reason to believe that the sprint goal is in jeopardy. The key stakeholder has expressed concern regarding the team achieving the sprint goal, but there is no information presented in this scenario to support the view that the goal is at risk. While stakeholders' concerns should not be ignored, the project leader might just need to explain the information provided by the burndown chart. Regardless, the question is asking what should be done to keep the team on track rather than how to address the stakeholder's concern. Given that the team is projected to achieve the sprint goal and that no information has been provided to suggest that the goal is at risk, the best course of action is to allow the project team to continue their work as planned.

Reference:
A Guide to the Project Management Body of Knowledge, (PMBOK® Guide) – Sixth Edition, Project Management Institute Inc., 2017, Page(s) 226

Agile Practice Guide – First Edition, Project Management Institute Inc., 2017, Page(s) 62

Question 2: Answer

iA2

A project manager meets with company executives to apprise them of value gain progress on the project. To make it easier for the executives to understand the various earned value metrics without complex formulas and calculations, the project manager draws a chart, as shown below. The date of the meeting is indicated by "Today" on the X-axis.

What is the schedule variance (SV) of the project?

(On the real PMP exam you may be asked to provide your answer by clicking the correct area in the image. But here in the book, we are asking you to select the answer below.)

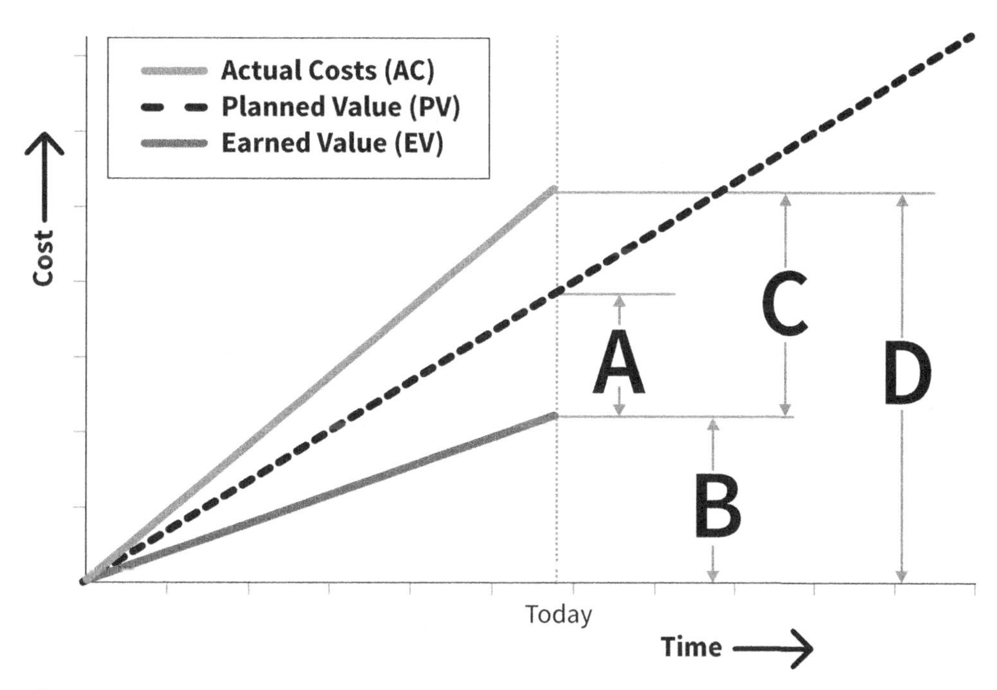

☑ **A) A**

Correct. Area A represents the difference between the earned value (EV) and the planned value (PV). The schedule variance (SV) of the project is a measure of schedule performance expressed as the difference between the earned value (EV) and the planned value (PV), making this choice the best answer to the question asked.

B) B

Incorrect. Area B represents the earned value (EV) as of "Today", the date of the meeting. The question is asking to determine the schedule variance (SV) of the project. The SV is the difference between the earned value (EV) and the planned value (PV), rather than just the earned value. Therefore, this choice is an incorrect answer.

C) C
Incorrect. Area C represents the difference between the earned value (EV) and the actual costs (AC). The difference between the earned value (EV) and the actual costs (AC) is the cost variance (CV), not the schedule variance (SV), as asked by the question. Hence, this choice represents an incorrect answer.

D) D
Incorrect. Area D represents the actual costs (AC) as of "Today", the date of the meeting. The question is asking to determine the schedule variance (SV) of the project. The SV is the difference between the earned value (EV) and the planned value (PV), rather than just the actual costs, making this choice an incorrect answer.

Explanation:
Earned value analysis (EVA) is an example of data analysis tools and techniques that can be used on a project to analyze its performance in terms of budget and schedule. The EVA compares the performance measurement baseline to the actual cost and schedule performance. Earned value analysis is typically associated with a more general term, earned value management (EVM), which is a methodology that combines scope, schedule, and resource measurements to assess project performance and progress.

To calculate its metrics, the EVA often uses various formulas. However, operating with the formulas and values that result from them may sometimes be difficult for project stakeholders (such as the executives in the scenario described) who are less familiar with the formulas. Therefore, to make it easier for such stakeholders, a visual representation of the value gain progress may be useful.

The question is asking to find the schedule variance (SV) of the project. SV is a measure of schedule performance expressed as the difference between the earned value (EV) and the planned value (PV):

SV = EV - PV

On the chart, the SV can be determined by the height of the section on the vertical dotted line (indicated by "Today") between the curves representing the planned value and the earned value. It can be seen that the EV is lower than the PV, making SV a negative number. A negative SV means the project is behind schedule.

Reference:
A Guide to the Project Management Body of Knowledge, (PMBOK® Guide) – Sixth Edition, Project Management Institute Inc., 2017, Page(s) 262

Question 3: Answer

iA3

Your project has a CV of -200.

This means:

- A) Your project is under budget
- B) Your SPI is also negative
- ☑ **C) Your project is above budget**
- D) CV cannot be negative and there must be an error in the calculation

Explanation:
Cost variance (CV) is calculated **CV = EV – AC.** Therefore, a negative cost variance means that you have spent more Actual Cost than you have Earned Value. Thus, you are spending more than is coming in and you are over budget.

Question 4: Answer

An agile team uses Scrumban as the development approach and, after completing four out of eight planned sprints, has established a stable velocity of 30 story points per sprint. The team is confident in maintaining this velocity for the remainder of the project. The current schedule performance index (SPI) is 0.91, and the project has a fixed deadline.

Which of the following actions would be most appropriate for the project leader to take? (Choose three.)

☑ **A) Ask the project sponsor if an additional developer can be added to the team**
Correct. An SPI of 0.91 indicates that the project is running behind schedule. Adding resources is an example of crashing. Crashing is a schedule compression technique that can shorten the schedule duration by adding resources. Note: adding resources might put the project over budget; however, the scenario is not concerned with this constraint.

☑ **B) Ask the product owner if they would be willing to cut scope to complete the project on time**
Correct. With an SPI less than 1.0, the project is behind schedule and will not likely complete the remaining work at the current velocity. One option to complete the project sooner is to reduce the project backlog. Given that the deadline is fixed, the product owner might be willing to sacrifice some functionality to meet the deadline.

C) Release one of the developers early to reduce cost since the project is ahead of schedule

Incorrect. The question provides an SPI of 0.91, which means the project is running behind schedule, and the current velocity is insufficient to complete the project on time. Releasing one of the developers early would likely decrease the team's velocity and further exacerbate the schedule issue, making this choice an incorrect answer.

☑ **D) Review the Kanban board and look for opportunities to reduce work in progress (WIP)**

Correct. The question states that the project management framework is Scrumban. Scrumban combines scrum and Kanban practices within a single project. One of the goals of Kanban is to minimize WIP to increase throughput. Incomplete work represents no value for the customer, and the greater the WIP, the greater the risk of rework and multitasking, which can slow velocity. Thus, looking for opportunities to reduce WIP would be a viable action when attempting to increase velocity.

E) Ask the product owner for additional features to take advantage of the excess capacity

Incorrect. With an SPI of 0.91, the project is behind schedule, implying there is no excess capacity. This means that the current velocity of 30 story points is insufficient to complete the project on time, let alone adding more features. Adding scope to the project would likely cause the project to run even further behind schedule.

Explanation:

The pertinent information provided in this scenario is that the schedule performance index (SPI) is 0.91, and the project deadline is fixed. An SPI of 0.91 means that the project team only works at 91% of the planned rate. Since the project is running behind schedule and the deadline is fixed, there are really only two options to complete the project on time: to increase the velocity or cut the project scope. Both of the incorrect answer choices represent actions that would likely delay the project further. One might have selected one or both incorrect answer choices if the SPI was incorrectly interpreted as the project running ahead instead of behind schedule. All three correct answer choices represent actions that might increase velocity or reduce scope, which should help bring the project to completion sooner.

Reference:

A Guide to the Project Management Body of Knowledge, (PMBOK® Guide) – Sixth Edition, Project Management Institute Inc., 2017, Page(s) 263, 267

Agile Practice Guide – First Edition, Project Management Institute Inc., 2017, Page(s) 69, 108

Question 5: Answer

iA5

You are the project manager of the Sterling project. The goal is to explore two possible new products for your company. Over €150,000 have been spent on this exploratory project. Market studies with focus groups show that there is a need for both products. Your sponsor is worried that only 60% of the project work has been completed so far. The current ETC tells you that another €175,000 is required to complete the project.

What should you do?

A) Stop the project because you are over budget
☑ **B) Ignore the sunk cost in the decision-making process**
C) The SPI is positive; therefore, the project can continue
D) Defer the decision to the project control board

Explanation:

A decision on whether to continue with a project should be based on forward-looking criteria. The sunk cost (= money that has been spent) should not be a factor in the decision-making process. Take your car as an analogy: If you learn that you need to have the flux capacitor replaced (at a cost of €750) then you should not be thinking "Gee... I just replaced the intake valve for €250 last month!" Instead you should look at the value of your car and whether this investment/repair is worth the future usage of the vehicle. It is the same with projects. Make forward-looking decisions and ignore sunk cost.

Question 6: Answer

iA6

A project team has completed four out of eight planned sprints. The initial project backlog consisted of 22 user stories of the same size and complexity, of which the team has completed 10. Each user story has a budgeted value of $1,000. $11,000 has been spent on the project thus far. A bottom-up estimate to complete the remaining work yields $15,000 for an estimated $26,000 at completion. The agile coach has been asked to provide an estimate at completion (EAC).

What options might the agile coach consider in deriving the estimate at completion (EAC)? (In your exam, on a question like this, you would be asked to drag and drop the items to create matching pairs. In this book, please arrange the answers in the correct order.)

Correct Answers:

Answer choices	Answers
Future work will be accomplished at the planned rate	**EAC = AC + BAC – EV**
The original plan is no longer valid	**EAC = AC + bottom-up ETC**
Both SPI and CPI influence the remaining work	**EAC = AC + [(BAC – EV) / (CPI * SPI)]**
The current CPI is expected to remain the same	**EAC = BAC / CPI**

Explanation:
The estimate at completion (EAC) is the expected total cost of completing all work expressed as the sum of the actual cost to date and the estimate to complete. There are various methods to determine the EAC for a project. The appropriate formula to use will depend upon the assumptions that one is willing to make regarding the project's future performance. Changing the assumptions may lead to a different value for EAC. In this scenario, the necessary metrics are provided to calculate EAC with various methods.

Answering this question correctly does not require performing any calculations. The numbers provided in the scenario are superfluous. Those who wish to practice the application of various EAC formulas may review the explanation provided below.

- When future work will be accomplished at the planned rate, an estimate at completion (EAC) can be calculated using the following formula: EAC = AC + BAC – EV. Based on the scenario, AC = $11,000 (provided in the scenario), BAC = $22,000 (22 user stories of the same size and complexity multiplied by their budgeted value of $1,000 per user story), EV = $10,000 (10 completed user stories multiplied by their budgeted value of $1,000 per user story). Therefore, EAC = $11,000 + $22,000 – $10,000 = $23,000.
- When the current plan is no longer valid, a new ETC can be determined by performing a bottom-up estimate. To derive EAC, one must include the actual expenditures to date. Thus, using the formula AC + bottom-up ETC would be the appropriate method to determine the EAC when the original plan is no longer valid: EAC = $11,000 + $15,000 = $26,000. Note: this value has already been provided in the scenario and, therefore, does not require a calculation (which is not required for this question anyway).

- In some cases, the current cost and schedule performance will continue to affect the project going forward. To adjust the EAC to account for cost and schedule performance, the cost performance index (CPI) and schedule performance index (SPI) can be incorporated into the formula: EAC = AC + [(BAC – EV) / (CPI * SPI)]. The CPI can be calculated as EV / AC. The EV was calculated above as $10,000, and the AC was stated in the question as $11,000. Thus, CPI = $10,000 / $11,000 = 0.91. The formula for SPI is EV / PV. Earned value was previously calculated at $10,000. Having completed four of eight planned sprints, the project is 50% complete. Thus, the PV at this point in the project would be half of the BAC or $11,000. Applying the formula for SPI would result in $10,000 / $11,000 = 0.91. Thus, EAC = $11,000 + [($22,000 – $10,000) / (0.91 * 0.91)] = $25,520.
- When the current cost performance is expected to remain the same for the remainder of the project, the current CPI must be included in the EAC calculation. Under this circumstance, the appropriate formula would be EAC = BAC / CPI. We have previously determined BAC at $22,000 and CPI at 0.91. Applying the formula yields $22,000 / 0.91 = $24,176.

Reference:
A Guide to the Project Management Body of Knowledge, (PMBOK® Guide) – Sixth Edition, Project Management Institute Inc., 2017, Page(s) 263-265, 267

Agile Practice Guide – First Edition, Project Management Institute Inc., 2017, Page(s) 61, 69

Question 7: Answer

iA7

Using the Payback Period as a means of project selection, which of the following projects would you select?

Project Name	Project Team	Investment	Yearly Income	Overall Risk
Gold	10 Resources	1,500,000	450,000	1.0
Silver	8 Resources	1,700,000	400,000	0.9
Platinum	15 Resources	2,000,000	640,000	1.3
Diamond	26 Resources	3,500,000	850,000	1.2

A) Gold
B) Silver
☑ **C) Platinum**
D) Diamond

Explanation:
To calculate the payback period, you divide the investment by the yearly income. In this question, project Platinum has the shortest payback period of 3.125 years, calculated as follows: **2,000,000 / 640,000 = 3.125.** The values in the other columns (project team size and overall risk) are irrelevant. You have to be able to spot the important information in the question and "tune out" the rest.

iA8

Question 8: Answer

A project team has established a stable velocity of 30 story points per sprint and has completed 15 of 30 planned sprints. The team is confident they can maintain this velocity for the remainder of the project. The project has an SPI of 0.8 and a CPI of 1.2. The sponsor asks the scrum master for recommendations to get the project back on track.

Which of the following actions would be most appropriate for the scrum master to take? (Choose two.)

☑ **A) Seek approval to add another developer to the project team**
Correct. A schedule performance index (SPI) of 0.8 indicates that the project is behind schedule. Adding resources to a project to expedite delivery is known as crashing. Crashing will increase costs, but with a CPI of 1.2, the project is running under budget and, as such, might be able to absorb the cost of an additional developer and still complete on budget.

B) Fast track some project activities that are off the critical path
Incorrect. The strategy of running tasks in parallel that were originally planned to be performed sequentially is known as fast tracking. Fast tracking is a viable option for shortening the schedule duration. However, fast tracking will only be effective for activities that are on, rather than off, the critical path.

☑ **C) Outsource some of the project deliverables to a vendor**
Correct. Outsourcing work to a vendor is another example of crashing. Resources that are added will likely increase cost but should also enhance velocity. Since the project is trending to finish well under budget with a CPI of 1.2, funds may be available to contract with a vendor for additional support without endangering the budget.

D) Release one of the project team members to reduce costs
Incorrect. With the earned value metrics provided in the scenario (SPI = 0.8, CPI = 1.2), the project is considered behind schedule and

under budget. Therefore, the goal is to bring the project back on schedule rather than reduce costs. Releasing a team member would only worsen the project schedule performance, making this choice an incorrect answer.

E) No action is needed since SPI and CPI even out one another
Incorrect. One would select this answer if one mistakenly thought that 0.2 "missing" from the SPI of 1.0 could be compensated by the "extra" 0.2 of the CPI. However, SPI and CPI are independent earn value metrics. Based on the scenario, the project is behind schedule and under budget. While no action is required to modify project cost performance, action should be taken to bring the project back on schedule.

Explanation:

With the schedule performance index (SPI) of 0.8 and a cost performance index (CPI) of 1.2 provided in the scenario, the project is considered behind schedule and under budget. Thus, the problem that needs to be addressed is how to increase velocity to complete the deliverables on time. Both of the correct answer choices are examples of crashing where resources are added to shorten the schedule duration. Crashing increases costs, but with the project running under budget, there is an opportunity to deploy some of the excess funds to shorten the schedule without endangering the budget.

Reference:

A Guide to the Project Management Body of Knowledge, (PMBOK® Guide) – Sixth Edition, Project Management Institute Inc., 2017, Page(s) 267

Agile Practice Guide – First Edition, Project Management Institute Inc., 2017, Page(s) 61, 69

Question 9: Answer

An agile coach is leading a project using Scrumban and has updated the Kanban board below. He is currently exploring options for reporting metrics that can be provided to key stakeholders.

How would the agile coach derive each of the metrics? (In your exam, on a question like this, you would be asked to drag and drop the items to create matching pairs. In this book, please arrange the answers in the correct order.)

Ready (WIP Limit = 8)	Development (WIP Limit = 4)	Unit Testing (WIP Limit = 2)	Integration Testing (WIP Limit = 3)	Final Approval (WIP Limit = 3)	Done
User story 21	User story 19	User story 17	User story 14	User story 11	User story 1
User story 22	User story 20	User story 18	User story 15	User story 12	User story 2
User story 23			User story 16	User story 13	User story 3
User story 24					User story 4
User story 25					User story 5
User story 26					User story 6
User story 27					User story 7
User story 28					User story 8
User story 29					User story 9
User story 30					User story 10

Correct Answers:

Answer choices	Answers
Track the number of days a user story spends in the "Ready" column	**Response time**
Track the time from when a user story is placed in the "Ready" column until it has been delivered to the customer	**Lead time**
Measure the number of days from when a user story is pulled into the "Development" column until it arrives in the "Done" column	**Cycle time**
Calculate the average number of user stories completed per iteration	**Velocity**
Divide the number of story points completed by the number of story points planned	**Schedule performance index (SPI)**

Explanation:

The question indicates that Scrumban is being used as a project management framework. As such, the project will be executed iteratively, and the work will be tracked with a Kanban board. Many metrics can be used to track project performance on an agile project. In this case, response time, lead time, cycle time, velocity, and the schedule performance index (SPI) have been specifically listed. To answer the question correctly, one must match the metric to a brief description of how the metric might be derived.

Note that in some cases, there might be more than one method to derive the metric, but only one example has been provided.

- Response time is the time a work item waits until work begins on that item. In this case, the "Ready" column lists user stories that are ready for work to begin. Once work begins on a user story, it will be pulled into the "Development" column. Thus, the response time can be represented as the number of days the user story spends in the "Ready" column.
- Lead time represents the total time it takes to deliver a work item. In other words, lead time can be measured from the moment a work item is placed on the board until the work item is delivered to the customer for deployment. In this case, lead time can be measured from the moment a user story is placed in the "Ready" column until the deliverable related to that user story is delivered to the customer. Note: the "Done" column does not necessarily indicate the deployment to the customer. It only suggests the work has been completed. Delivery to the customer is typically outside the Kanban board boundaries. Each team/project may implement the Kanban board differently.
- Cycle time can be measured from the moment work begins on a work item until the work is completed. In this example, cycle time can be derived from the time a user story is pulled into the "Development" column until it arrives in the "Done" column.
- Velocity can be defined as the sum of story points completed during an iteration or the average number of story points completed per iteration. Since the project management framework used in this example is Scrumban (a combination of Scrum and Kanban), it is reasonable to assume that the relative size of each user story will be measured using story points, and the work will be completed iteratively. Thus, velocity would be a viable metric to use.
- Traditional earned value metrics can also be applied to agile projects. The schedule performance index (SPI) can be calculated as the earned value (EV) divided by the planned value (PV). When incorporating scrum practices, the sprint goal will represent a certain number of story points or planned value, and the number of story points completed by the team would be the earned value. Dividing the number of story points completed by the number of story points planned would be one method of calculating the SPI on an agile project.

The contents of the Kanban board are irrelevant for matching the items correctly. The various user stories are provided for illustration purposes only.

Reference:
Agile Practice Guide – First Edition, Project Management Institute Inc., 2017, Page(s) 61-69
https://www.projectmanagement.com/blog-post/7502/Kanban-is-the-new-Scrum

Question 10: Answer

Using the internal rate of return as a means of project selection, which of the following projects would you select?

Project Name	Project Team	IRR	Investment	Bank loan needed?	Overall Risk
Gold	10 Members	6.0%	4,500,000	Yes	1.0
Silver	8 Members	5.8%	1,700,000	No	0.9
Platinum	15 Members	5.9%	2,000,000	No	1.3
Diamond	26 Members	3.0%	3,500,000	Yes	1.2

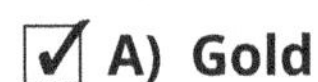

A) Gold
B) Silver
C) Platinum
D) Diamond

Explanation:
Project Gold has the highest internal rate of return (IRR), which is the project selection criteria requested to be used by the scenario provided. Therefore, other values can be ignored.

Question 11: Answer

A scrum master creates the burnup chart below for the sprint that was just completed.

During the sprint retrospective, what might be said of the sprint?

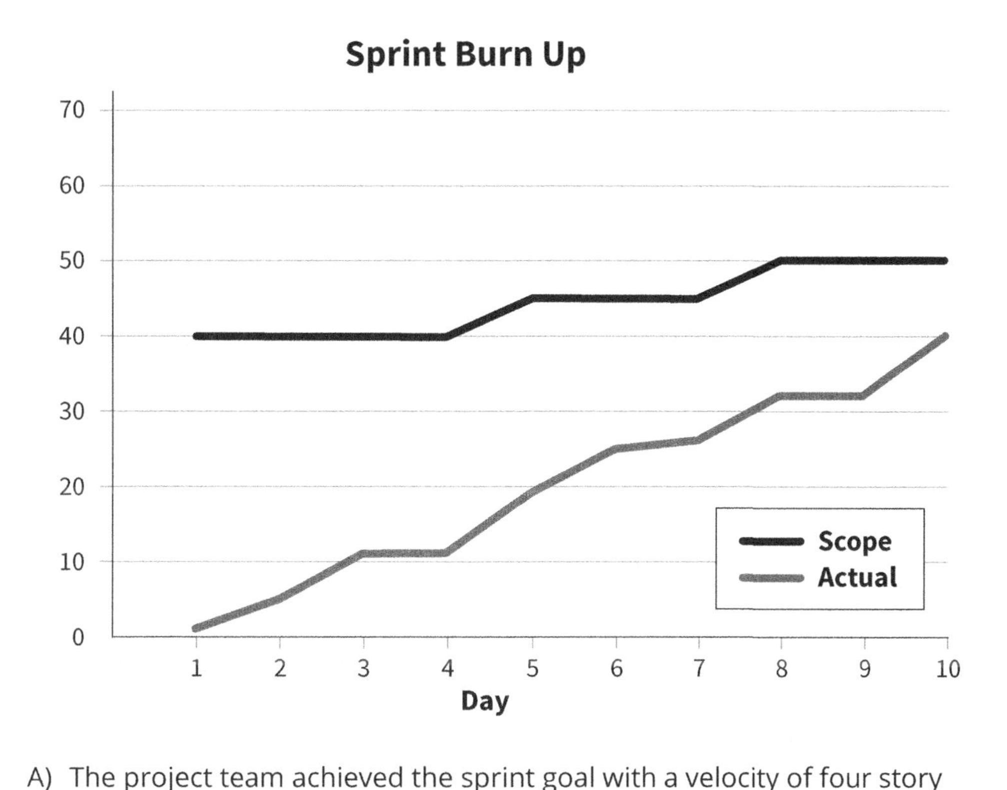

A) The project team achieved the sprint goal with a velocity of four story points per day.
Incorrect. Although the team completed four story points per day for a total of 40 story points, the sprint failed because the final sprint goal for the sprint was 50 story points. One may argue that the team reached the sprint goal by completing the original sprint scope of 40 story points. However, the sprint scope has been increased (for whatever reason) but not achieved, making this answer incorrect.

B) The sprint failed with a velocity of four story points per day because the team did not do any project work on Days 4 and 9.
Incorrect. The team achieved a velocity of four story points per day. However, from the burnup chart, what work was actually accomplished on Days 4 and 9 cannot be determined. The team might have completed some tasks associated with one or more user stories but just could not complete a user story to gain credit for the points assigned to that user story.

C) The sprint succeeded by attaining a velocity of five story points per day versus a target of four.
Incorrect. The project team completed 40 story points over a 10-day sprint. To calculate the velocity for the sprint, one must divide the story points completed by the number of days in the sprint. In this case, 40 story points / 10 days = four story points per day, not five. Additionally, the final sprint goal was 50 points, while the team only completed 40.

☑ **D) The team achieved a velocity of four story points per day, but the sprint failed because the scope was increased.**
Correct. The team achieved a velocity of four story points per day, which can be calculated by dividing the total completed story points by the number of days in the sprint: 40 / 10 = 4 points per day. The blue line on the chart represents the target story points for the sprint, which indicates that the sprint scope was increased from 40 story points to 45 points and then 50 points. Had the original scope of 40 points not been increased, the project team would likely have achieved the sprint goal.

Explanation:
The blue line on the burnup chart represents the target number of story points for the sprint. The orange line represents a running total of the number of story points actually earned by the project team. On the last day of the sprint (Day 10), the orange line terminates at 40, indicating that the team completed a total of 40 story points for the sprint. To calculate the daily velocity for the sprint, divide the number of total completed story points by the number of days in the sprint, which would be 40 points / 10 days = four points per day. The blue line indicates that on Day 10, the target was 50 points. Since the team did not reach the 50 story points, the sprint has failed. In addition, the blue line indicates that the target increased during the sprint from 40 points to 45 and then to 50. Had the scope not been increased and remained at 40 story points for the entire sprint, the team would likely have achieved the sprint goal since they completed 40 story points.

Note: typically, sprint scope (number of story points to be completed in a sprint) remains unchanged. However, under some circumstances, the scope may change, such as implied by the burnup chart provided in the scenario.

Reference:
Agile Practice Guide – First Edition, Project Management Institute Inc., 2017, Page(s) 63-64

https://www.projectmanagement.com/blog-post/40731/Burndown-vs-Burnup-Chart

Question 12: Answer

iA12

Inspection shows that roughly 72% of your products are produced defect free.

What sigma level does this finding represent?

- **A) 1 sigma**
- B) 2 sigma
- C) 3 sigma
- D) 4 sigma

Explanation:
1 sigma = 68.27%, 2 sigma = 95.45%, 3 sigma =99.73%, 6 sigma = 99.99%. Even though 72% is not an exact sigma value, it is the closest value to the choice A. Therefore, of the choices provided, 1 sigma is the best answer to the question asked.

Question 13: Answer

iA13

A project manager meets with company executives to apprise them of value gain progress on the project. To make it easier for the executives to understand the various earned value metrics without complex formulas and calculations, the project manager draws a chart, as shown below. The date of the meeting is indicated by "Today" on the X-axis.

What is the cost variance (CV) of the project?

(On the real PMP exam you may be asked to provide your answer by clicking the correct area in the image. But here in the book, we are asking you to select the answer below.)

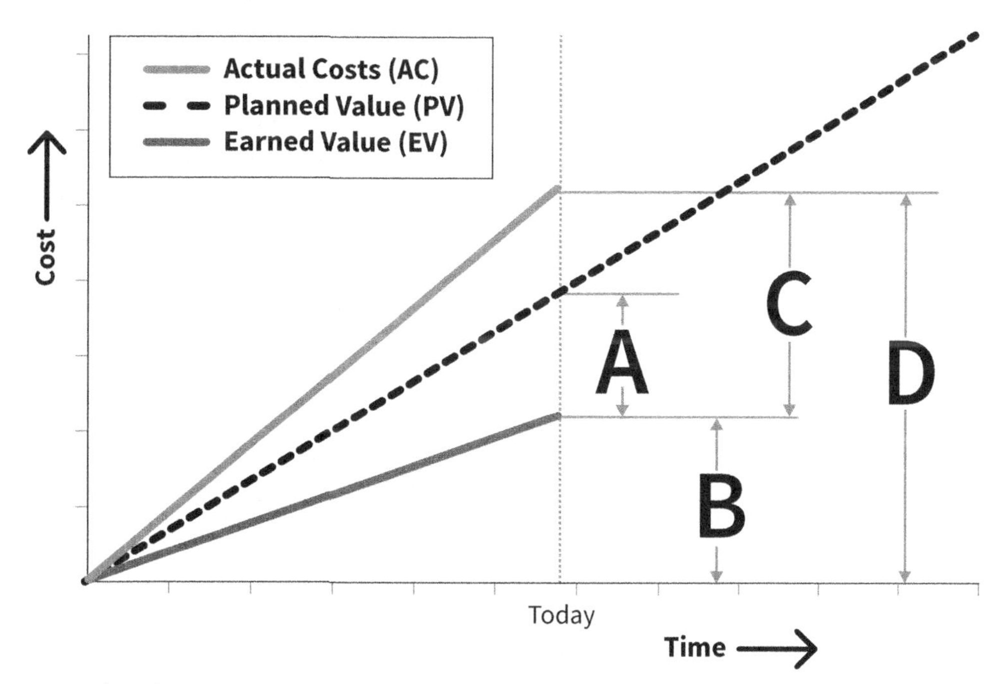

A) A
Incorrect. Area A represents the difference between the earned value (EV) and the planned value (PV). The difference between the earned value (EV) and the planned value (PV) is the schedule variance (SV), not the cost variance (CV), as asked by the question. Hence, this choice represents an incorrect answer.

B) B
Incorrect. Area B represents the earned value (EV) as of "Today", the date of the meeting. The question is asking to determine the cost variance (CV) of the project. The CV is the difference between the earned value (EV) and the actual costs (AC), rather than just the earned value. Therefore, this choice is an incorrect answer.

☑ **C) C**
Correct. Area C represents the difference between the earned value (EV) and the actual costs (AC). The cost variance (CV) of the project is the amount of budget deficit or surplus at a given point in time, expressed as the difference between the earned value (EV) and the actual cost (AC), making this choice the best answer to the question asked.

D) D
Incorrect. Area D represents the actual costs (AC) as of "Today", the date of the meeting. The question is asking to determine the cost variance (CV) of the project. The CV is the difference between the earned value (EV) and the actual costs (AC), rather than just the actual costs, making this choice an incorrect answer.

Explanation:
Earned value analysis (EVA) is an example of data analysis tools and techniques that can be used on a project to analyze its performance in terms of budget and schedule. The EVA compares the performance measurement baseline to the actual cost and schedule performance. Earned value analysis is typically associated with a more general term, earned value management (EVM), which is a methodology that combines scope, schedule, and resource measurements to assess project performance and progress.

To calculate its metrics, the EVA often uses various formulas. However, operating with the formulas and values that result from them may sometimes be difficult for project stakeholders (such as the executives in the scenario described) who are less familiar with the formulas. Therefore, to make it easier for such stakeholders, a visual representation of the value gain progress may be useful.

The question is asking to find the cost variance (CV) of the project.

CV is the amount of budget deficit or surplus at a given point in time, expressed as the difference between the earned value (EV) and the actual cost (AC):

CV = EV - AC

On the chart, the CV can be determined by the height of the section on the vertical dotted line (indicated by "Today") between the curves representing the actual costs and the earned value. It can be seen that the EV is lower than the AC, making CV a negative number. A negative CV means the project is over budget.

Reference:
A Guide to the Project Management Body of Knowledge, (PMBOK® Guide) – Sixth Edition, Project Management Institute Inc., 2017, Page(s) 262

Question 14: Answer

iA14

An agile coach facilitates a project retrospective and reviews the project performance metrics attained at various points throughout the project life cycle.

How can the agile coach describe each of the metrics? (In your exam, on a question like this, you would be asked to drag and drop the items to create matching pairs. In this book, please arrange the answers in the correct order.)

Correct Answers:

Answer choices	Answers
The cost performance index (CPI)	**The ratio of earned value to the actual cost**
A schedule performance index (SPI)	**The ratio of earned value to planned value**
The schedule variance (SV)	**The amount by which the project is ahead or behind schedule**
The cost variance (CV)	**The amount of budget surplus or deficit at a given point in time**
The project team's velocity	**The sum of story points completed for a particular iteration**

Explanation:

There are many performance metrics that can be applied to a particular project. Understanding the metrics and what they mean for the project allows a project leader to take the appropriate action in a timely manner. With this question, a particular metric is provided, and one must match the metric to a brief description of that metric.

- The cost performance index (CPI) is a measure of cost efficiency on a project and can be expressed as the ratio of earned value (EV) to actual cost (AC). The formula to calculate the CPI is EV / AC.
- The schedule performance index (SPI) is a measure of schedule efficiency for a project and can be expressed as the ratio of earned value (EV) to the planned value (PV). The formula for SPI is EV / PV.
- The schedule variance (SV) quantifies the amount by which a project is ahead or behind schedule. The SV can be calculated as earned value (EV) – planned value (PV). Negative SV means the project is behind schedule, positive SV indicates the project is ahead of schedule.
- The cost variance (CV) is the amount by which a project is over or under budget at a given point in time and can be obtained by comparing the earned value (EV) versus the actual cost (AC). The CV can be calculated as EV – AC.
- Velocity represents the units of work completed during a given timeframe. The most common unit of measure on agile projects is a story point, and the typical timeframe is an iteration (or sprint). For example, if a team completed 23 story points for an iteration, their velocity for that iteration would be 23. Alternatively, velocity could be expressed as the average number of story points completed per iteration.

Reference:

A Guide to the Project Management Body of Knowledge, (PMBOK® Guide) – Sixth Edition, Project Management Institute Inc., 2017, Page(s) 261-267

Agile Practice Guide – First Edition, Project Management Institute Inc., 2017, Page(s) 61, 69

iA15

Question 15: Answer

Every sprint planning meeting, the team commits to 40 story points. However, after completing the first five sprints, the team's velocity is only 35 story points per sprint. An agile coach determines that the earned schedule exceeds the actual time.

What is the best course of action for the agile coach? (Choose two.)

A) Ask the project sponsor for approval to add another developer to the project team
Incorrect. The fact that the earned schedule (ES) exceeds the actual time (AT) means that the project is running ahead of schedule. Adding

resources will increase costs for the project. Since the project deadline is not currently at risk, there is no reason to incur the incremental expense of adding another developer.

B) Allow the testers to begin testing partially completed user stories and not to wait until they are finished
Incorrect. This answer choice describes fast tracking, a schedule compression technique that involves running tasks in parallel that were originally planned to be run sequentially. Fast tracking can shorten the schedule duration but also increases risk. Testing partially completed deliverables would increase the risk of rework. The fact that earned schedule (ES) exceeds actual time (AT) means that the project is running ahead of schedule. Thus, there is no reason to increase project risk by fast tracking the testing.

☑ **C) Discuss the topic during the next retrospective and suggest being less aggressive during sprint planning**
Correct. Earned schedule (ES) exceeding the actual time (AT) means the team is trending to complete the project ahead of schedule. The real issue is that the team has failed to achieve the sprint goal, implying the team members are overcommitting when establishing the sprint goal. This issue should be brought up during the retrospective with a recommendation to be less aggressive with their commitments.

☑ **D) Stress the importance of achieving the sprint goal and suggest committing to fewer story points during sprint planning**
Correct. During sprint planning, an agile team commits to a sprint goal – the number of story points to be completed during the sprint. Meeting this commitment is imperative. In the scenario, the earned schedule (ES) exceeds the actual time (AT), meaning the team is trending to complete the project ahead of schedule. This situation suggests that the team overcommits during sprint planning and should consider being less aggressive with their commitments.

E) Inform the stakeholders that the project is running behind schedule and request that the product owner reduce the scope
Incorrect. When using the concept of earned schedule, the schedule variance (SV) can be calculated as earned schedule (ES) less the actual time (AT). A positive SV means the project is ahead of schedule. Therefore, there is no reason to believe that the scope will need to be reduced in order to complete the project on time.

Explanation:
Earned schedule is an alternative method used in earned value management to evaluate schedule performance. When using the earned schedule methodology, the schedule variance (SV) can be expressed as earned schedule (ES) less actual time (AT). The scenario states that the ES exceeds AT. Thus, the schedule variance is a positive value, which means the team is running ahead of schedule. With a velocity of 35 story points per sprint, the team is completing fewer story points than committed but more story points than is required to complete the project on time. The only real problem inferred from the scenario is that the team members have been failing to achieve the sprint goals they set for themselves.

The fact that the team's velocity is greater than required and that the team consistently failed to achieve its sprint goal suggests that the team members are overcommitting when determining their sprint goal. It would be appropriate for the agile coach to encourage the team to be less aggressive when establishing their sprint goal, which is reflected in the two correct answer choices. The incorrect answer choices misidentify the core issue by mistakenly assuming that the project is running behind schedule while, in fact, it's running ahead of schedule.

Reference:
A Guide to the Project Management Body of Knowledge, (PMBOK® Guide) – Sixth Edition, Project Management Institute Inc., 2017, Page(s) 231, 47

Agile Practice Guide – First Edition, Project Management Institute Inc., 2017, Page(s) 61, 69

Question 16: Answer

Your project has an SPI of 1.1 and a CPI of 0.9.

What does this mean?

☑ **A) The project is over budget and ahead of schedule**
B) The project is ahead of schedule but under budget
C) The project is over budget and behind schedule
D) The project is behind schedule and under budget

Explanation:
A schedule performance index (SPI) of greater than 1 means that we are ahead of schedule because the work is progressing at a rate of greater than what was planned. A cost performance index (CPI) of <1 means that the project is over budget because we are getting less value for the money spent than what we had planned.

Question 17: Answer

The following burnup chart shows the team's progress for the project. At Sprint 9 review, the product owner rejects the deliverables.

What can be said of the project's velocity per sprint between Sprints 8 and 9?

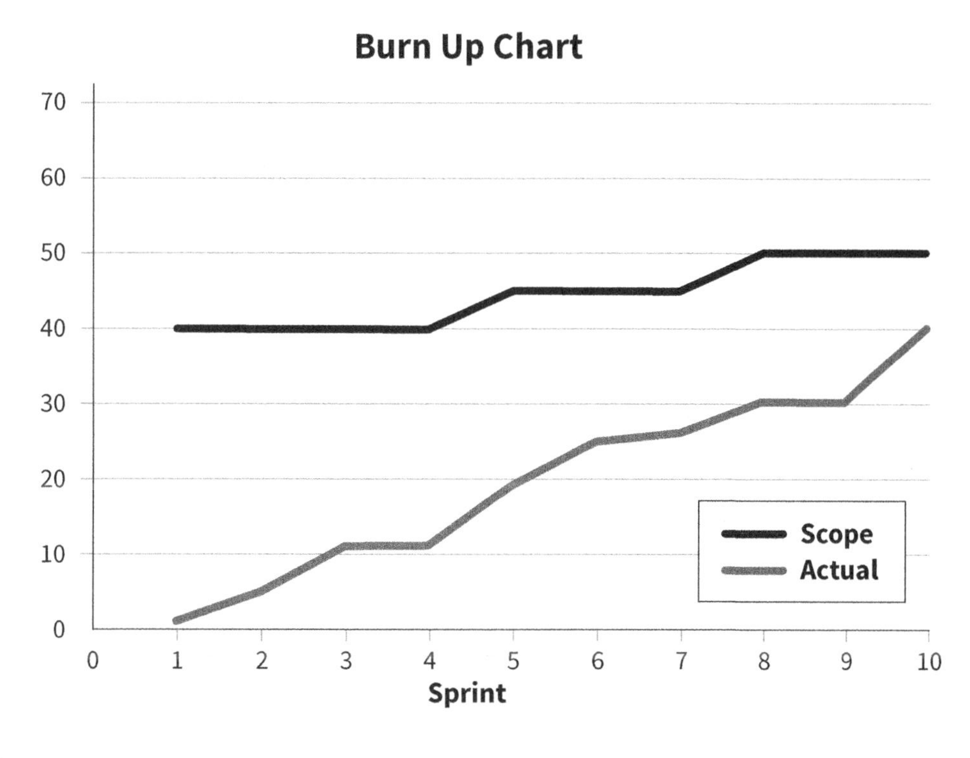

☑ **A) Decreased from 3.75 to 3.33**
Correct. The velocity can be calculated as the number of story points successfully completed by the project team divided by the number of sprints. The team had completed 30 story points by the end of Sprint 8 and remained at 30 points for Sprint 9. 30 / 8 = 3.75; and 30 / 9 = 3.33. Thus, between Sprints 8 and 9, velocity decreased from 3.75 to 3.33.

B) Remained the same at 30 story points
Incorrect. The team had completed 30 story points by this point in the project. However, the 30 story points represent the total number of story points completed rather than the velocity per sprint. Velocity per sprint is calculated as the number of story points successfully completed by the project team divided by the number of sprints.

C) Decreased from 6.25 to 5.56
Incorrect. If one used the story points associated with the curve that represents the planned scope for Sprints 8 and 9, then the result might have been 6.25 and 5.56. However, velocity calculations should be based

upon the actual results produced by the project team rather than the planned scope.

D) Remained stable at 50 story points
Incorrect. It is the planned scope, not velocity per sprint, that was stable at 50 story points between Sprint 8 and 9. The velocity should be based upon the actual performance rather than the planned scope. Velocity per sprint is the number of story points completed divided by the number of sprints over which these points have been completed.

Explanation:
In order to answer this question correctly, one must calculate the velocity for Sprints 8 and 9. Velocity can be calculated as the story points completed divided by the number of sprints. The burnup chart indicates that by Sprint 8, the team completed 30 story points, and for Sprint 9, the team remained at 30 story points. For Sprint 8, the velocity can be calculated as 30 / 8, which is 3.75. For Sprint 9, the velocity can be calculated as 30 / 9, which is 3.33. Therefore, the velocity decreased from 3.75 to 3.33.

Note: the fact the product owner rejected the deliverables produced during Sprint 9 does not affect the selection of the correct answer. This fact only confirms the point already reflected on the burnup chart that the number of story points completed by the team between Sprint 8 and 9 was zero. Reason: only those deliverables (user stories) accepted by the relevant stakeholders (the product owner in the scenario provided) can be counted towards velocity.

Reference:
Agile Practice Guide – First Edition, Project Management Institute Inc., 2017, Page(s) 63-64
https://www.projectmanagement.com/blog-post/40731/Burndown-vs-Burnup-Chart

Question 18: Answer

Using the Benefit Cost Ratio, which of the following projects do you select?

A) Project Gold with a BCR of 0.9
B) Project Silver with a CBR of 0.9 and cost of $100,000
C) Project Diamond with a cost of $100,000 and benefits of $110,000
☑ **D) Project Platinum with a BCR of 1.2**

Explanation:
The higher the BCR the better. Project Platinum has the highest BCR of 1.2 and should be selected if you rely only on the BCR. Here is why:

Project Gold has a BCR of 0.9, so it is clearly less than Project Platinum's 1.2.

Project Silver has a CBR of 0.9 and a cost of 100,000. We cannot compare a CBR to a BCR. We have to first calculate its BCR. This is a two-step process: First, you have to calculate the benefits by dividing the cost by the ratio: 100,000 / 0.9 = 111,111. Now you calculate the BCR by dividing the benefits by the cost: 111,111 / 100,000 = 1.11. Now we see that project Silver has a BCR of 1.11 which is less than Project Platinum's 1.2.

Project Diamond doesn't give us the BCR. So, we have to calculate it by dividing the benefits by the cost: 110,000 / 100,000 = 1.1. Now we see that project Diamond has a BCR of 1.1 which is less than Project Platinum's 1.2.

Question 19: Answer

iA19

After four sprints, an agile project has completed five features worth 80 story points. Each story point has a budgeted value of $900 for a BAC of $144,000. The agile coach believes the current cost performance will continue for the remainder of the project and, based on this assumption, calculates a variance at completion (VAC) of -$5,000.

Of the following, which actions should the agile coach consider taking? (Choose two.)

A) Take no action as the project is trending to complete all planned features under budget
Incorrect. The formula to calculate the variance at completion (VAC) is budget at completion (BAC) – estimate at completion (EAC). In this scenario, the VAC is a negative value, which means that EAC exceeds BAC. Thus, the project is running over budget, and action needs to be taken in order to complete the project within the established budget.

☑ **B) Apply value stream mapping to eliminate waste and reduce actual cost (AC)**
Correct. A negative value for the VAC means that the project is trending to run over budget. Hence, the cost performance needs to be improved. The CPI can be calculated using the formula CPI = EV / AC. Increasing EV and/or decreasing AC will improve cost performance. Reducing waste to reduce AC is a viable strategy to improve cost performance.

C) Maintain the current cost performance index (CPI) for the remainder of the project
Incorrect. VAC can be calculated as VAC = BAC – EAC. In this scenario, the VAC is a negative value, meaning that EAC exceeds BAC, i.e., the project is running over budget. The CPI is a measure of cost performance. Therefore, maintaining the current CPI would likely mean that the project will not be completed within the current budget.

D) Submit a change request to increase the budget at completion (BAC)
Incorrect. Agile projects, like the one implied by the scenario, do not typically use a formal change management system. Regardless, increasing the BAC would not address the issue at hand, i.e., cost overruns. Project leaders should seek proactive solutions to resolve problems rather than adjust project parameters to submit to poor performance.

☑ **E) At the sprint retrospective, ask the team for suggestions to increase the earned value (EV)**
Correct. With the provided negative VAC, the project is running over budget. Hence, to complete on budget, the cost performance must be improved. Since the CPI = EV / AC, increasing EV or decreasing AC would improve the result. Using the retrospective to brainstorm strategies to increase EV would be a viable option to bridge the budget gap.

Explanation:
The question provides a great deal of project performance information, most of which is not needed to answer the question correctly. It is important to remember that questions on the real exam may contain superfluous information, and the aspirant will need to determine what information is relevant and what is not. In this case, what is relevant in answering the question is that the variance at completion (VAC) is negative. VAC calculation formula is:

VAC = budget at completion (BAC) - estimate at completion (EAC)

A negative value for VAC means that EAC exceeds BAC and the project is running over budget.

Since the project is running over budget, action needs to be taken to improve the project's cost performance. The cost performance index (CPI) can be calculated using the formula **CPI = earned value (EV) / actual cost (AC).**

Increasing EV and/or decreasing AC will improve cost performance. The correct answer choices represent strategies that might increase EV or reduce AC and are viable options to get the project's cost performance back into alignment with the project objectives.

Reference:
A Guide to the Project Management Body of Knowledge, (PMBOK® Guide) - Sixth Edition, Project Management Institute Inc., 2017, Page(s) 262, 267

Agile Practice Guide - First Edition, Project Management Institute Inc., 2017, Page(s) 61, 69

Question 20: Answer

iA20

In preparation for the meeting with the company executives, a program manager reviews the cost and schedule performance metrics for the projects in the program she is overseeing.

What shall the program manager report to the company executives? (In your exam, on a question like this, you would be asked to drag and drop the items to create matching pairs. In this book, please arrange the answers in the correct order.)

Correct Answers:

Answer choices	Answers
Project Alpha has a CPI of 0.8	**The project is running over budget**
Project Bravo has an SPI of 0.9	**The project is at risk of jeopardizing its deadline**
Project Charlie has a CV of $2,000	**The project currently has a budget surplus**
Project Delta has an SPI of 1.0	**The project is on track to complete on time**
Project Echo has an SV of 25 story points	**The project will likely be completed early**

Explanation:

There are many performance metrics that can be applied to a particular project. Understanding the metrics and what they mean for the project allows a project leader to take the appropriate action in a timely manner. With this question, a particular metric is provided, and one must match the metric to what it means for the project's performance.

- Project Alpha has a CPI of 0.8. The cost performance index (CPI) is a measure of cost efficiency on a project and can be expressed as the ratio of earned value (EV) to actual cost (AC). The formula to calculate the **CPI is EV / AC.** With a CPI of 0.8, the project has only earned $0.80 on the dollar (assuming the project is denominated in dollars), which means the project is running over budget.
- Project Bravo has an SPI of 0.9. The schedule performance index (SPI) is a measure of schedule efficiency for a project and can be expressed as the ratio of earned value (EV) to the planned value (PV). The formula for determining **SPI is EV / PV.** In this case, project Bravo has only earned 90% of the planned value. Thus, if the current schedule performance continues unchanged, the project will not complete all of

the planned work by the deadline. In other words, the project is at risk of jeopardizing its deadline.

- Project Charlie has a CV of $2,000. The cost variance (CV) is the amount by which a project is over or under budget at a given point in time by comparing the earned value (EV) versus the actual cost (AC). The **CV can be calculated as EV - AC.** In this case, project Charlie has earned $2,000 more of the budget than has actually been spent. Therefore, the project currently has a budget surplus of $2,000.
- Project Delta has an SPI of 1.0. The schedule performance index (SPI) is a measure of schedule efficiency for a project and can be expressed as the ratio of earned value (EV) to the planned value (PV). The formula for calculating the **SPI is EV / PV.** When a project has an SPI of 1.0, the earned value is equal to the planned value, which means the project is trending to complete on time.
- Project Echo has an SV of 25 story points. A story point represents a unit of measure for work. Story points are commonly used in agile projects. The schedule variance (SV) quantifies the amount by which a project is ahead or behind schedule. The **SV can be calculated as earned value (EV) - planned value (PV).** In this case, project Echo has completed 25 story points more than planned for this point in the project. Thus, the project is running ahead of schedule and is trending to be completed early.

Reference:

A Guide to the Project Management Body of Knowledge, (PMBOK® Guide) – Sixth Edition, Project Management Institute Inc., 2017, Page(s) 261-267

Agile Practice Guide – First Edition, Project Management Institute Inc., 2017, Page(s) 61, 69

https://www.projectmanagement.com/blog-post/39925/Earned-Value-Management--EVM--in-Scrum

iA21

Question 21: Answer

Which of the following two projects should be selected if the goal of the company is to maximize the return on investment?

Project	NPV	IRR
A	2,581	29%
B	4,313	25%

☑ **A) Project A because the IRR is 29%**
B) Project A because the NPV is 2,581
C) Project B because the IRR is 25%
D) Project B because the NPV 4,313

Explanation:
Since the selection criteria is a higher return on investment, in other words higher IRR, the project with higher IRR should be selected. In this case, project A should be selected as it has the highest IRR.

Question 22: Answer

iA22

An agile coach needs to provide a revised estimate at completion (EAC) to the sponsor. The project backlog consists of user stories totaling 300 story points. The budget at completion (BAC) was initially established at $300,000. The development team has completed 100 story points with expenditures totaling $100,000 and a cost performance index (CPI) of 1.0.

What options for determining the EAC should the agile coach consider? (Choose three.)

☑ **A) Assuming that the cost performance will remain the same for the remainder of the project, divide the BAC by the CPI**
Correct. One method of calculating the EAC is BAC / CPI. When using this formula, the assumption is that the cost performance will not change for the remainder of the project. With the numbers provided in the scenario: EAC = $300,000 / 1.0 = $300,000. The EAC is equal to BAC because the project is proceeding exactly on budget with a CPI of 1.0.

☑ **B) Assuming the remaining work will be completed at the planned rate, subtract the earned value from the BAC and add the actual cost**
Correct. Estimate at completion (EAC) can be calculated as actual cost (AC) + budget at completion (BAC) – earned value (EV). This formula should be used when one assumes that the remaining work will be completed at the planned rate. Although performing the calculations is not necessary to answer the question correctly, the EAC can be expressed as $100,000 + $300,000 – $100,000, which would be an EAC of $300,000.

C) Assuming the work is proceeding according to the original plan, subtract the actual cost from the estimate at completion
Incorrect. This answer choice describes a formula to determine the estimate to complete (ETC), which is estimate at completion (EAC) – actual cost (AC). Although this is the correct formula for ETC with

the assumption that the work will proceed according to the plan, the question asks for a method to calculate EAC rather than ETC.

☑ **D) If the original budget is no longer valid, re-estimate the cost for the remaining backlog items and add the actual costs**
Correct. When the original budget is fundamentally flawed, or conditions have changed, the estimate at completion (EAC) can be calculated as a bottom-up estimate to completion (ETC) + actual cost (AC). Once the cost for the remaining work has been estimated (ETC), the actual cost can be added to the ETC to determine the EAC.

E) Re-estimate the cost associated with the work items remaining in the project backlog and report this estimate as the EAC
Incorrect. This answer choice describes the estimate to complete (ETC) rather than the estimate at completion (EAC), as asked by the question. Re-estimating the cost associated with the remaining work is a valid method for determining the ETC. But to determine the EAC, one would need to include the money already spent (actual cost).

Explanation:
The *PMBOK® Guide* identifies four different methods for determining the estimate at completion (EAC). The decision for which method to use is based on the assumptions one is willing to make regarding future project performance. The correct answer choices describe assumptions and the correct formula that can be used to calculate the EAC based on those assumptions. The incorrect answer choices describe methods for calculating the estimate to complete (ETC) rather than the estimate at completion (EAC).

Note: answering this question correctly does not require any calculations. Rather, one only needs to identify valid methods for calculating the estimate at completion (EAC). The reason some of the explanations to the answer choices use the numbers provided in the scenario is solely to illustrate how the various formulas for calculating the EAC can be applied with the corresponding assumptions.

Reference:
A Guide to the Project Management Body of Knowledge, (PMBOK® Guide) – Sixth Edition, Project Management Institute Inc., 2017, Page(s) 264-265, 267

https://www.projectmanagement.com/blog-post/21177/A-Simple-Explanation-of-the-Earned-Value-Management-technique

Question 23: Answer

iA23

Your company has a very elaborate project selection method. You use multiple factors to determine if a project will be undertaken.

Which of the following factors is unlikely to be a part of this system?

A) Internal Rate of Return
B) Present Value
☑ **C) Pareto Analysis**
D) Benefit Cost Ratio

Explanation:
The Pareto Analysis cannot be used in project selection. It is an excellent tool to show distribution but has nothing to do with the problem at hand.

Question 24: Answer

iA24

A senior leader reviews the business cases for three different software development projects (Alpha, Beta, and Gamma). Project Alpha has an NPV of $100,000 and will take 10 sprints to complete. Project Beta has an NPV of $25,000 and will take 9 sprints to complete. Project Gamma has an NPV of -$125,000 and will take eight sprints to complete.

Assuming resources are available, what is the best course of action?

A) Approve project Alpha
Incorrect. Project Alpha should be approved as it has the highest NPV. However, since there are no resource constraints, project Beta should also be approved based on a positive NPV. Therefore, while this choice represents a correct answer, another answer choice addresses the question better and more complete.

☑ **B) Approve projects Alpha and Beta but reject Gamma**
Correct. Projects Alpha and Beta both have a positive net present value (NPV) and should be approved. Project Gamma has a negative NPV and should be rejected. Note: the scenario does not set any limitations of organizational resources. It says that resources are available, meaning approving all projects with positive NPV makes the most sense.

C) Approve project Gamma
Incorrect. Project Gamma has a negative net present value (NPV). A negative NPV means that the project will lose money. Thus, the company would most likely be better off financially by not moving forward with the project (unless there is a legal requirement, compliance issue, etc., which is unclear from the scenario provided).

D) Approve all three projects
Incorrect. Approving all three projects means going ahead with two projects that will likely make money because they have positive NPV and one that will lose because of a negative NPV. Therefore, based on NPV provided in the scenario, projects Alpha and Beta should be approved, while project Gamma should be rejected.

Explanation:
The net present value (NPV) represents the present value of all cash inflows minus the present value of all cash outflows. A positive NPV means the project would be financially advantageous for the organization and should be approved if the organization has the resources and ability to complete the project. A negative NPV means that the project is unprofitable and should be rejected unless there are special circumstances such as a legal requirement. In the scenario described, projects Alpha and Beta each have a positive NPV and should be approved since there are no resource constraints. Project Gamma should be rejected even if resources are available based on a negative NPV.

Note that the question also provides the number of sprints to complete the project. This information is superfluous as the time value of money is already taken into account with the NPV formula. Also, note that the actual formula to calculate NPV is complex and not likely to be required for the real exam.

Reference:
A Guide to the Project Management Body of Knowledge, (PMBOK® Guide) – Sixth Edition, Project Management Institute Inc., 2017, Page(s) 34, 152
https://www.pmi.org/learning/library/net-present-value-project-scheduling-5743

Question 25: Answer

An organization considers two projects but only has the resources to support one of them. Project Alpha will provide $100,000 in revenue annually for 10 years with an investment of $500,000. Project Beta will produce $75,000 in annual revenue for 10 years and will cost $500,000. Based on this information, the organization approves project Alpha and rejects Beta.

How did the organization most likely derive the metrics used in its decision-making process? (In your exam, on a question like this, you would be asked to drag and drop the items to create matching pairs. In this book, please arrange the answers in the correct order.)

Correct Answers:

Answer choices	Answers
$500,000 / ($100,000 * 10) = 0.5	**Cost-benefit ratio (CBR) of project Alpha**
$750,000 – $500,000 = $250,000	**Opportunity cost**
$500,000 / $100,000 = 5 years	**Payback period for project Alpha**
($100,000 * 10) / $500,000 = 2	**Benefit-cost ratio (BCR) of project Alpha**
$500,000 / ($75,000 * 10) = 0.67	**Cost-benefit ratio (CBR) of project Beta**
($75,000 * 10) / $500,000 = 1.5	**Benefit-cost ratio (BCR) of project Beta**
$500,000 / $75,000 = 6.67 years	**Payback period for project Beta**

Explanation:
When evaluating potential projects, various project success measures can be used to determine the best use of an organization's limited resources. Among these measures are the benefit-cost ratio (BCR), cost-benefit ratio (CBR), payback period, and opportunity cost. There are other metrics that an organization would likely review before approving a project, but those are beyond the scope of this particular question.

Correctly matching the pairs does not require performing any calculations. The calculations below are provided for illustration purposes.

- The cost-benefit ratio (CBR) describes the benefits versus the costs of a potential project. The CBR can be calculated as the cost of a project divided by the benefit. In this scenario, the cost for projects Alpha and Beta are both $500,000. The benefit would be the financial gain from completing the project. In the case of project Alpha, the project will generate $100,000 in revenue annually for 10 years, which is $1,000,000. Thus the CBR for project Alpha would be $500,000 / $1,000,000 = 0.5. The benefit for project Beta would be $75,000 in annual revenue for 10 years or $750,000. Applying the formula for CBR for project Beta would result in $500,000 / $750,000 = 0.67.
- The benefit-cost ratio (BCR) is just the reciprocal of the cost-benefit ratio (CBR). Thus, the BCR can be derived by taking the benefit divided by the cost. For project Alpha, the benefit would be the annual revenue of $100,000 for 10 years or $1,000,000. The cost is stated at $500,000. Therefore, $1,000,000 / $500,000 would be a BCR of 2 for project Alpha.

Similarly, the BCR for project Beta can be calculated as ($75,000 * 10) / $500,000 = 1.5.

- The opportunity cost is the benefit forgone by selecting one option over another. In this scenario, project Beta has been rejected in favor of project Alpha because the organization can only support one of the potential projects. The benefit of project Beta was the $75,000 in annual revenue for 10 years for a total of $750,000. However, it will cost $500,000 to gain the $750,000, so the net profit of project Beta is $750,000 – $500,000 or $250,000. Thus, the organization is giving up $250,000 in profit as an opportunity cost for selecting project Alpha.
- Payback period is the time it takes to recover the initial investment by adding up all future cash flows until they are equal to the initial investment. In this scenario, the payback period for the selected project (project Alpha) can be calculated by dividing the project cost by the annual revenue, which would be $500,000 / $100,000 per year = 5 years. Similarly, the payback period for project Beta (assuming it was selected) would be $500,000 / $75,000 per year = 6.67 years.

Reference:

A Guide to the Project Management Body of Knowledge, (PMBOK® Guide) – Sixth Edition, Project Management Institute Inc., 2017, Page(s) 34

https://www.projectmanagement.com/blog-post/4677/What-is-Payback-Period-

https://www.projectmanagement.com/blog-post/4081/What-is-BCR-

Question 26: Answer

A project manager meets with company executives to apprise them of value gain progress on the project. To make it easier for the executives to understand the various earned value metrics without complex formulas and calculations, the project manager draws a chart, as shown below. The date of the meeting is indicated by "Today" on the X-axis.

What is the earned value (EV) of the project?

(On the real PMP exam you may be asked to provide your answer by clicking the correct area in the image. But here in the book, we are asking you to select the answer below.)

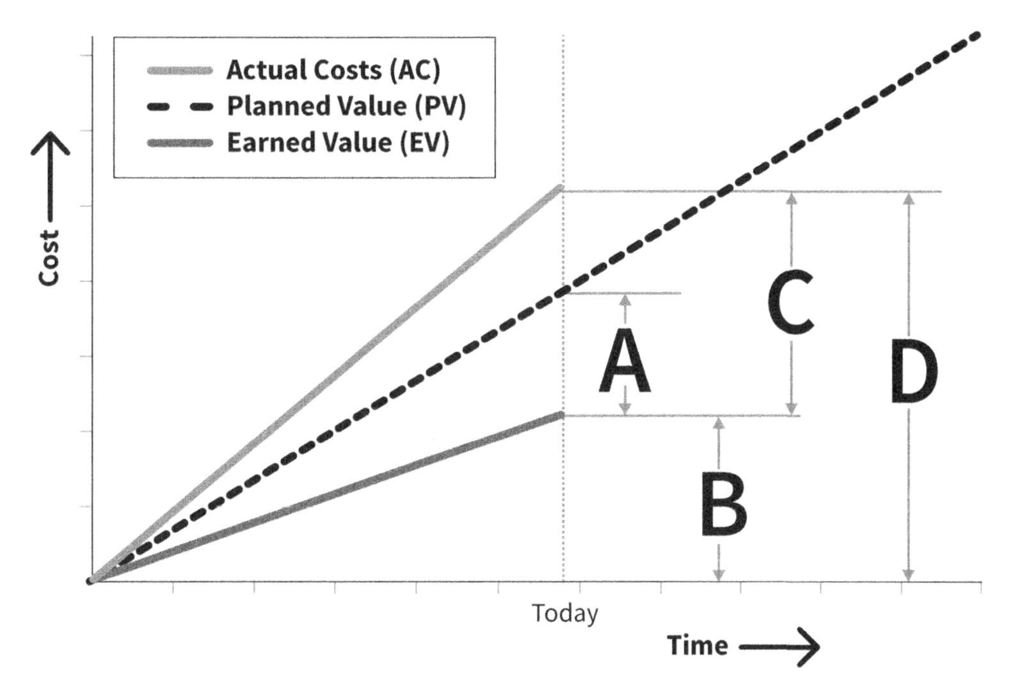

A) A
Incorrect. Area A represents the difference between the earned value (EV) and the planned value (PV). The difference between the earned value (EV) and the planned value (PV) is the schedule variance (SV), not the earned value, as asked by the question. Hence, this choice represents an incorrect answer.

☑ **B) B**
Correct. Area B represents the earned value (EV) as of "Today", the date of the meeting. The question asks to find the earned value on the chart, which is exactly what this answer choice represents, making it the best answer to the question asked.

C) C
Incorrect. Area C represents the difference between the earned value (EV) and the actual costs (AC). The difference between the earned value (EV) and the actual cost (AC) is the cost variance (CV) of the project. However, the question simply asks to find the current earned value of the project. Hence, this choice is an incorrect answer.

D) D
Incorrect. Area D represents the actual costs (AC) as of "Today", the date of the meeting. The question asks to find the current earned value (EV) of the project rather than the actual costs (AC), making this choice an incorrect answer.

Explanation:
Earned value analysis (EVA) is an example of data analysis tools and techniques that can be used on a project to analyze its performance in terms of budget and schedule. The EVA compares the performance measurement baseline to the actual cost and schedule performance. Earned value analysis is typically associated with a more general term, earned value management (EVM), which is a methodology that combines scope, schedule, and resource measurements to assess project performance and progress.

To calculate its metrics, the EVA often uses various formulas. However, operating with the formulas and values that result from them may sometimes be difficult for project stakeholders (such as the executives in the scenario described) who are less familiar with the formulas. Therefore, to make it easier for such stakeholders, a visual representation of the value gain progress may be useful.

The question is asking to find the earned value (EV) of the project. The EV is a measure of work performed expressed in terms of the budget authorized for that work. Finding the earned value does not require any calculations or formulas. The earned value is already given on the chart: it is simply the height of the section on the vertical dotted line (indicated by "Today") between the X-axis and the curve representing the earned value.

Reference:
A Guide to the Project Management Body of Knowledge, (PMBOK® Guide) – Sixth Edition, Project Management Institute Inc., 2017, Page(s) 262

Question 27: Answer

You are in the procurement process for a high-tech product that is needed for your current project. You have sent out an RFP to several vendors and you expect a target price of about £10,000. The first estimate has arrived this morning. You open the envelope and you see that the vendor is offering the product to you at a cost of £9,500 – £11,000.

What type of estimate have you received from this vendor?

A) Preliminary estimate
✓ **B) Definitive estimate**
C) Rough order of magnitude estimate
D) Final estimate

Explanation:
For the PMP exam you must know the following estimate types as well as percent ranges:

- Rough order of magnitude estimate -25% to +75 *(PMBOK® Guide)*
- Preliminary estimate -15% to +50%
- Budget estimate -10% to +25%
- Definitive estimate -5% to +10%
- Final estimate 0%

Since your expected target price was around £10,000 you can easily see that the definite estimate of -5% and +10% is what you received from the vendor.

Question 28: Answer

iA28

An agile project is being performed by a virtual team. The project manager calculates the schedule and cost efficiency and finds that the schedule performance index (SPI) is 0.85 and the cost performance index (CPI) is 1.35.

What actions should the project manager consider to meet the project goals? (Choose two.)

A) Do nothing because the project is behind schedule but well under budget
Incorrect. Completing a project on schedule and budget are among the typical project goals. An SPI of 0.85 and a CPI of 1.35 means the project is running behind schedule but under budget. If no action is taken and the SPI does not change for the remainder of the project, one of the project goals, being on schedule, won't be achieved.

☑ **B) Colocate the development team for a limited time in order to increase velocity**
Correct. The SPI less than 1.0 means the project is running behind schedule. By facilitating better collaboration and shortening feedback loops, colocation can improve the team's productivity and velocity, thus bringing the project back on track. While colocation will likely increase cost, with the project running under budget (CPI is greater than 1.0), there should be additional funds available to pay for the colocation expense for some period of time.

☑ **C) Add another developer to the team to expedite the completion of project work**
Correct. With a CPI of 1.35 and an SPI of 0.85, the project is trending to complete late but under budget. Adding another developer should increase the velocity to help complete the project on time. Since the project is running under budget, cost savings may be used to cover (completely or partially) the cost of the additional resources.

D) Ask the product owner to add scope to take advantage of the team's excess capacity
Incorrect. The metrics provided in the scenario imply the project is trending behind schedule and under budget. Therefore, while there are excess funds, the project schedule is at risk. Hence, adding scope will likely delay project completion even further, making this choice an incorrect answer.

E) Reduce cost by releasing one of the project team members early
Incorrect. This answer would be a plausible option if one incorrectly interpreted the metrics provided in the scenario. The CPI of 1.35 means the project is under budget and does not need to reduce costs. Releasing a developer would only further delay the project's completion, which is already behind schedule as indicated by the SPI of less than 1.0.

Explanation:
The first step in answering this question correctly is to determine the current status of the project. The provided schedule performance index (SPI) and cost performance index (CPI) indicates that the project is running behind schedule and under budget. Thus, the project manager should be investigating options that will speed up delivery and bring the project completion in alignment with its original schedule. The fact that the project is under budget represents an opportunity to apply some of the excess budgeted funds to actions that might increase velocity. Both correct answer choices describe options that might increase velocity and are viable options at the expense of increased costs. The incorrect answer choices are based on an incorrect interpretation of the project status.

Reference:
A Guide to the Project Management Body of Knowledge, (PMBOK® Guide) – Sixth Edition, Project Management Institute Inc., 2017, Page(s) 263, 267

Agile Practice Guide – First Edition, Project Management Institute Inc., 2017, Page(s) 69

Question 29: Answer

A company reviews the various projects that are currently underway as well as potential projects under consideration. Projects A, B, and C are all roughly halfway complete. Projects D and E are both at the pre-project stage.

Based only on the metrics provided, what is the best course of action for the company? (In your exam, on a question like this, you would be asked to drag and drop the items to create matching pairs. In this book, please arrange the answers in the correct order.)

Correct Answers:

Answer choices	Answers
Project A has a CPI of 1.2 and an SPI of 0.8	**Approve the use of overtime**
Project B has a CPI of 0.8 and an SPI of 1.2	**Release a member of the project team early**
Project C has a CPI of 1.0 and an SPI of 1.0	**No action is needed at this time**
Project D has a cost-benefit ratio (CBR) of 0.8	**Approve the project**
Project E has a benefit-cost ratio (BCR) of 0.8	**Reject the project**

Explanation:

Various project performance metrics can be utilized to gain insight into how a current project is progressing or a potential project is evaluated. This information can be used to determine what actions are appropriate to take. In this scenario, performance metrics have been provided for current projects and evaluation metrics for potential projects. To answer this question correctly, one must review the information provided, interpret what the metric indicates about the project, and then select the most appropriate response of the options provided.

- Project A has a CPI of 1.2 and an SPI of 0.8. These metrics indicate that the project is currently trending under budget and behind schedule. To get the project back on track with project objectives, action should be taken to increase productivity. Adding resources, which may include the use of overtime, should improve productivity and shorten the project schedule. The fact that the project is running under budget suggests that the project can absorb some increase in expenditures without running over budget.
- Project B has a CPI is 0.8 and an SPI of 1.2. This situation indicates that the project is running over budget and ahead of schedule. As a result, action needs to be taken to reduce expenses. Reducing the size of the project team should reduce cost, but this will likely negatively impact the schedule. Since the project is running ahead of schedule, the schedule can be delayed to some extent without risking the planned delivery date.

- Project C has both the CPI and SPI equal to 1.0, which means the project is currently running exactly on schedule and budget. This situation implies that no immediate action is necessary to keep the project on track.
- Projects D and E are both stated as being in the pre-project stage, which means that the projects have yet to be initiated. Various project success measures can be used to determine whether to approve or reject a particular project. Included among these common project success measures are the cost-benefit ratio (CBR) and the benefit-cost ratio (BCR). Both of these metrics describe cost versus benefit, with one just being the reciprocal of the other. The CBR can be calculated as cost divided by benefit (C/B), whereas the BCR would be the benefit divided by the cost (B/C). In financial terms, a CBR of less than 1.0 would mean that the cost is less than the benefit, i.e., the project is profitable. A BCR of less than 1.0 would indicate that the benefit is less than the cost, i.e., the project would not be profitable. Therefore, of these two projects, it would make the most sense to approve project D and reject project E.

Reference:
A Guide to the Project Management Body of Knowledge, (PMBOK® Guide) – Sixth Edition, Project Management Institute Inc., 2017, Page(s) 34, 263

iA30

Question 30: Answer

What information does the EAC contain?

A) The cost of the work to be performed to finish the project
B) The value of the work that has already been performed
C) The cost of the work that was completed
☑ **D) The expected total cost of our project once it is finished**

Explanation:
The EAC is the estimate at completion. It represents the estimated cost of the total project upon completion.

Question 31: Answer

A project has completed six sprints. The entire project backlog has been estimated at 250 story points, and each point is worth $1,200 of budgeted value. The project leader has calculated a cost performance index (CPI) of 0.92.

Based on this information, what else can be said of the project's performance? (Choose three.)

☑ **A) The CV must be a negative value**
Correct. The CPI is calculated as EV / AC. In the scenario, the CPI is 0.92. A CPI less than 1.0 means the project is running over budget. The cost variance (CV) is also calculated using EV and AC: CV = EV – AC, but provides a monetary amount for the variance rather than a ratio. To have a CPI of less than one, EV must be less than AC, implying the CV must be a negative value.

☑ **B) The TCPI is most likely greater than 1.0**
Correct. The to-complete performance index (TCPI) provides a measure for the cost performance that must be achieved for the remainder of the project to meet the project budget. The CPI of 0.92 means that the project is running over budget. Thus, to meet the budget, the project must run under budget to some extent for the remainder of the project. Since the project must achieve a cost performance greater than 1.0 for the remainder of the project, the TCPI should be greater than 1.0.

C) The SPI must be less than 1.0
Incorrect. The schedule performance index (SPI) can be expressed as earned value (EV) divided by the planned value (PV). In the scenario, there are 250 story points in the backlog, and each point is worth $1,200. However, no information is available about the completed story points. Without this information, there is no way to determine the SPI.

☑ **D) The VAC should be a negative value**
Correct. The variance at completion (VAC) is the difference between the budget at completion (BAC) and the current estimate at completion (EAC): VAC = BAC – EAC. With a CPI of 0.92, we know the project is trending to complete over budget, or, in other words, the EAC exceeds BAC. If EAC is greater than BAC, then the VAC would be a negative value.

E) The project is trending to complete under budget.
Incorrect. The cost performance index (CPI) is the ratio of earned value (EV) and actual cost (AC) or CPI = EV / AC. The scenario provides a CPI of 0.92, which means that the project has only earned $0.92 for every dollar spent. With the project earning less than is being spent, the project is trending to complete over budget rather than under budget.

Explanation:
The cost performance index (CPI) is the ratio of earned value (EV) and actual cost (AC). The formula to calculate CPI can be expressed as:

CPI = EV / AC

In the scenario, the CPI is stated as 0.92, which means that the project has only earned $0.92 for every dollar spent. With the project earning less than is being spent, the project is currently running over budget. The correct answer choices all represent metrics that are consistent with a project that is trending to finish over budget. The incorrect responses either mischaracterize the project as running under budget or are a metric that cannot be determined from the limited information provided.

Note that the only relevant information to answering this question correctly is the CPI of 0.92. The information provided regarding the number of sprints completed, total story points, and budgeted value per story point is superfluous. Questions on the real exam may contain superfluous information, and the aspirant will need to determine what information is and is not relevant.

Reference:
A Guide to the Project Management Body of Knowledge, (PMBOK® Guide) – Sixth Edition, Project Management Institute Inc., 2017, Page(s) 263, 267

Agile Practice Guide – First Edition, Project Management Institute Inc., 2017, Page(s) 69

iA32

Question 32: Answer

You are behind schedule when...

A) SPI = 1
B) SPI = -1
C) SPI > 1
☑ **D) SPI < 1**

Explanation:
The interpretation of the SPI is as follows:

- SPI = 1: The project is progressing at the planned rate.
- SPI = -1: There should never be negative SPIs; however, negative SPIs do on occasion occur when accounting adjustments are made. If observed, they should be questioned.
- SPI > 1: The project is progressing at a faster rate than planned.
- SPI < 1: The project is progressing at a slower rate than planned.

Question 33: Answer

A manufacturing company is considering two potential projects. Project A will streamline production based on a recent Kaizen event and provide an estimated ROI of $15,000. Project B will reduce downtime by replacing equipment on the production line and yield an estimated ROI of -$20,000. Project A has a backlog of 300 story points, and project B has a backlog of 250 story points. The company has sufficient resources to support both of the projects.

What is the company's best course of action?

A) Approve both projects
Incorrect. Even though the company has sufficient resources to support both projects, not all projects are profitable. In this case, project A has a positive return on investment (ROI), which means that it is profitable and should be approved. However, project B has a negative ROI, which means that the project is unprofitable and should be rejected.

☑ **B) Approve project A and reject project B**
Correct. Based solely on the provided return on investment (ROI) for each project, project A should be approved, and project B should be rejected. Project A has a positive ROI, which means that it will be financially beneficial for the company. Project B should be rejected as the negative ROI means that the project would be unprofitable to undertake.

C) Reject both projects
Incorrect. Project A has a positive return on investment (ROI) and should be approved if resources are available. Project B should be rejected as it is unprofitable with a negative ROI. Therefore, there is no reason to reject both projects since project A has a positive ROI, and the organization does have the resources to support the project.

D) Approve project B and reject project A
Incorrect. Even though the company has sufficient resources to fund project B, it should be rejected since it has a negative ROI, meaning the project is unprofitable. The company is financially better off incurring downtime as opposed to investing the money to replace the equipment. Project A should be accepted based on its positive ROI of $15,000.

Explanation:
When considering projects based on the return on investment (ROI), the organization should select the project(s) with the highest positive ROI. Projects with a negative ROI should be rejected as they would be unprofitable for the organization. In this case, project A should be approved based on the ROI of $15,000 and project B should be rejected based on the ROI of -$20,000 even though the company has the resources to support both projects. The question also provides the number of story points for each project, but that information is superfluous to answering the question correctly.

Note that there are circumstances in which a project with a negative ROI should be accepted such as for compliance with legal requirements, safety systems, social concerns, etc. However, in this case, there is no information to suggest that the company has a legal or ethical obligation to undertake project B.

Reference:
A Guide to the Project Management Body of Knowledge, (PMBOK® Guide) – Sixth Edition, Project Management Institute Inc., 2017, Page(s) 34
https://www.pmi.org/learning/library/measuring-project-management-roi-3562

iA34

Question 34: Answer

At the project retrospective, the project manager reviews each of the monthly status reports produced over the course of the project. Included in the reports are the various performance metrics.

What could be said of the project's past performance at those points? (In your exam, on a question like this, you would be asked to drag and drop the items to create matching pairs. In this book, please arrange the answers in the correct order.)

Correct Answers:

Answer choices	Answers
Month 1: SPI = 1.1	**The project was running ahead of schedule**
Month 2: CV = $0.00	**The project was progressing on budget**
Month 3: TCPI = 1.1	**The project was trending over budget**
Month 4: TCPI = 0.9	**The project was running under budget**
Month 5: SV = -$1,000	**The project was behind schedule**

Explanation:
In this scenario, the results of several different performance metrics are provided for the project's past performance. To answer the question correctly, one must interpret what the performance level means for the project as it relates to cost or schedule.

- The schedule performance index (SPI) can be calculated as earned value (EV) divided by the planned value (PV): **SPI = EV / PV.** An SPI of greater than 1.0 would mean that the project has earned more value than had been planned, which means the project is running ahead of schedule.
- The formula for cost variance (CV) is earned value (EV) minus actual cost (AC): **CV = EV – AC.** A CV of $0.00 means that the project has earned the

same amount as it has spent, and, therefore, the project is trending exactly on budget.

- The to-complete performance index (TCPI) is a measure of the cost performance that will be required for the remainder of the project to finish the remaining work within the budget. The formula for calculating TCPI is **TCPI = (BAC – EV) / (BAC – AC)** or **TCPI = (BAC – EV) / (EAC – AC)**, depending on whether the calculation is based on BAC or EAC. A TCPI of greater than 1.0 would mean that the project has been underperforming with respect to the budget and, to meet the budget, will need to over-perform going forward. Conversely, a TCPI of less than 1.0 would mean that the project is overperforming relative to the budget.
- The schedule variance (SV) can be calculated as earned value (EV) minus planned value (PV): **SV = EV – PV.** A negative value for SV means that the completed work was of less value than had been planned, which indicates that the project is behind schedule.

Reference:

A Guide to the Project Management Body of Knowledge, (PMBOK® Guide) – Sixth Edition, Project Management Institute Inc., 2017, Page(s) 261-267

https://www.projectmanagement.com/videos/550420/RPI---The-Third-Musketeer-in-the-Earned-Value-Framework

Question 35: Answer

iA35

How do you calculate the estimate to complete (ETC)?

A) You subtract the actual cost from estimate at completion

B) You subtract the budget at completion from the actual cost
C) You divide the budget at completion by the schedule performance index
D) You subtract the actual cost from the budget at completion

Explanation:

There are two formulas used in the *PMBOK® Guide* to calculate ETC and two orphan formulas* that are not used by *PMBOK® Guide* any longer to calculate ETC.

- **ETC = EAC – AC:** estimate at completion minus the actual cost to date. The result is a monetary value that tells us how much more the project will cost.
- **ETC = Re-estimate** (re-estimate the remaining work from the bottom up.)
- ***ETC = BAC – EV:** the planned budget minus the earned value. The result is a monetary value that tells us how much more the project will cost.

- ***ETC = (BAC – EV) / CPI:** the product of planned budget minus the earned value divided by cost performance index. Result is a monetary value that tells us how much more the project will cost.

* Orphaned formulas are formulas that do not appear in *PMBOK® Guide*. However, as the *PMBOK® Guide* is not the only reference source used by the PMI® to design their PMP exam questions, we have decided to keep the questions that use these formulas.

iA36

Question 36: Answer

A project team has completed eight sprints. The project backlog consists of 350 story points, and each point is worth $800 of budgeted value. The team has calculated a schedule performance index (SPI) of 0.87.

Based on this information, what else can be said of the project's performance? (Choose two.)

A) The CV must be a positive value
Incorrect. The cost variance (CV) can be calculated as the earned value (EV) less the actual cost (AC). The scenario does not provide information on how much of the project work has been completed nor how much funds have been spent. Without this information, there is no way to determine a value for the cost variance.

B) The CPI is greater than 1.0
Incorrect. The cost performance index (CPI) is a ratio of earned value (EV) and actual cost (AC): CPI = EV / AC. In the scenario, no information has been provided on how many of the 250 story points have been completed nor how much money has been spent. Without knowing the AV and AC values, calculating the CPI would be impossible.

C) The VAC must be a negative value
Incorrect. The variance at completion (VAC) is the difference between the budget at completion (BAC) and the estimate at completion (EAC): VAC = BAC – EAC. While we can calculate the BAC based on the total number of story points and budgeted value of each story point, we are not provided with any information regarding the cost performance.

☑ **D) The SV must be a negative value**
Correct. The schedule variance (SV) measures schedule performance and is calculated as SV = EV – PV. While EV and PV are unknown, the SPI is given as 0.87. The formula for SPI is EV / PV. An SPI of less than 1.0 means the project has earned less than planned at this point in the project, i.e., EV is less than PV. Since the EV is less than PV, the schedule variance must be a negative value.

☑ **E) The project is running behind schedule**
Correct. The scenario indicates that the schedule performance index (SPI) is 0.87. The formula to calculate SPI is SPI = earned value (EV) / planned value (PV). An SPI of less than 1.0 suggests that the project team has earned less than the planned value at this point in the project, meaning that the project is currently running behind schedule.

Explanation:
The schedule performance index (SPI) is a measure of schedule efficiency for the project. The question states that the SPI is 0.87 for the project. The formula to calculate SPI is SPI = earned value (EV) / planned value (PV):

SPI = EV / PV

An SPI less than 1.0 means the project team has completed (or earned) fewer story points than had been planned by this point in the project, which, in turn, indicates that the project is currently running behind schedule. The schedule variance (SV) also uses EV and PV in the calculation as follows:

SV = EV – PV

Since we know that EV is less than PV, the SV must be a negative value.

The incorrect answer choices all have to do with the cost performance of the project, and not enough information has been provided in the scenario to draw any conclusions regarding cost performance.

Reference:
A Guide to the Project Management Body of Knowledge, (PMBOK® Guide) – Sixth Edition, Project Management Institute Inc., 2017, Page(s) 263, 267

Agile Practice Guide – First Edition, Project Management Institute Inc., 2017, Page(s) 69

Question 37: Answer

iA37

Your project is to manufacture screws. Your production control limits are set from 2.51 grams to 2.58 grams. Your customer informs you that they would like to have the control limits set from 2.54 grams to 2.57 grams.

What do you tell your customer?

A) Thank you, we will change the control limits as required
B) I am sorry, but your specifications have to be =2.51 and =2.58
C) Please change your specifications to be less than 2.51 and less than 2.58
☑ **D) Please provide your specifications and we will statistically determine the appropriate control limits**

Explanation:
Control limits and specification limits are used in the context of a control chart, sometimes also called a Shewhart chart. The customer provides the specification limits, while the control limits are statistically determined and are based on the specification limits. As a general rule, customer specification limits have to be "looser" (or outside) of these limits.

Here is a sample of such a chart:

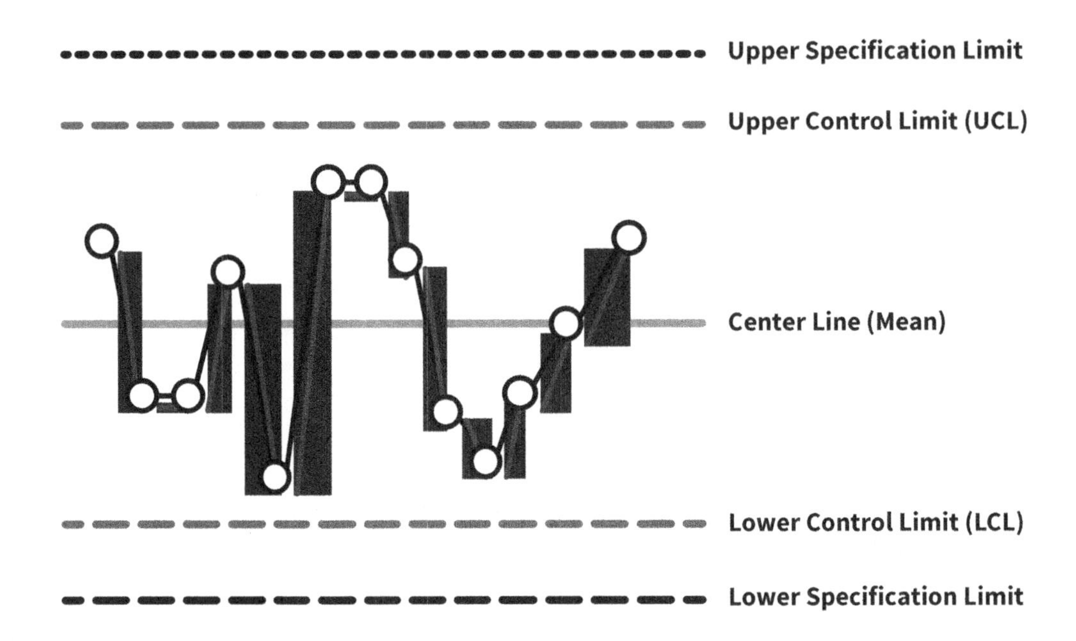

The red lines are the upper and lower control limits. We expect that any production variations will fall in between these lines. Therefore, the specification limits must be outside (or looser) than the control limits.

Question 38: Answer

During a sprint retrospective, the agile coach presents the burndown chart as shown below. The team discusses what went well during the sprint and what improvements might be applied to the following sprint.

What did the team members most likely find about their performance while analyzing the chart? (Choose three.)

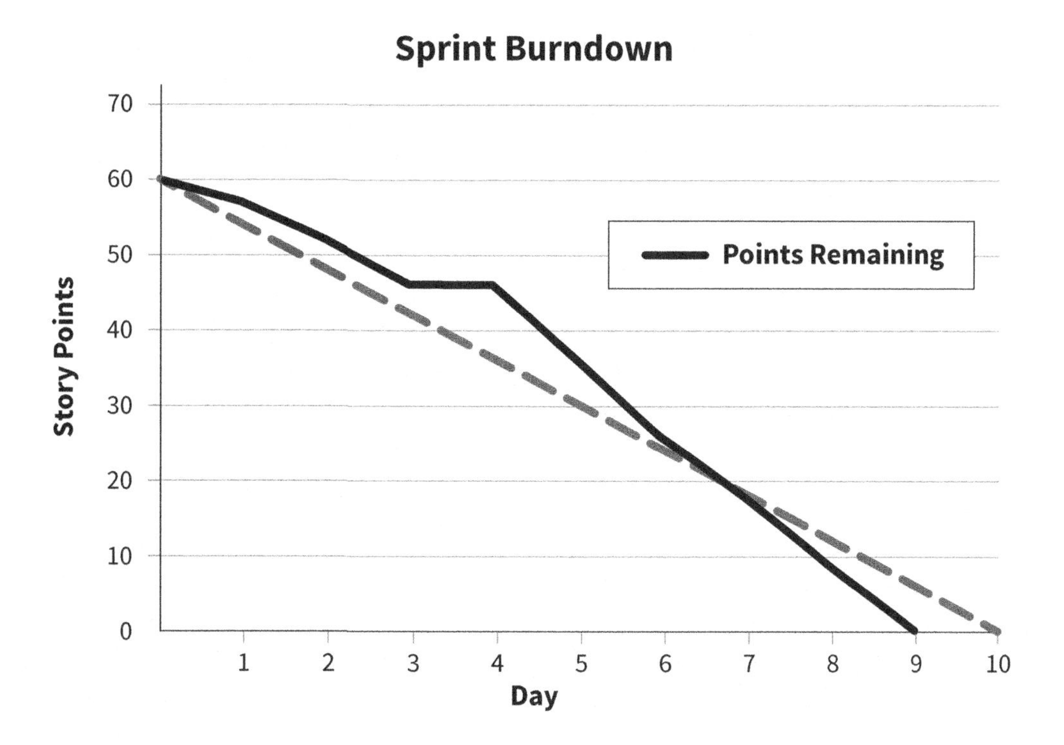

A) The team's velocity slowed, and they failed to achieve the sprint goal
Incorrect. The project team did get off to a slow start, as evidenced by the points remaining curve riding above the dashed line representing the sprint plan until day seven of the sprint. However, on day nine, zero story points remained to be completed for the sprint, meaning that the team successfully completed the sprint goal a day ahead of schedule.

☑ **B) To meet the sprint goal, the team's velocity had to be at least six story points per day**
Correct. The sprint goal is represented by the number of story points on day zero, which, in the burndown chart provided, is provided as 60 points. There are ten days in the sprint. Dividing 60 story points by the 10 days results in 6 story points per day. Therefore, to meet the sprint goal, the team needs to average at least six story points per day.

C) Scope was added to the sprint on day four which caused the sprint to fail
Incorrect. The horizontal part of the solid blue line between days three and four may indicate that either scope was added or the team completed zero story points. Regardless, this answer choice can be eliminated because the project team completed all 60 story points planned for the sprint on day nine, which means the sprint goal was met.

☑ **D) The team had finished all of the deliverables for the sprint by day nine**

Correct. On day nine, the solid blue line representing the story points remaining in the sprint reaches the zero mark on the burndown chart. With zero story points remaining to be completed by the project team, the sprint goal of 60 story points was achieved. Thus, all of the deliverables have been completed by day nine of the sprint.

☑ **E) The SPI on day seven of the sprint would have been 1.0**

Correct. On day 7, the solid blue line representing the story points remaining and the dashed line representing the story points planned intersect. This means the story points remaining are equal to those planned for that particular day, suggesting the team is exactly on track to complete the sprint goal on time, which, in turn, means the SPI = 1.0.

Explanation:

To answer this question correctly, one must understand how to interpret a burndown chart. A burndown chart graphically represents the story points remaining to be completed for the sprint or project. In this case, the solid blue line represents the points remaining for the sprint, and the dashed line represents the sprint plan. When the solid line is above the dashed line, the project runs behind schedule for the sprint. When the blue and dashed lines intersect, which in this scenario occurs on day seven, the project is running exactly on schedule. When the solid line is below the dashed line, the project runs ahead of schedule for this particular sprint. Once the blue line reaches zero story points remaining, which happens on day nine of the sprint, there is no work remaining to be completed for the sprint, and the sprint goal has been successfully achieved.

Reference:

A Guide to the Project Management Body of Knowledge, (PMBOK® Guide) – Sixth Edition, Project Management Institute Inc., 2017, Page(s) 267

Agile Practice Guide – First Edition, Project Management Institute Inc., 2017, Page(s) 61-62, 69

Question 39: Answer

A project manager meets with company executives to apprise them of value gain progress on the project. To make it easier for the executives to understand the various earned value metrics without complex formulas and calculations, the project manager draws a chart, as shown below. The date of the meeting is indicated by "Today" on the X-axis.

What is the actual cost (AC) of the project?

(On the real PMP exam you may be asked to provide your answer by clicking the correct area in the image. But here in the book, we are asking you to select the answer below.)

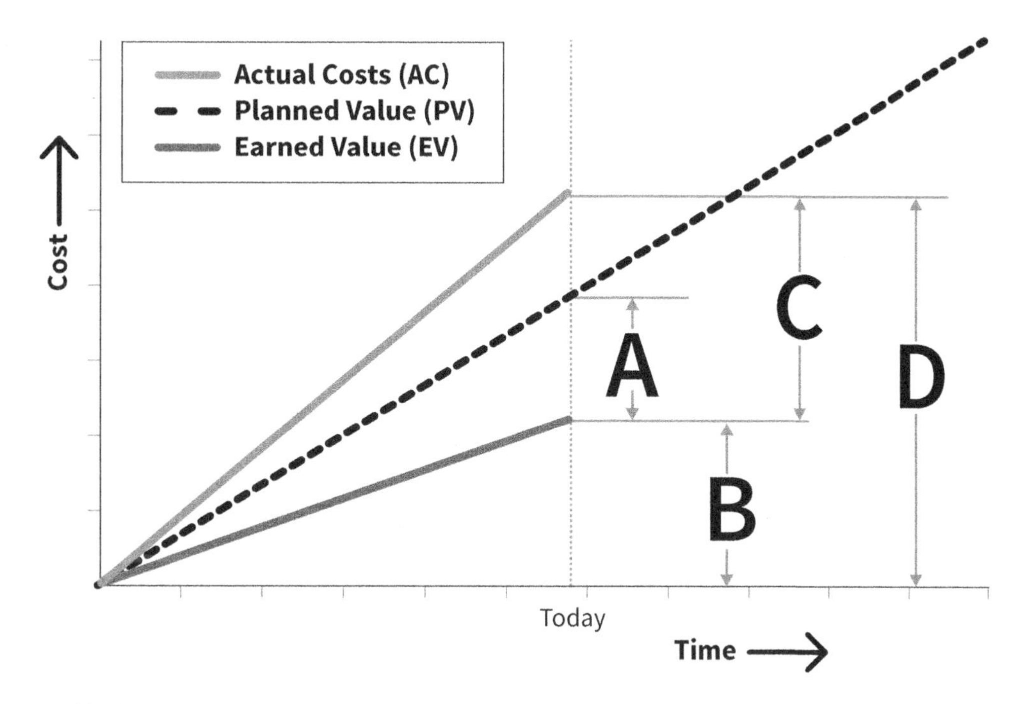

A) A
Incorrect. Area A represents the difference between the earned value (EV) and the planned value (PV). The difference between the earned value (EV) and the planned value (PV) is the schedule variance (SV), not the actual costs, as asked by the question. Hence, this choice represents an incorrect answer.

B) B
Incorrect. Area B represents the earned value (EV) as of "Today", the date of the meeting. The question asks to find the actual costs (AC) on the chart rather than the earned value (EV), making this choice an incorrect answer.

C) C
Incorrect. Area C represents the difference between the earned value (EV) and the actual costs (AC). The difference between the earned value (EV) and the actual cost (AC) is the cost variance (CV) of the project. However, the question simply asks to find the actual cost of the project. Hence, this choice is an incorrect answer.

☑ **D) D**

Correct. Area D represents the actual costs (AC) as of "Today", the date of the meeting, which is exactly what this answer choice represents, making it the best answer to the question asked.

Explanation:

Earned value analysis (EVA) is an example of data analysis tools and techniques that can be used on a project to analyze its performance in terms of budget and schedule. The EVA compares the performance measurement baseline to the actual cost and schedule performance. Earned value analysis is typically associated with a more general term, earned value management (EVM), which is a methodology that combines scope, schedule, and resource measurements to assess project performance and progress.

To calculate its metrics, the EVA often uses various formulas. However, operating with the formulas and values that result from them may sometimes be difficult for project stakeholders (such as the executives in the scenario described) who are less familiar with the formulas. Therefore, to make it easier for such stakeholders, a visual representation of the value gain progress may be useful.

The question is asking to find the actual cost (AC) of the project. The AC is the realized cost incurred for the work performed on an activity during a specific time period. Finding the actual cost does not require any calculations or formulas. The actual cost is already given on the chart: it is simply the height of the section on the vertical dotted line (indicated by "Today") between the X-axis and the curve representing the actual costs.

Reference:

A Guide to the Project Management Body of Knowledge, (PMBOK® Guide) – Sixth Edition, Project Management Institute Inc., 2017, Page(s) 262

Question 40: Answer

You have just received an email from your customer that contains the specification limits that they expect from your production process. You add these specification limits to your chart. The chart also contains the control limits.

What do the control limits represent?

A) 1 standard deviations above and below the mean
B) 2 standard deviations above and below the mean
☑ **C) 3 standard deviations above and below the mean**
D) 6 standard deviations above and below the mean

Explanation:
Control limits are set at 3 standard deviations above and below the mean. Control limits reflect the maximum allowed variation in a process. For the process to be under control, data points should fall within the control limits.

Question 41: Answer

iA41

A project has completed 11 of 22 planned sprints. The team has finished 200 of 500 story points, with each point having a budgeted value of $1,000. The EV is $200,000, the BAC is $500,000, and the CPI is 0.8. $250,000 has been spent on the project thus far. The steering committee has asked the project manager to provide an estimate for the final and total project cost at completion.

Which options might you consider in preparing the estimate for the steering committee? (Choose three.)

A) Assuming that the original plan is still valid, take the earned value of $200,000 and subtract the actual cost of $250,000
Incorrect. This answer choice describes the formula for cost variance (CV), which can be calculated as earned value (EV) – actual cost (AC). Applying the formula to this example would be $200,000 – $250,000 for a CV of -$50,000. However, the question is asking for the estimate at completion rather than the schedule variance.

B) Assuming that plan is fundamentally flawed, reestimate the remaining work from the bottom up
Incorrect. When the original plan is fundamentally flawed, or conditions have changed, it is appropriate to reestimate the remaining work from the bottom up. The result would be a revised estimate to complete (ETC). However, the question asks for an estimate at completion (EAC). To derive the EAC, one would need to add the actual cost to the ETC.

☑ **C) Assuming the cost performance will remain the same for the remainder of the project, use the formula EAC = BAC / CPI**
Correct. One method of calculating the EAC is budget at completion (BAC) divided by cost performance index (CPI). Using this formula presumes that the current cost performance will continue for the remainder of the project. While no calculations are required, if one wants to calculate the EAC, the result would be $500,000 / 0.8 = $625,000.

☑ **D) Assuming that conditions have changed and the original plan is no longer valid, develop a new cost estimate for the work remaining and add $250,000**
Correct. When the original plan is no longer valid, a new cost estimate for the remaining work should be developed. Providing a bottom-up estimate for the work remaining will be the new estimate to complete the project (ETC). To obtain the project's total cost at completion (EAC), the money already spent, $250,000, needs to be added to the ETC.

☑ **E) Assuming that the remaining work will be completed at the planned rate, use the formula EAC = AC + BAC – EV**
Correct. If one assumes that the remainder of the project will be completed at the planned rate, one can use the formula:
EAC = AC + BAC – EV. Although to answer the question correctly, performing the calculations is not necessary, applying this formula for EAC would result in EAC= $250,000 + $500,000 – $200,000 = $550,000.

Explanation:
The way the question is worded implies one is requested to calculate the estimate at completion (EAC). There are four different methodologies for calculating the EAC, with each one providing a different result. The appropriate formula to use in calculating the EAC depends on the assumptions one is willing to make. The correct answer choices provide the appropriate formulas to apply based on the provided assumptions. The incorrect answer choices describe how to calculate a metric other than EAC.

Note that answering this question correctly does not require performing any calculations. Rather one only needs to understand the correct assumptions and formulas to determine the EAC. Calculations provided in the explanations to some of the answer choices are given merely to illustrate the application of the formula using the values provided in the scenario.

Reference:
A Guide to the Project Management Body of Knowledge, (PMBOK® Guide) – Sixth Edition, Project Management Institute Inc., 2017, Page(s) 264-265, 267

Agile Practice Guide – First Edition, Project Management Institute Inc., 2017, Page(s) 69

iA42

Question 42: Answer

As the project progresses, the project manager collects work performance data and calculates the various earned value metrics, such as the variance at completion (VAC) and to-complete performance index (TCPI). The results of the calculations along with their interpretations are published for the stakeholders on the company's internal website.

How should the stakeholders read the results? (In your exam, on a question like this, you would be asked to drag and drop the items to create matching pairs. In this book, please arrange the answers in the correct order.)

Correct Answers:

Answer choices	Answers
Variance at completion (VAC) is positive	**The project is under budget**
Variance at completion (VAC) is equal to zero	**The project is on budget**
Variance at completion (VAC) is negative	**The project is over budget**
To-complete performance index (TCPI) is greater than 1.0	**Completing the project will be harder**
To-complete performance index (TCPI) is equal 1.0	**Completing the project will be neither harder nor easier**
To-complete performance index (TCPI) is less than 1.0	**Completing the project will be easier**

Explanation:

Earned value analysis is an example of data analysis tools and techniques that can be used on projects, both traditional and agile/hybrid. The analysis compares the performance measurement baseline to the actual schedule and cost performance. The earned value analysis is typically followed by the variance analysis, which often focuses on cost and schedule variances. This analysis allows project managers to determine the cause and degree of variance relative to the cost baseline and schedule baseline and, in turn, to decide on what action, corrective or preventive, is best to take to bring the project back on track.

Variance at completion (VAC) is not as often used as the schedule variance (SV) or the cost variance (CV). However, understanding this metric may be helpful in some situations, for example, when there is insufficient data to calculate SV or CV. The VAC is the projection of the amount of budget deficit or surplus, expressed as the difference between the budget at completion (BAC) and the estimate at completion (EAC): **VAC = BAC – EAC.** Positive VAC values mean that the BAC is greater than the EAC. In other words, at any given point in time when the VAC is measured, the project is running under planned costs, or the project is under budget. Negative VAC values mean that the EAC is greater than the original BAC, suggesting the project is over budget. And, finally, when the VAC is equal to zero (or neutral), which is the case when BAC is equal to EAC, the project is running on budget.

Of all the earned value metrics, the to-complete performance index (TCPI) is perceived by many students as the most complicated. However, when looked at closely, the TCPI is not that "scary". Its formal definition is the measure of the cost performance required to be achieved with the remaining resources to meet a specified management goal. The TCPI is expressed as the ratio of the cost to finish the outstanding work to the remaining budget: **TCPI = (BAC - EV) / (BAC - AC)**. When the BAC is no longer attainable, and a new budget, estimate at completion (EAC), is determined, the EAC replaces BAC in the equation: **TCPI = (EAC - EV) / (EAC - AC)**.

Unlike the cost performance index (CPI) or the schedule performance index (SPI), TCPI values greater than 1.0 are considered unfavorable, while TCPI values less than 1.0 are considered favorable. To demonstrate how TCPI works, let's assume that up until a given point in time, cost efficiency in completing one unit of project work was measured as 1.0. Therefore, values above 1.0 mean a higher efficiency is needed to complete the same amount of work, while values below 1.0 mean lower efficiency is needed to complete a unit of project work. Therefore, TCPI > 1.0 means that completing the project from now on will be harder than until the point in time the TCPI was measured. TCPI < 1.0 means that completing the project work from now on will be easier compared to the efficiency required to carry out the same amount of work before the point in time the TCPI was measured. Finally, TCPI = 1.0 means completing the project work will be neither harder nor easier, i.e., efficiency that must be maintained to complete as planned may remain the same.

Reference:
A Guide to the Project Management Body of Knowledge, (PMBOK® Guide) – Sixth Edition, Project Management Institute Inc., 2017, Page(s) 261-267

iA43

Question 43: Answer

Which of the following represent the work that has been completed on the project so far?

A) PV
B) SV
☑ **C) EV**
D) CPI

Explanation:
Earned value (EV) is the amount (usually in a currency) for the work that has been completed on a project so far.

Question 44: Answer

An organization is conducting a meeting to determine the budget for the next fiscal year. Under discussion are several proposed software development projects. Since the organization only has one scrum team available, just the most profitable project can move forward.

Which project should the organization select?

A) The project with the highest cost-benefit ratio
Incorrect. The cost-benefit ratio (CBR) is a ratio that describes the benefits versus the cost of a project. The formula can be stated as CBR = Cost / Benefit. A project with a lower cost-benefit ratio is better than a project with a higher cost-benefit ratio, making this choice an incorrect answer.

B) The project with the lowest benefit-cost ratio
Incorrect. The benefit-cost ratio (BCR) is a ratio that describes the cost versus benefits of a project. The BCR is the inverse of the cost-benefit ratio (CBR) and can be expressed as following: BCR = Benefit / Cost. From this formula, one can see that it is the project with the highest BCR, not the lowest BCR, that is the most financially advantageous.

☑ **C) The project with the highest discounted cash flow**
Correct. The discounted cash flow (DCF) is a valuation method for potential investment that utilizes future free cash flow projections and discounts them, typically using the simple or weighted average cost of capital (WACC). Therefore, the project with the highest DCF is the most financially beneficial.

D) The project with the lowest internal rate of return
Incorrect. The internal rate of return (IRR) represents the interest rate at which the present value of all future cash flows equals the initial investment. When selecting a project based on the IRR, the project with the highest, rather than the lowest, internal rate of return should be selected.

Explanation:

The cost-benefit ratio (CBR), benefit-cost ratio (BCR), internal rate of return (IRR), and discounted cash flow (DCF) are all financial metrics that can be used in the selection of a project. The actual exam is not likely to expect the aspirant to perform the financial calculations (with the exception of the BCR and CBR, which are relatively straightforward). However, the aspirant should understand the concepts and how they pertain to the project selection process. Based on the scenario described, all of the incorrect answer choices represent the worse financial option. However, a project with a higher DCF is more financially advantageous compared to a project with a lower DCF, making this choice the best answer to the question asked.

Reference:
A Guide to the Project Management Body of Knowledge, (PMBOK® Guide) – Sixth Edition, Project Management Institute Inc., 2017, Page(s) 34
https://www.pmi.org/learning/library/financing-project-planned-value-6866

Question 45: Answer

At a meeting to communicate the project status to stakeholders, the project manager uses the various earned value metrics. Some stakeholders are unfamiliar with the various terms and their meanings and request clarification.

How should the project manager respond? (In your exam, on a question like this, you would be asked to drag and drop the items to create matching pairs. In this book, please arrange the answers in the correct order.)

Correct Answers:

Answer choices	Answers
Schedule variance (SV) is positive	**The project is ahead of schedule**
Schedule variance (SV) is equal to 0	**The project is on schedule**
Schedule variance (SV) is negative	**The project is behind schedule**
Cost variance (CV) is positive	**The project is under budget**
Cost variance (CV) is equal to 0	**The project is on budget**
Cost variance (CV) is negative	**The project is over budget**

Explanation:
Earned value analysis is an example of data analysis tools and techniques that can be used on projects, both traditional and agile/hybrid. The analysis compares the performance measurement baseline to the actual schedule and cost performance. The earned value analysis is typically followed by the variance analysis, which often focuses on cost and schedule variances. This analysis allows project managers to determine the cause and degree of variance relative to the cost baseline and schedule baseline and, in turn, to decide on what action, corrective or preventive, is best to take to bring the project back on track.

Schedule performance is typically represented by schedule variance (SV) and schedule performance index (SPI). The SV is a measure of schedule performance expressed as the difference between the earned value (EV) and the planned value (PV): **SV = EV – PV.** At a given point in time, the SV shows the amount by which the project is ahead, on, or behind the planned delivery date. In other words, the SV shows whether the project is ahead, on, or behind schedule. Positive values of the SV mean that the EV is greater than the PV, which suggests the project is ahead of schedule. Negative SV values mean the project is behind schedule. If the SV is equal to zero, the project is earning exactly as planned, meaning the project is on schedule.

Cost performance is typically represented by cost variance (CV) and cost performance index (CPI). The CV is the amount of budget deficit or surplus at a given point in time, expressed as the difference between the earned value (EV) and the actual cost (AC): **CV = EV – AC.** Positive CV values mean that the EV is greater than the AC, in other words, the project is running under the planned costs, or under budget. Negative CV values indicate that the actual costs are higher than planned, in other words, the project is over budget. When the CV is equal to zero, the project is on budget.

Note that determining whether or not being under budget and/or ahead of schedule is good or bad depends on how accurate the original estimates were. For example, if the original schedule estimate was too high (whether intentionally or not), the project being ahead of schedule does not necessarily reflect positively on the project manager and the team. Similarly, if the cost estimate was too low, then the project being over budget does not necessarily mean the project manager and/or team are doing a bad job.

Reference:
A Guide to the Project Management Body of Knowledge, (PMBOK® Guide) – Sixth Edition, Project Management Institute Inc., 2017, Page(s) 261-267

Question 46: Answer

iA46

You are on the phone with your project sponsor discussing the most recent project figures. There are slight variances to the original budget. Your project sponsor says: "If I look at the budget at completion and the cost performance index, then our estimate to complete should still be around 200,000. So, we are OK."

Based on this information, what do you know?

A) The sponsor doesn't know how to calculate the ETC
☑ **B) The sponsor thinks that the variances will remain**
C) The sponsor thinks that the variances will not happen again
D) The sponsor thinks that our budget is flawed

Explanation:
There are a few ways in which you can calculate the ETC and each is based on a particular assumption on how the project is progressing. Your interpretation of the assumptions is required. The formulas to calculate ETC are:

- ETC = EAC - AC
- ETC = New estimate, when it is thought that the original estimate was flawed.
- However, neither formula seems to deal with the sponsor's belief that the variances are minor. To do that, you need to look at the EAC formulas and determine which one would work with the values the sponsor used to arrive at the ETC.
- **EAC = BAC / CPI:** use this formula if current variances *will remain.*
- **EAC = AC + BAC – EV:** use this formula if current variances are thought to *not happen again.*
- **EAC = AC + [(BAC – EV) / (CPI * SPI)]:** use this formula if currently over budget and deadline.

In this question, the sponsor said that she looks at the BAC and CPI and thereby figures that the ETC = 200,000. There is only one EAC formula that allows her to do that, and that is the formula that assumes that variances will remain. The other ways of arriving at the EAC require additional / different information.

It is important to realize that the actual numbers of the BAC and CPI are irrelevant to solve the puzzle. You know from the question that the sponsor used the two variables BAC and CPI and "somehow" calculated that the ETC must be = 200,000. Your task is to realize that he used the formula **EAC = BAC / CPI,** which is the EAC formula used when you think that current variances will remain.

Question 47: Answer

A project has been carried out using 10 two-week sprints. The project is now complete, and, as part of its closure, the project manager uses the following feature chart to analyze the project's performance that will be included in the final report.

What will most likely be included in the report? (Choose three.)

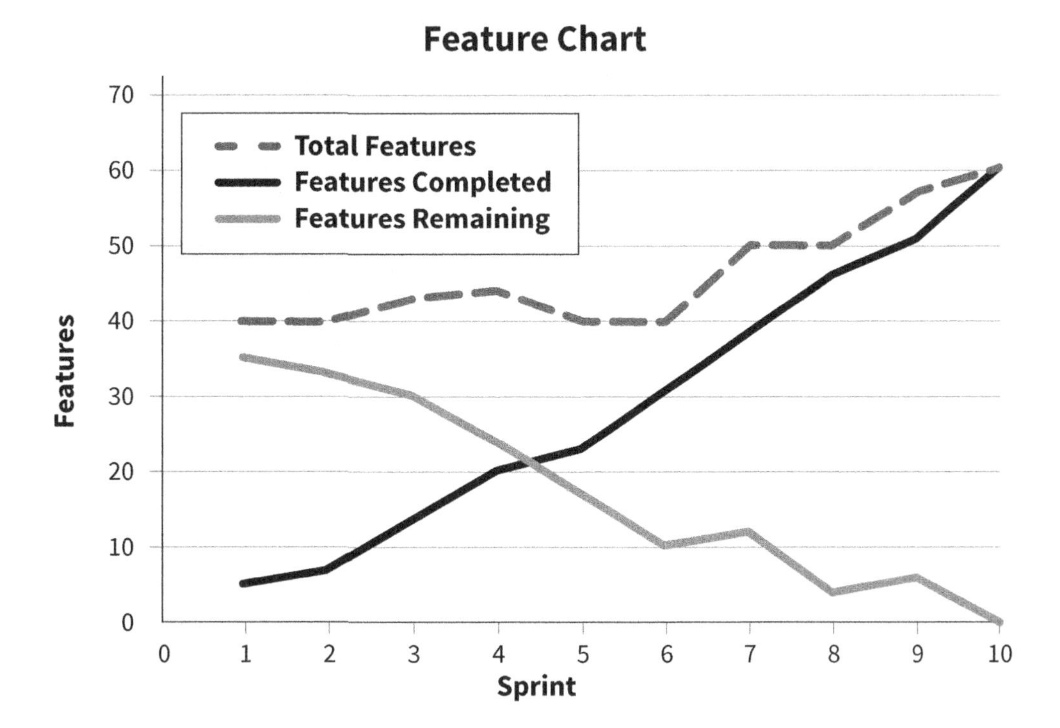

☑ **A) The project team completed the project with a velocity of six features per sprint**

Correct. Velocity can be calculated as the number of features divided by the number of sprints. The solid blue line representing the number of features completed terminates at 60 features after 10 sprints. Thus, the team completed a total of 60 features after 10 sprints, which means the team's velocity was: 60 / 10 = 6 features per sprint.

B) The project team met the project's objectives and ended with a CPI of 1.0

Incorrect. The formula for calculating the cost performance index (CPI) is earned value (EV) / actual cost (AC). The feature chart described in the scenario does not provide any information regarding the project budget or expenditures from which to derive the CPI. Therefore, no determination can be made regarding the CPI.

☑ **C) The project scope increased over the course of the project**

Correct. The dashed line on the chart represents the total number of features to be built (project scope). The starting point of the dashed line at sprint one indicates a project scope of 40 features. The dashed line terminates at 60 features during sprint 10. Therefore the project scope increased from 40 features to 60 features by the end of the project.

D) The project team failed to complete all of the features due to added scope
Incorrect. The dashed line representing the number of planned features does indicate that the project scope increased from 40 to 60 features as the project progressed. The solid blue line representing the number of completed features terminates at 60, indicating that the team completed all 60 planned features. Additionally, the green line shows zero features remaining to be completed. Hence, the project team succeeded in completing the project scope despite the increase in the number of features.

☑ **E) At the end of the project, the project team attained an SPI of 1.0**
Correct. An SPI of 1.0 means that the earned value (EV) is equal to the planned value (PV). Since the team completed all 60 of the planned features in the final sprint, the SPI must have been 1.0 at the end of the project. One might argue that the SPI exceeded 1.0 because the project started with only 40 features. While this is a valid point, this answer choice refers to the SPI at the end of the project.

Explanation:
Although burnup and burndown charts typically utilize story points to measure project scope, another method of tracking project performance is using a feature chart. The feature chart tracks features rather than story points, but the concept is still the same. In this case, the feature chart indicates that the project was initially planned with 40 features, and the scope increased over the course of the project to 60 features. Despite the increase in scope, the project team was able to complete all 60 of the features by the end of the 10 planned sprints. The incorrect answer choices can be eliminated because the project team successfully completed all of the planned features, and the feature chart provides no information on cost performance.

Reference:
A Guide to the Project Management Body of Knowledge, (PMBOK® Guide) – Sixth Edition, Project Management Institute Inc., 2017, Page(s) 263, 267

Agile Practice Guide – First Edition, Project Management Institute Inc., 2017, Page(s) 67, 69

Question 48: Answer

iA48

To communicate project progress to stakeholders, the project manager assigns a team member to prepare a weekly presentation. The team member is supposed to calculate the various earned value metrics and provide their interpretation in the presentation.

How should the team member interpret the following metrics? (In your exam, on a question like this, you would be asked to drag and drop the items to create matching pairs. In this book, please arrange the answers in the correct order.)

Correct Answers:

Answer choices	Answers
Cost performance index (CPI) is greater than 1.0	**The project is under budget**
Cost performance index (CPI) is equal to 1.0	**The project is on budget**
Cost performance index (CPI) is less than 1.0	**The project is over budget**
Schedule performance index (SPI) is greater than 1.0	**The project is ahead of schedule**
Schedule performance index (SPI) is equal to 1.0	**The project is on schedule**
Schedule performance index (SPI) is less than 1.0	**The project is behind schedule**

Explanation:

Earned value analysis is an example of data analysis tools and techniques that can be used on projects, both traditional and agile/hybrid. The analysis compares the performance measurement baseline to the actual schedule and cost performance. The earned value analysis is typically followed by the variance analysis, which often focuses on cost and schedule variances. This analysis allows project managers to determine the cause and degree of variance relative to the cost baseline and schedule baseline and, in turn, to decide on what action, corrective or preventive, is best to take to bring the project back on track.

Cost performance is typically represented by cost variance (CV) and cost performance index (CPI). The CPI is a measure of the cost efficiency of budgeted resources, expressed as a ratio of earned value (EV) to actual costs (AC): **CPI = EV / AC.** A CPI value greater than 1.0 indicates that the AC is less than EV, which means the project is spending less budget than planned to complete the work, which, in turn, suggests the project is under budget. A CPI value equal to 1.0 means the project is on budget. A CPI value less than 1.0 means the project is over budget.

Schedule performance is typically represented by schedule variance (SV) and schedule performance index (SPI). The SPI measures the schedule efficiency, expressed as a ratio of earned value (EV) to planned value (PV): **SPI = EV / PV.** An SPI value greater than 1.0 indicates that the EV is greater than PV, which means that at the point in time when the measurements have been taken, the project earned more value than planned, or, in other words, the project is ahead of schedule. An SPI value equal to 1.0 means the project is on schedule. An SPI value less than 1.0 means the project is behind schedule.

Note that determining whether or not being under budget and/or ahead of schedule is good or bad depends on how accurate the original estimates were. For example, if the original schedule estimate was too high (whether intentionally or not), the project being ahead of schedule does not necessarily reflect positively on the project manager and the team. Similarly, if the cost estimate was too low, then the project being over budget does not necessarily mean the project manager and/or team are doing a bad job.

Reference:
A Guide to the Project Management Body of Knowledge, (PMBOK® Guide) – Sixth Edition, Project Management Institute Inc., 2017, Page(s) 261-267

Question 49: Answer

You are a consultant specializing in recovery of troubled projects. Your latest assignment is on a project where the CPI = 0.78 and the SPI = 0.65.

Without knowing anything else about this project, which of the following could be the root cause of the situation?

A) The project manager did not create a resource-loaded schedule
B) 35% of the tasks were not finished on time
C) The construction machines used were too expensive
☑ **D) This project has been staffed with a team that was not sufficiently experienced**

Explanation:
To answer this question correctly, you must first analyze and understand that CPI = 0.78 and SPI = 0.65 means that this project is **both** over budget and behind schedule. So, you need to pick an answer that could explain why there are problems with both the budget and the schedule. Let's analyze the available answers together:

- A) The project manager did not create a resource-loaded schedule.
  This answer does not address either budget or schedule problems.
  It just shows that the PM forgot to perform a particular action during scheduling.

- B) 35% of the tasks were not finished on time
  This answer can explain why the project is behind schedule, but not why it is above budget.

- C) The construction machines used were too expensive
  This answer can explain why the project is above budget, but not why it is behind schedule.

- D) This project has been staffed with a team that was not sufficiently experienced
  An inexperienced staff can explain both. Because of their lack of experience tasks will take a lot longer to finish. This will cause a delay in the schedule and because the tasks take longer to finish they will also cost more. This explains both the CPI and SPI and is therefore, of the choices provided, the best answer to the question asked.

Note that answer D is "the best" answer of the four, because it is the only one that can address both the budget and cost variance on this project. We won't really know if it is the true until we talk to the project team and get more information about the project. But based on the information available in the question, choice D is the best answer.

Question 50: Answer

iA50

To track project performance, a project manager creates a feature chart. Each feature is of the same size and value. The project has a budget of $600,000 and is carried out using two-week sprints. The project was planned to be completed in 16 weeks but ended up taking 20. The project manager facilitates the project retrospective.

What can the project manager tell about the project? (Choose three.)

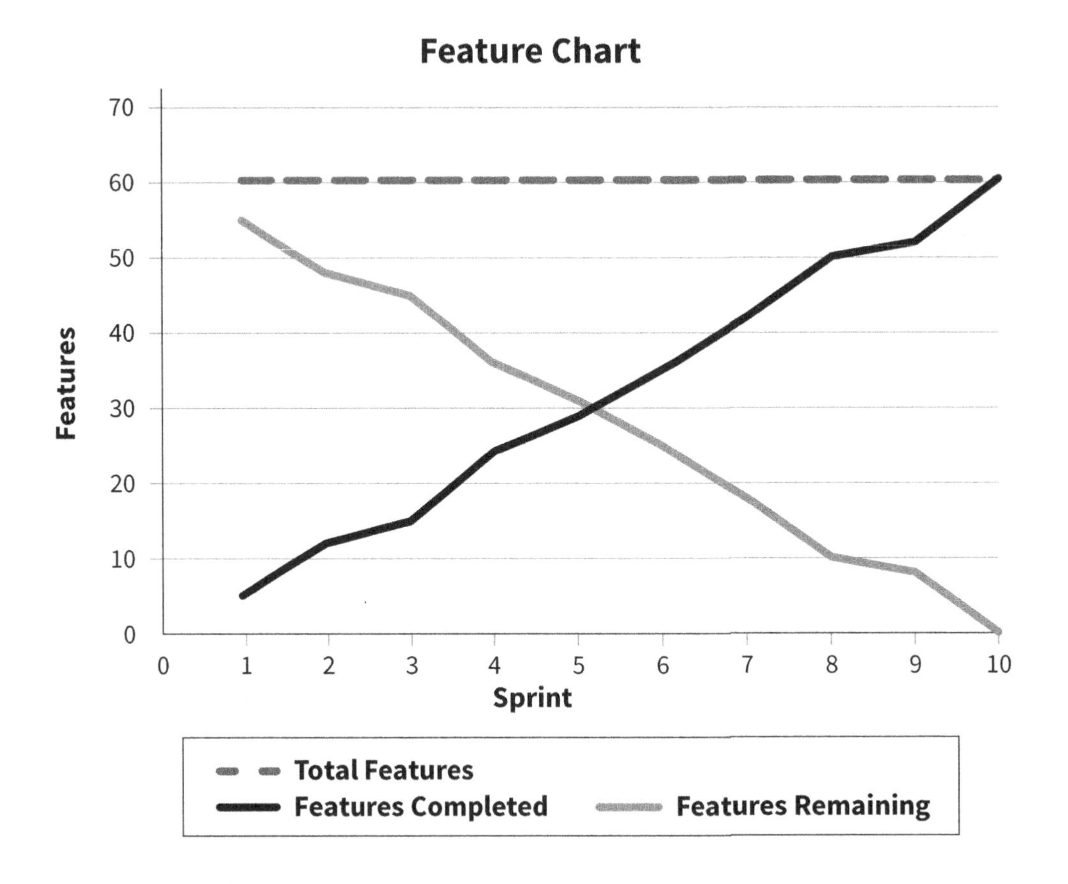

☑ **A) After eight sprints, the project's schedule performance index (SPI) was less than 1.0**
Correct. The scenario states that the project was planned to be completed in 16 weeks, representing 8 two-week sprints, but eventually completed in 10 sprints. Thus, the project ran behind schedule, meaning the schedule performance index (SPI) would have been less than 1.0.

☑ **B) The project scope remained at 60 features throughout the project**
Correct. The dashed line representing the total number of features in the project scope starts at 60 and never deviates from the 60 feature line. Therefore, the project scope of 60 features remained the same throughout the project. While it is possible that some features were replaced with other features, the total number of features did not change.

☑ **C) To complete on time, the team had to achieve a velocity of 7.5 features per sprint**
Correct. Using a feature chart, velocity can be calculated by dividing the total number of features by the number of sprints. In the scenario, the project consisted of 60 features and was originally planned for

8 two-week sprints. Thus, velocity is 60 / 8 = 7.5 features per sprint. Note that the team actually completed 60 features after 10 sprints which would be a velocity of 6 features per sprint. But this answer choice describes what was planned rather than what was actually achieved.

D) After eight sprints, the schedule variance (SV) was a positive value
Incorrect. According to the scenario, the project was initially planned to be completed in 8 two-week sprints. However, the feature chart indicates that after 8 sprints, the team only completed 50 of the planned 60 features. Thus, the project ran behind schedule, meaning the SV was a negative value. Although not necessary, one can determine the SV after 8 sprints. SV = EV – PV. Each feature has a budgeted value of: $600,000 / 60 = $10,000. The team completed 50 features worth $10,000 each, i.e., EV = $500,000 after 8 sprints while it should have completed all 60 features, i.e., PV = $600,000. Applying the formula for SV results in SV = $500,000 – $600,000 = -$100,000.

E) The project ran over budget with a cost performance index (CPI) of less than 1.0
Incorrect. The formula for CPI is EV / AC. While we can calculate the EV for the project, there is no information in the scenario regarding expenditures. Without being able to determine AC, there is no way to determine the CPI. Note: the fact that it took the team two additional sprints to complete the entire project scope means that it is more likely than not that the project ran over budget. However, since determining cost performance cannot be done accurately, and the question only permits three correct answer choices, this option should be eliminated.

Explanation:
One method of tracking a project's schedule performance when using an agile framework is the use of a feature chart. According to the scenario, the project was initially planned to be completed within 16 weeks, i.e., eight two-week sprints. The dashed line on the feature chart indicates that a total of 60 features were planned for the project and remained unchanged throughout the course of the project. As stated in the scenario and depicted on the feature chart, it took the project team ten sprints instead of the eight originally planned to complete the project scope of 60 features. Since it took longer than, the project ran behind schedule, which means the schedule performance index (SPI) would have been less than 1.0, and the schedule variance (SV) would have been a negative value. The incorrect answer choices either suggest that schedule performance was better than planned or cannot be determined with the information provided.

Reference:
A Guide to the Project Management Body of Knowledge, (PMBOK® Guide) – Sixth Edition, Project Management Institute Inc., 2017, Page(s) 263, 267

Agile Practice Guide – First Edition, Project Management Institute Inc., 2017, Page(s) 67, 69

iA51

Question 51: Answer

If the cost variance is negative and the SPI is less than one, what does this indicate?

A) Your project is under budget but behind schedule
B) Your project is under budget but on schedule
C) Your project is over budget and ahead of schedule
✓ **D) Your project is over budget and behind schedule**

Explanation:
A negative cost variance means that you are spending more than planned, which means that you are over budget. If the SPI is less than one, this means that you are progressing slower than planned, which means that you are behind schedule.

iA52

Question 52: Answer

As the project progresses, the product owner reviews the various earned value metrics. The data indicates that the schedule variance (SV) is -15 story points and the cost variance (CV) is $1,200. The team members believe that their velocity of 20 story points per sprint has stabilized.

What actions might the product owner consider taking? (Choose two.)

✓ **A) Ask the team for suggestions on increasing earned value (EV)**
Correct. Schedule variance (SV) is calculated as SV = EV – PV. A negative value for SV means that the project team has earned less than what was planned and is running behind schedule. In this case, the team has completed fewer story points than was planned. Increasing EV and/or reducing PV will be necessary to address the gap.

✓ **B) Reprioritize the product backlog to lower planned value (PV)**
Correct. PV is part of the formula for the SV, which is calculated as SV = EV – PV. In the scenario, the SV is negative, which means that the project is running behind schedule. Cutting the project's scope by reprioritizing the backlog should lower PV, which would make it more likely for the project team to complete the remaining work on time.

C) No action is needed as the current team's velocity is sufficient
Incorrect. Since the SV is the difference between EV and PV, negative SV of -15 story points provided in the scenario means that the project team has earned 15 story points fewer than originally planned and is running behind schedule. Therefore, if no action is taken, as suggested by this answer choice, the project is unlikely to be completed on time.

D) Search for strategies to reduce actual cost (AC)
Incorrect. The problem statement presented by the scenario describes a project that is currently running behind schedule. The question provides a cost variance (CV) of $1,200, which means the project is trending under budget. Therefore, there is no compelling reason to search for strategies to reduce costs.

E) Look for opportunities to reduce the earned value (EV)
Incorrect. Earned value (EV) refers to the total value of work completed. In this case, given the formula SV = EV – PV, the schedule variance (SV) indicates that the project has earned 15 story points fewer than was planned for this point in the project. Therefore, the project team needs to look for opportunities to increase, not reduce, the earned value.

Explanation:
The formula to calculate the schedule variance (SV) is **SV = earned value (EV) – planned value (PV).** An SV of -15 story points means that the project team has earned 15 story points fewer than was planned and is running behind schedule. In order to bring the schedule performance back into alignment with project goals, the project team needs to increase EV and/or decrease PV. The correct answer choices represent actions that would either increase EV or decrease PV.

Note: with the exception of the backlog prioritization, some of the answer choices represent actions that are typically the responsibility of the scrum master, agile coach, or another project leader rather than the product owner. However, the idea behind this question is 'what' should be done rather than 'who' should do it. PMP aspirants should keep in mind that questions on the real exam may have ambiguous scenarios and/or answer choices. Making reasonable assumptions before selecting an answer is an approach that proved to work well.

Reference:
A Guide to the Project Management Body of Knowledge, (PMBOK® Guide) – Sixth Edition, Project Management Institute Inc., 2017, Page(s) 262, 267

Agile Practice Guide – First Edition, Project Management Institute Inc., 2017, Page(s) 61, 69

iA53

Question 53: Answer

What rule is the Pareto Diagram based on?

A) The 50/50 rule
☑ **B) The 80/20 rule**
C) The rule of diminishing returns
D) The 90/10 rule

Explanation:
Vilfredo Pareto was the first to realize that 80% of his country's wealth (Italy) was owned by 20% of the people. Statisticians rediscovered his findings making them widely used nowadays. It's called the 80/20 rule, or Pareto principle.

iA54

Question 54: Answer

Your company is considering three potential agile projects. The first project will cost $25,000 and has an NPV of $35,000. The second project will cost $30,000 and has an NPV of $37,000. The third project will cost $40,000 and has an NPV of $20,000. The company only has the resources to approve two of the projects.

What is the opportunity cost of only selecting two of the projects?

A) $72,000
Incorrect. The first and second projects are the most profitable. If one added the NPV of these projects, the result would be $72,000. However, this would be the benefit of the two selected projects rather than the opportunity cost. The opportunity cost is the profit or gain of the project not selected.

B) $35,000
Incorrect. $35,000 represents the net present value (NPV) of the first project, which should be one of the selected projects because, of the three projects described in the scenario, the first project has the second-largest NPV. Opportunity cost relates to the value of the project that has not been selected, making this choice an incorrect answer.

☑ **C) $20,000**
Correct. The third project has a net present value of $20,000, which is the lowest of the three projects provided in the scenario and, therefore, will likely be rejected. Since this project will not be selected, the company will not receive the benefit of the $20,000 in NPV. Thus, the opportunity cost of not selecting this project would be $20,000.

D) $40,000
Incorrect. $40,000 represents the cost of the third project rather than the opportunity cost, as asked by the questions. Opportunity cost relates to the benefit of the option (project) that has not been selected. $40,000 would simply be the cost of the third project, not its benefit.

Explanation:
The question stipulates that the company can only approve two of the three proposed projects. All other things being equal, the company should select the two projects with the highest net present value (NPV) and reject the project with the lowest NPV. Thus, in this case, the company will likely reject the third project that has an NPV of $20,000. Opportunity cost can be described as the profit or gain of the project not chosen. Since the $20,000 NPV would represent the value of the third project, this would be the opportunity cost.

Note that the project cost would be included in determining the NPV and is not relevant to answering this question correctly.

Reference:
A Guide to the Project Management Body of Knowledge, (PMBOK® Guide) – Sixth Edition, Project Management Institute Inc., 2017, Page(s) 34

https://www.project-management-prepcast.com/free/pmp-exam/articles/691-what-is-opportunity-cost-and-why-do-you-need-to-understand-it

Question 55: Answer

iA55

The project is over budget when...

A) CPI = 0
B) CPI = 1
C) CPI > 1
☑ **D) CPI < 1**

Explanation:

The interpretation of the cost performance index (CPI) is as follows:

- CPI = 0 does not exist
- CPI = 1: The project is getting $1 for every $1 spent. Funds are being used as planned. The project is on budget.
- CPI > 1: The project is getting >$1 for every $1 spent. Funds are being used less than planned. The project is under budget.
- CPI < 1: The project is getting <$1 for every $1 spent. Funds are being used more than planned. The project is over budget.

iA56

Question 56: Answer

After 10 sprints, 100 of the planned 200 story points have been completed. Based on the current velocity, the project scope can be completed after 15 of the originally planned 20 sprints. The project was budgeted at $1,000 per story point but only consumed $750 per story point. A stakeholder requests three new features to be included in the final product and wants to know if the project can be delivered within the original budget.

What should the project manager do?

☑ **A) Develop a revised ETC based on a bottom-up estimate and add the actual cost**
Correct. With the addition of the three new features, the existing BAC has been invalidated. A revised estimate at completion (EAC) can be determined by reestimating the remaining work and adding the actual cost. The scenario does not provide information about the relative size of the new features upon which the new EAC can be calculated. Thus, to determine the new EAC, the remaining work, including the new features, needs to be estimated.

B) Calculate a new EAC by applying the formula EAC = AC + BAC – EV
Incorrect. One method of determining the estimate at completion (EAC) is EAC = AC + BAC – EV. This formula should be used when the remaining work will be accomplished at the planned rate. However, the remaining work has just been increased, and this formula will not take into account the cost associated with the expanded scope.

C) Reject the new features since new features can only be requested by the product owner
Incorrect. The product owner's main responsibility is to maximize the value of the product. This is typically achieved by working with the relevant stakeholders and grooming the backlog accordingly. However, any stakeholder can reach out to the product owner and request adding new features or changing the existing ones.

D) Determine a new EAC by dividing the BAC by the current CPI
Incorrect. Although the BAC and CPI have not been provided, they can be calculated based on the information given. However, using this information would not take into account the additional features that are being requested. One should know the relative size of the new features before any determination for revised earned value metrics can be made.

Explanation:
The scenario indicates that the existing scope should be completed after only 15 of the planned 20 sprints, and the project has only consumed $750 per story point versus the planned $1,000 per story point. This situation means that the project is trending to finish significantly ahead of schedule and under budget. As a result, a stakeholder requests to expand the project scope and wants to know if the project can still be delivered on budget after adding the new features. The most logical way to answer the stakeholder's question is to develop a new estimate at completion (EAC) based on the expanded scope and see if the new EAC is less than or equal to the existing budget at completion (BAC). There are several methods for determining a new EAC. When the original plan is no longer valid (as is the case when the project scope is being increased), the appropriate action would be to develop a new estimate to complete (ETC) by performing a bottom-up estimate of the work remaining and then add in the actual cost to determine the new EAC. Knowing the EAC based on a re-estimation of the remaining work, including the additional features, the project leader can determine if it would be feasible to complete the new project scope within the original budget.

Reference:
A Guide to the Project Management Body of Knowledge, (PMBOK® Guide) – Sixth Edition, Project Management Institute Inc., 2017, Page(s) 264-265, 267

Agile Practice Guide – First Edition, Project Management Institute Inc., 2017, Page(s) 61, 69

Question 57: Answer

iA57

Which of the following projects would you select?

☑ **A) Project A with an Internal Rate of Return of 13%**
B) Project B with a Future Value of $300,000
C) Project C with Benefit Cost ratio of 1:1.1
D) Project D with an estimated income of $310,000

Explanation:
Let us first analyze the answers:

- Project A will give us an IRR of 13%. This means that our investment will give us a 13% return.
- Project B shows that it has a future value of 300,000, but there is no additional information and as such we cannot calculate how "good" this future value is compared to the other projects.
- Project C has a BCR of 1:1.1. This means that the cost is higher than the benefits, which is bad.

- Project D lists an income of $310,000 but just like project B, there are no other numbers to put this income into perspective – it could be excellent, it could be bad.

Based on this analysis you can make the following statements:

- We cannot determine how good project B or D really are because we don't have enough information
- Project C will cost us more than the benefits it will bring
- Project A has a clearly specified IRR of 13%

Therefore, of the choices provided, based on the information available in the question, project A is the *best* answer to the question asked.

Question 58: Answer

A project team has established a stable velocity of 50 story points per two-week iteration, and there are 500 story points remaining in the project backlog. As the team is about to begin the next sprint, the project sponsor informs the project manager that due to market conditions the remaining scope must be completed in 18 weeks.

What is the best course of action for the project manager?

A) Recommend project termination so that the team can fail fast
Incorrect. If a project is going to fail, it is best for it to fail earlier rather than later. Failing fast will save some financial resources and allow other resources to be redeployed sooner. However, before taking this course of action, other options should be explored. Terminating the project would be premature based on the minimal information provided.

☑ **B) Ask the product owner which user stories can be eliminated**
Correct. Given the team's current velocity and the work remaining in the project backlog, it is unlikely that the entire project backlog will be delivered by the new project deadline. Either the velocity will need to be increased or the scope reduced. The product owner should work with relevant stakeholders to decide what user stories can be sacrificed to deliver by the new deadline. While reducing the scope might or might not be a viable option, it is an alternative that should be explored.

C) Change development cadence from two-week iterations to weekly
Incorrect. According to the scenario, the iterations are currently two weeks in length. Once an iteration length is determined at the start of the project, changing it in the middle of the project would be highly unusual. Shortening the iteration length might improve feedback loops, but would also result in the team spending more time conducting the

agile ceremonies. Therefore, it is unclear if shortening the iteration length would significantly improve velocity.

D) Request that the project sponsor reprioritize the backlog
Incorrect. The project sponsor may provide some inputs regarding the user stories that he/she thinks need to remain in the project backlog under the changing market conditions. However, it's the product owner's, not the project sponsor's, responsibility to prioritize the project backlog.

Explanation:
With a stable velocity of 50 points per two-week iteration, the team is trending to complete the remaining 500 story points in 10 iterations (500 / 50 = 10), which represents 20 weeks. With the deadline being moved up to 18 weeks remaining, it is not likely that the team will be able to complete the entire scope. For the team to complete the project in 18 weeks instead of 20, the velocity will need to be increased, or the scope must be reduced. It is possible that the project backlog includes features that may have value but are not imperative. Reducing the scope may not be a viable option, but it is a valid option that should be explored. Since none of the answer choices are likely to increase velocity, asking the product owner to "eliminate" some user stories (or, in other words, to reprioritize the backlog) is the best answer to the question asked.

Reference:
A Guide to the Project Management Body of Knowledge, (PMBOK® Guide) – Sixth Edition, Project Management Institute Inc., 2017, Page(s) 131, 133

Agile Practice Guide – First Edition, Project Management Institute Inc., 2017, Page(s) 61

Question 59: Answer

Project A has an IRR of 15% and an NPV of $26,000 for a 2-year duration. Project B has an IRR of 14% and an NPV of $28,000 for a 4-year duration.

What is the opportunity cost, if you select project A instead of project B?

A) -2,000
B) 2,000
C) 26,000
☑ **D) 28,000**

Explanation:

When selecting between two options (or projects), the opportunity cost is simply the value of the option (or project) that was not selected. In this case, we selected project A over project B. This means that an opportunity cost is the value of project B which is $28,000. The IRR and duration of the projects are irrelevant.

iA60

Question 60: Answer

Halfway through the project, the project manager is informed by the program manager that all projects in the program will have an immediate 10% cut in their budgets. Based on the revised budget at completion (BAC), the project manager calculates a to-complete performance index (TCPI) of 0.96.

What is the best course of action for the project manager to comply with the revised budget?

A) Cut costs by reducing the size of the project team
Incorrect. A TCPI of less than 1.0 (as given by the scenario) means the project is trending under budget. Hence, there is no reason to cut costs to meet the revised budget. Although no schedule performance information has been provided, reducing the size of the team would likely delay the completion of the project and might put its deadline at risk.

B) Add resources to the project team in order to shorten the schedule duration
Incorrect. The question does not provide any information regarding schedule performance and specifically asks about meeting the revised budget. Adding resources might shorten the schedule duration but will increase costs. Increasing costs will make it less likely that the project will be completed within budget.

C) Submit a change request to reduce the project scope
Incorrect. There is no information presented by the scenario to suggest that the project goals cannot be met and that cutting scope would be required. Since the project has a TCPI of less than one, the project is trending to finish within the revised budget without reducing the project scope, making this answer choice an overreaction.

☑ **D) Work with the project team to maintain their cost performance for the remainder of the project**
Correct. TheTCPI represents the cost performance that must be maintained for the remainder of the project to meet the budget. Even with the reduced budget, the TCPI is still less than 1.0, which indicates that the project is trending to finish under budget. If the team can maintain their cost performance for the remainder of the project, the project will be completed slightly under budget.

Explanation:
The scenario indicates that the to-complete performance index (TCPI) is 0.96 based on the revised budget at completion (BAC). TCPI represents the cost performance that must be achieved for the remainder of the project to complete on budget. A TCPI greater than 1.0 means that completing the project on budget will be harder. A TCPI of less than 1.0 means that completing the project on budget will be easier. Thus, a TCPI of 0.96 indicates that the project is trending to complete slightly under budget. If the project team can maintain its current cost performance, the project will be delivered within the revised budget. The incorrect answer choices represent actions that are unnecessary for a project that is trending to complete within budget.

Reference:
A Guide to the Project Management Body of Knowledge, (PMBOK® Guide) – Sixth Edition, Project Management Institute Inc., 2017, Page(s) 266-267

https://www.projectmanagement.com/blog-post/2734/PMP-Exam-Tip--What-is-the-To-Complete-Performance-Index--TCPI--

Question 61: Answer

iA61

Your project engineer has just been fired. It turned out that he had lied about his professional experience. He had claimed to have worked on several similar projects such as yours, but it turned out that this was not the case. Your project sponsor is now understandably nervous and would like to know how much more the project will cost. You promise that you will get back to him in two days with a new estimate to complete. You set up a meeting with the two junior engineers on the project to work your way through the original estimates. You know already that the current project figures are as follows: EAC = 2,100,000; AC = 230,000; BAC = 2,140,000; EV = 233,000; CPI = 1.01 and SPI = 1.03.

How will you calculate the new ETC for your sponsor?

A) ETC = BAC – EV
✓ **B) We will create a new bottom up ETC**
C) ETC = EAC – AC
D) ETC = (BAC – EV) / CPI

Explanation:
There are two accepted ways in which you can calculate the ETC, and each is based on a particular assumption on how the project is progressing. Your interpretation of the assumptions is required. The formulas are:

ETC = EAC – AC: Use this formula when no variances are given.
ETC = New estimate when it is thought that the original estimate was flawed.

The other two formulas are considered orphan formulas. Orphaned formulas are formulas that do not appear in *PMBOK® Guide.* However, as the *PMBOK® Guide* is not the only reference source used by the PMI® to design their PMP exam questions, we have decided to keep the questions that use these formulas. Reference your Study Guide for an expanded explanation.

ETC = BAC - EV
ETC = (BAC - EV) / CPI

In this question the facts are clear: your engineer did not calculate properly the original budget for this project. Therefore, your original estimate was flawed. As such, you must create a new estimate for the project.

iA62

Question 62: Answer

An agile team is working within a comprehensive overarching project management plan. The team has completed 140 story points of the planned 150. The project budget is $150,000, and each story point is worth $1,000. Based on the money spent to date, the agile coach calculates a cost variance (CV) of -$2,000.

What is the best course of action to ensure the project achieves its goals?

A) Crash the schedule
Incorrect. Crashing is a schedule compression technique that will shorten the schedule duration by adding resources. While crashing might help complete the project sooner, it will also increase costs. Since a negative CV means the project is already over budget, taking this course of action will not help bring the project back into alignment with the budget.

B) Return the cost savings to the organization
Incorrect. According to the scenario, the project has a negative CV. The formula for CV is earned value (EV) less actual cost (AC). While no calculations are required for this question, the formula tells us that the project has spent more than it has earned, meaning it's over budget and will unlikely have any cost savings to return to the organization.

C) No action is necessary
Incorrect. The scenario indicates that the project has a negative cost variance (CV). A negative CV means that the project is running over budget. To bring the project back into alignment with its goals, the project leader will need to cut costs or secure additional capital for the project. If no action is taken, meeting project goals would be improbable.

☑ **D) Check the risk register for reserves**
Correct. The way the scenario is worded implies the project is hybrid, making it reasonable to assume the risk register exists on the project. A negative CV means the project is running over budget. If planned properly, the risk register should identify a response plan in case the project is running over budget, which may include contingency reserves.

Explanation:
The question asks to determine the appropriate action for the project to achieve its goals. While not much information has been provided, the fact that the cost variance (CV) is a negative value indicates that the project is running over budget. Therefore, of the available choices, one should identify the action that might address a budget shortfall. In this case, none of the incorrect answer choices represent an action that directly addresses the budget issue.

The fact that an agile team is working within an overarching project management plan makes this a hybrid project. Since a project management plan exists, it is reasonable to assume that a risk register with response plans is also part of the project documentation. As such, with the project running over budget, the first step would be to review the risk register to gain an understanding of what response plans have been established for cost overruns. A common approach to address risks associated with increased costs would be to establish a contingency reserve. Therefore, of the available choices, the best course of action for the project leader would be to check the risk register for contingency reserves that can be applied to bring the project back into alignment with the budget.

Reference:
A Guide to the Project Management Body of Knowledge, (PMBOK® Guide) – Sixth Edition, Project Management Institute Inc., 2017, Page(s) 262, 267

Agile Practice Guide – First Edition, Project Management Institute Inc., 2017, Page(s) 61

Question 63: Answer

iA63

Which of the following is correct?

☑ **A) EAC = AC + [(BAC – EV) / (CPI * SPI)], when project schedule and budget is a factor**
B) EAC = AC + BAC – EV, when variances will remain
C) EAC = BAC / CPI, when what the project has experienced to date will not continue
D) ETC = EAC – AC, when the original estimate was flawed

Explanation:
There are many ways to calculate the EAC depending on how the project is progressing. The key phrases *will remain, will not happen again,* and *fundamentally flawed* (or any variation of their meaning) indicate which formula to use. Therefore, to answer this question correctly, you not only need to know the correct formulas, but you also need to know which formula to use in combination with the correct keyword. In this question, we have listed four correct formulas, but three of them have been paired with the **wrong keyword.** Only answer A is paired with the **correct keyword.**

Here are the answers again, but we have included the **correct keywords** for you:

A) EAC = AC + [(BAC – EV) / (CPI * SPI)], when the project is over budget and you must meet a schedule deadline
B) EAC = AC + BAC – EV, when variances **will not happen again**
C) EAC = BAC / CPI, when variances **will remain**
D) ETC = EAC – AC, this formula cannot be used if the original estimate is flawed.

It is important to know which formula to use in what given situation.

iA64

Question 64: Answer

During project execution, the sponsor is concerned whether the project will be completed on time and requests the project manager to provide an update on the schedule performance metrics.

What data should the project manager collect to perform the calculations? (Choose two.)

A) The sum of all project expenditures to date
Incorrect. The sum of all project expenditures to date represents the actual cost (AC) of the project. AC is used to calculate a project's cost performance but not to determine the schedule performance. Therefore, data related to AC is neither relevant nor required for evaluating project schedule performance.

B) The expected cost to finish all of the remaining work
Incorrect. The expected cost to finish all of the remaining work describes the estimate to complete (ETC). This metric provides information regarding the project's cost performance rather than its schedule performance. Therefore, knowing the expected cost to finish all remaining work would not be relevant for schedule performance.

☑ **C) The authorized budget assigned to the scheduled work**
Correct. This answer choice provides a description of planned value (PV). PV is one of the variables that is used to calculate schedule performance. Therefore, the project manager will need to know the budgeted value for the scheduled work in order to provide the information requested by the project sponsor.

☑ **D) The planned value of all the work completed to date**
Correct. The planned value of all the work completed to date refers to the earned value (EV) of the project. EV is a metric that is used in the formulas to determine schedule performance. In order to calculate schedule performance, one needs to have some measure of the work that has already been completed.

E) A bottom-up estimate for the work remaining plus the actual cost
Incorrect. A bottom-up estimate for the work remaining is one method for calculating the estimate to complete (ETC). When actual cost (AC) is added to the ETC, the result is an estimate at completion (EAC). EAC provides information regarding cost performance rather than schedule performance, as requested by the question.

Explanation:
The schedule performance index (SPI) and schedule variance (SV) are the most common metrics that are used to assess project schedule performance. SPI can be derived by dividing earned value (EV) by the planned value (PV). SV can be calculated by subtracting PV from EV. In either case, one needs to know EV and PV in order to derive the schedule performance metrics. The correct answer choices provide a description for EV and PV. The incorrect answer choices are components that might be used to determine the cost, rather than schedule, performance.

Reference:
A Guide to the Project Management Body of Knowledge, (PMBOK® Guide) – Sixth Edition, Project Management Institute Inc., 2017, Page(s) 261-263, 267

Agile Practice Guide – First Edition, Project Management Institute Inc., 2017, Page(s) 69

Question 65: Answer

iA65

You work for the PMO of a Fortune 1000 company. Every month you are a member of a panel that grills project teams about their proposed projects. You ask them to provide more background on their data and calculations for the NPV. You want to know why they chose the double declining balance depreciation method. You point out errors in the cost benefit ratio formulas and watch their reactions. You also ask them to explain the PTA calculations for government contracts.

What is this type of project selection called?

A) Constrained optimization methods
B) Mathematical model
☑ **C) Murder board**
D) Economic model

Explanation:
This question injects formulas and calculations into the scenario, making you think that the formulas and calculations are important. They are not. What is described in the question is a project murder board, which is defined as *a panel of people who try to shoot down a new project idea.* The other answers are also project selection methods, but they don't explain why there is a panel of people that asks all of these questions.

Question 66: Answer

A project has a budget of $300,000. After four iterations, 200 story points have been completed versus 220 planned. By this point, the project has spent $25,000 and earned $30,000. To bring the project back on track, a developer has been added to the project team. Based on a new bottom-up estimate, it's expected that the project will meet its original goals.

What can be said of the current project performance? (Choose three.)

A) The schedule variance (SV) is zero
Incorrect. The formula for the schedule variance is SV = EV – PV. With 200 completed story points (EV) versus 220 planned story points (PV), the SV is: 200 – 220 = -20 story points. The SV is a negative value rather than zero. This determination can be made without any calculations: when EV is less than PV, the SV is negative.

☑ **B) The schedule performance index (SPI) is less than 1.0**
Correct. The schedule performance index is calculated as SPI = EV / PV. In the scenario, the project has completed 200 of 220 planned story points. Completing less than planned means the project is running behind schedule, which, in turn, suggests that the SPI is less than 1.0. Although not needed, the SPI can be calculated as 200 / 220 = 0.91.

☑ **C) The cost variance (CV) is a positive value**
Correct. The formula for the cost variance is CV = EV – AC. With $30,000 earned (EV) versus $25,000 spent (AC), the cost variance can be calculated as follows: CV = $30,000 – $25,000 = $5,000. The CV is a positive value, making this choice one of the correct answers.

D) The cost performance index (CPI) is equal to 1.0
Incorrect. The CPI is calculated as CPI = EV / AC. In this scenario, the

project has earned $30,000 and spent $25,000. Completing more than spending means the project is running under budget, which, in turn, suggests that the CPI is greater than 1.0, rather than equal to 1.0. While not required, one may find that: CPI = $30,000 / $25,000 = 1.2.

☑ **E) The estimate at completion (EAC) is $300,000**
Correct. The question indicates that a new bottom-up estimate has been calculated for the remainder of the project. Based on the new estimate, the project is projected to meet its original goals. BAC is one of the original goals and is given as $300,000. Therefore, it can be inferred that the newly calculated EAC is $300,000.

Explanation:
The information provided by the question indicates that the project is currently running behind schedule but under budget. This determination can be made based on the schedule performance index (SPI) and cost performance index (CPI), which can be calculated using the following formulas:

SPI = EV / PV
CPI = EV / AC

In the scenario, 200 story points have been completed (EV) versus 220 planned (PV). Therefore:

SPI = EV / PV = 200 / 220 = 0.91

Since the SPI is less than 1.0, the project is behind schedule. An SPI less than 1.0 also means the schedule variance (SV) is negative.

In the scenario, $30,000 has been earned (EV) versus $25,000 spent (AC). Therefore:

CPI = $30,000 / $25,000 = 1.2

Since the CPI is greater than 1.0, the project is under budget. A CPI greater than 1.0 also means the cost variance (CV) is positive.

According to the scenario, to bring the project back on track, a developer has been added to the project team. While the scenario does not explicitly mention this, one can assume that "back on track" refers to the project running behind schedule. Adding resources should improve productivity with a tradeoff of added cost, which the project can afford since it's running under budget. The cost performance and schedule performance metrics are based upon the current project performance rather than what might be anticipated in the future.

As far as the estimate at completion (EAC), there are several methods for making this determination. In this scenario, a bottom-up estimation has already been completed, and it's expected that the project will meet its original goals. BAC is one of the project's original goals. Therefore, it can be inferred that the EAC is equal to the BAC, which is given as $300,000.

Note: to answer this question correctly, no calculation is necessary. The calculations described above, as well as in the per-choice explanations, are provided for illustration purposes only.

Reference:

A Guide to the Project Management Body of Knowledge, (PMBOK® Guide) – Sixth Edition, Project Management Institute Inc., 2017, Page(s) 261-267

Agile Practice Guide – First Edition, Project Management Institute Inc., 2017, Page(s) 69

iA67

Question 67: Answer

What is the required level of accuracy for a budget estimate?

A) -10% – +10%
☑ **B) -10% – +25%**
C) -15% – +10%
D) -15% – +25%

Explanation:

The percentages for the various estimates that you need to know for the exam are as follows: rough order of magnitude estimate = -25% to +75% *(PMBOK® Guide);* preliminary estimate = -15% to +50%; **budget estimate = -10% to +25%;** definitive estimate = -5% to +10%; final estimate = 0%.

iA68

Question 68: Answer

Your company's accountant informs you that she will be using a 40% depreciation rate one of your project assets. You know that the asset costs $24,650, has been used on the project for less than three months and that it has an expected life of five years.

Which of the following depreciation methods is the accountant most likely using?

☑ **A) Double-declining balance**
B) Straight-line depreciation
C) Sum-of-the year's digits
D) Units of time depreciation

Explanation:

This is an example of a question that gives you more information than what is needed. The cost of $24,650 as well as the 3 months of usage can be ignored.

The most important value is "life span of 5 years". Based on this you calculate that the asset has a yearly straight-line depreciation rate of 20%. The formula for this is:

Depreciation Rate = 100% / Useful Life = 100% / 5 years = 20%

Next, we know that the accountant is depreciating 40% every year. This is a clear indicator that she is using double the straight-line percentage, which leads us to the answer of the double-declining balance method.

Question 69: Answer

iA69

The to-complete performance index (TCPI) is calculated by:

A) Multiplying the estimate at completion by the cumulative cost performance index
B) Adding the estimate at completion to the actual costs to date and multiplying by the cumulative cost performance index
☑ **C) Dividing the budgeted cost of the remaining work by the difference between the estimate at completion and actual costs to date**
D) Subtracting the actual costs to date from the estimate at complete

Explanation:
There are two formulas to calculate the TCPI

Based on BAC: **TCPI = (BAC – EV) / (BAC – AC)**
Based on EAC: **TCPI = (BAC – EV) / (EAC – AC)**

This question is referring to the 2nd of these formulas and it requires you to understand both the formula and what it is that you actually calculate:

BAC – EV = Budgeted remaining work
EAC – AC = The difference between the two

Question 70: Answer

As the project progresses, the project manager and the team determine that the estimate at completion (EAC) is higher than the initial budget at completion (BAC).

What can be concluded about this project?

A) The initial cost estimate for the project was wrong
Incorrect. It is possible that the initial cost estimate for the project was wrong. However, to make this determination, additional information is required. Since no specific information concerning the cost estimate is

provided in the scenario, asserting that the initial cost estimate for the project was wrong would be incorrect.

B) The project is running behind schedule
Incorrect. One way to determine whether the project is running ahead, on, or behind schedule, is to calculate the schedule variance (SV) or the schedule performance index (SPI). The SV and SPI, in turn, can be calculated using the earned value (EV) and planned value (PV). However, none of those are provided, making the calculation impossible.

C) Due to unforeseen issues, EAC is always higher than BAC
Incorrect. It is true that most projects experience unforeseen issues throughout their life cycle. However, drawing a conclusion that unforeseen issues 'always' result in the EAC being higher than the BAC would not be accurate. Besides, absolute statements like 'always', 'never', 'only', etc. typically represent incorrect answer choices.

☑ **D) No definitive conclusion can be made**
Correct. Various reasons could result in the estimate at completion (EAC) being higher than the initial budget at completion (BAC). Finding the reason behind this difference requires additional earned value measurements. Since this information is missing in the scenario, no definitive conclusion can be made about this project.

Explanation:
The initial budget at completion (BAC) is the project's total planned value (PV). Planned value, in turn, is the authorized budget assigned to scheduled work. The planned value is determined during project planning based on the information available at that time. However, as the project progresses, various factors can influence project performance, resulting in deviations from the original plan. These may include deviations from the BAC. When this happens, the project manager and team may develop a forecast for the estimate at completion (EAC) that is typically different from the initial BAC. In the scenario, the EAC is higher than the BAC. However, no additional information is provided. Therefore, making a definitive conclusion about the project would not be possible.

Reference:
A Guide to the Project Management Body of Knowledge, (PMBOK® Guide) – Sixth Edition, Project Management Institute Inc., 2017, Page(s) 264

PART THREE

Computational Questions

Recent lessons learned from those who have taken the exam indicate that there are fewer formula-based questions. Exam takers report it being more common to get the type of computational question where they had to perform a simple calculation, sometimes not even requiring a calculator.

However, PMI regularly updates the exam. New questions are added several times per year, and no one can predict precisely what you will see on your test.

That is why here, in Part Three, we give you a good number of easy, medium, hard and very hard computational questions to put your teeth into. Being able to identify the right formula and calculate the correct answer is a good indicator that you have mastered the theory. And that is the first step to passing your exam.

Once you review the answers, you will notice that the explanations for the computational questions are shorter than those for the interpretational questions in Part Two. This is because computational questions usually only have one correct answer. Once you know your formulas and understand how to apply them in a given situation, there is only one correct answer. And because 1 + 1 = 2, that means the explanations need to be less elaborate.

Computational Questions

cQ1

Question 1

A scrum master is leading a project with a total budget of $335,000. Up until now, out of 335 story points planned for the entire project, the team has completed 12 user stories worth 74 story points. The team has begun to work on a user story, which is worth six story points.

What is the current earned value for the project?

- [ ] A) $12,000
- [ ] B) $74,000
- [ ] C) $80,000
- [ ] D) $335,000

cQ2

Question 2

Your sponsor would like to know how long it takes to build the prototype on your project. The sponsor tells you that a similar project last year produced a prototype in 28 days. Your engineer tells you that the design of the prototype will take anywhere from 25 to 45 days and based on the design changes, the engineer thinks it will probably be close to about 32 days.

What is the three-point estimate (beta distribution) of the activity duration?

- [ ] A) 31 days
- [ ] B) 32 days
- [ ] C) 33 days
- [ ] D) 34 days

cQ3

Question 3

The activity "Ship Container" in your network diagram has an early start of Day 17, a late start of Day 22 and a late finish of Day 37.

What is the activity duration?

- [ ] A) 15 days
- [ ] B) 16 days
- [ ] C) 59 days
- [ ] D) 14 days

Question 4

cQ4

After the last project meeting your sponsor has asked you to give her a new estimate of the cost at the end of the project. This is because during the meeting it was found that so much has gone wrong until now, that the numbers are probably off. It is expected that from now on things will progress normally. You gather all the necessary numbers from your PMIS.

Which formula will you use to create the expected total cost of the project?

- [ ] A) EAC = BAC / CPI
- [ ] B) EAC = AC + ETC
- [ ] C) EAC = AC + BAC – EV
- [ ] D) ETC = EAC – AC

Question 5

cQ5

You are managing a project using Kanban as the development framework. The project has consumed $9,000 of the $30,000 budgeted for the planned work.

Based on the Kanban board below and assuming that each user story is of the same size and value, what can be said of the project's current status?

To Do (WIP Limit = 8)	**Development (WIP Limit = 4)**	**Unit Testing (WIP Limit = 2)**	**Integration Testing (WIP Limit = 3)**	**Final Approval (WIP Limit = 3)**	**Deployed to Production**
User story 21	User story 19	User story 17	User story 14	User story 11	User story 1
User story 22	User story 20	User story 18	User story 15	User story 12	User story 2
User story 23			User story 16	User story 13	User story 3
User story 24					User story 4
User story 25					User story 5
User story 26					User story 6
User story 27					User story 7
User story 28					User story 8
User story 29					User story 9
User story 30					User story 10

- [ ] A) The project is running under budget
- [ ] B) The CPI is less than 1.0
- [ ] C) The project needs to be re-baselined
- [ ] D) The CV is a negative value

cQ6

Question 6

Your project is budgeted at £500,000 with a schedule duration of eight months. You are currently at the end of Month 4 and you know that you are £20,000 ahead of schedule. Your estimated earned value is £350,000.

How much of the project budget is complete?

- [ ] A) 70%
- [ ] B) 42%
- [ ] C) 5%
- [ ] D) 50%

cQ7

Question 7

PV = 100, EV = 105, BAC = 400, AC = 102, CV = 3, EAC = 390.

How much is the VAC?

- [ ] A) VAC = 205
- [ ] B) VAC = 10
- [ ] C) VAC = 3
- [ ] D) VAC = -10

cQ8

Question 8

PV = 100, EV = 105, BAC = 400, AC = 102, CV = 3, ETC = 300.

How much is the EAC if the variances from the BAC are expected to continue at the same rate?

- [ ] A) 388
- [ ] B) 402
- [ ] C) 397
- [ ] D) 400

cQ9

Question 9

Your development team just completed the first sprint. Based on the burndown chart below, what can be said about the project's schedule performance?

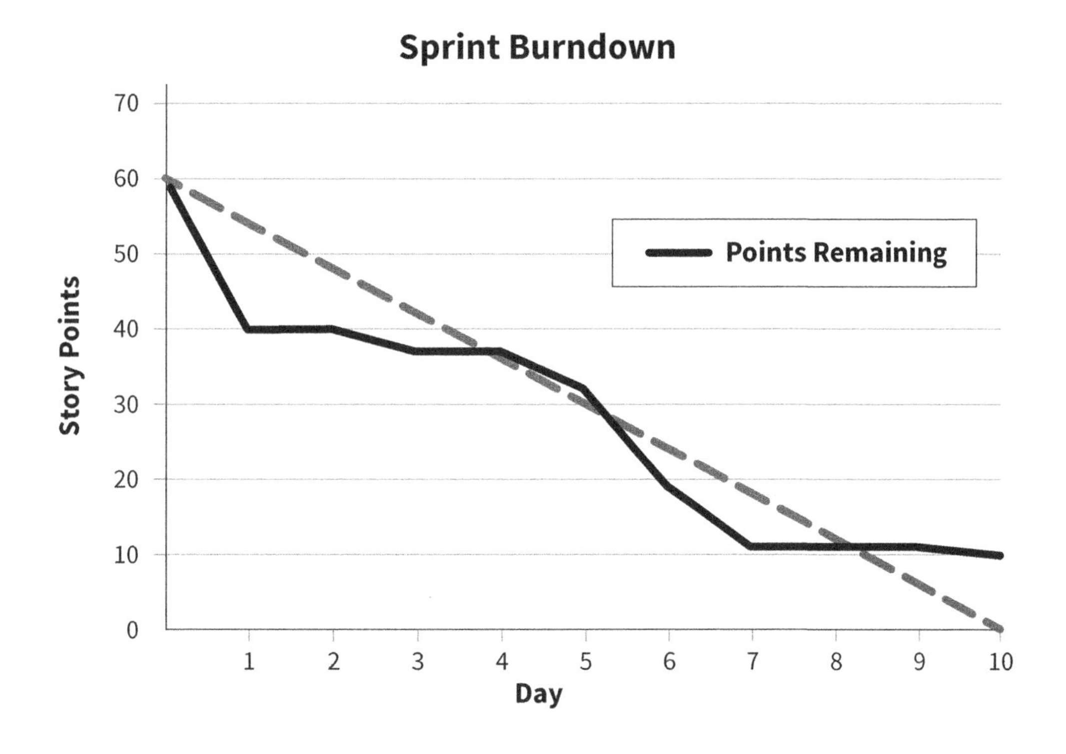

- [ ] A) The SPI is 0.83 and the team failed to meet the sprint goal
- [ ] B) The SPI is 1.0 and the team members met their commitment for the sprint
- [ ] C) The SPI is 1.17 and the team is ahead of schedule
- [ ] D) The SPI is 0.83 and the team completed the sprint backlog before the end of the sprint

Question 10

cQ10

You are planning a networking event. The idea is to bring 50 top executives from local companies who don't know each other together into one room and give them three minutes to talk with each other and then move on to the next person in the room. At the end of the event each attendee will have spoken to each of the other attendees. The event begins at 5pm.

When will the event end?

- [ ] A) About 61 hours later
- [ ] B) At 7:27pm
- [ ] C) At 7:30pm
- [ ] D) About 40 hours later

cQ11

Question 11

A project will be carried out using one-week sprints. The steering committee wants an estimate of how long the project will take. The project backlog has been estimated at 500 story points. The team estimates the velocity per sprint in the worst-case scenario as 10 story points, the best-case scenario with 25 story points, and the most likely scenario as 20 points.

Using a triangular distribution, how long will the project take?

- [ ] A) 25 weeks
- [ ] B) 32 weeks
- [ ] C) 50 weeks
- [ ] D) 64 weeks

cQ12

Question 12

PV = 100, EV = 105, BAC = 400, AC = 102, CV = 3.

What is the Estimate to Complete (ETC) if work will continue at the planned rate?

- [ ] A) 298
- [ ] B) 300
- [ ] C) 305
- [ ] D) 295

cQ13

Question 13

The plan for the first iteration was to complete 100 story points. However, the team was only able to complete 80. Each story point earns $1,000 for the project. The actual cost of the iteration was $90,000. As the iteration retrospective approaches, the scrum master requests that the team prepares all the data required to calculate the various earned value metrics.

At the retrospective, the team determines that the project is ________________ budget.

(On the real PMP exam you may be asked to provide your answer by filling in the blank with the letter representing the correct answer. But here in the book, we are asking you to select the answer below.)

- [ ] A) On
- [ ] B) Under
- [ ] C) Over
- [ ] D) Cannot be determined

Question 14

cQ14

PV = 100; EV = 105; BAC = 400; AC = 102; CV = 3; ETC = 300; EAC = 407.

How much is the Actual Cost?

- ☐ A) 100
- ☐ B) 102
- ☐ C) 7
- ☐ D) 2

Question 15

cQ15

You are the project manager of the Gutenberg project. One major activity in this project is the purchase of a printing press at a cost of CHF 2,500,000. The printing press has an expected life of 25 years, but it will only be used for the project for five years.

Using straight-line depreciation, what is the book value of the printing press at the end of its usage for the project?

- ☐ A) CHF 500,000
- ☐ B) CHF 1,500,000
- ☐ C) CHF 2,000,000
- ☐ D) CHF 2,500,000

Question 16

cQ16

You have received the following values from your statistical sampling: 80, 83, 85, 90, 82, 88, 90, 91, 94, 79.

What is the mean of this number set?

- ☐ A) 10
- ☐ B) 86.5
- ☐ C) 90
- ☐ D) 86.2

Question 17

cQ17

Your company is holding their annual employee get together. This year 123 employees have attended. Let's assume that each employee had a brief conversation with each of the other employees.

How many conversations took place?

- ☐ A) 15,006
- ☐ B) 123
- ☐ C) 7,503
- ☐ D) 15,129

cQ18

Question 18

A scrum master needs to provide a duration estimate for a project that is about to start its first two-week sprint. The team provides a pessimistic estimate of 50 sprints, a most likely estimate of 25 sprints, and an optimistic estimate of 20 sprints. The scrum master uses a beta distribution to calculate the estimated project duration.

How many weeks will it take for the team to complete the project based on the scrum master's calculation?

- ☐ A) 58 weeks
- ☐ B) 29 weeks
- ☐ C) 64 weeks
- ☐ D) 56 weeks

cQ19

Question 19

You have received the following values from your statistical sampling: 80, 83, 85, 90, 82, 88, 90, 91, 94, 79.

What is the median of this number set?

- ☐ A) 10
- ☐ B) 86.5
- ☐ C) 90
- ☐ D) 86.2

cQ20

Question 20

Your friend Joe is planning to retire 20 years from today. He is investing $200,000 in a long-term investment at 3.5%.

How much will this money be worth in 20 years?

- ☐ A) $399,757
- ☐ B) $401,627
- ☐ C) $379,597
- ☐ D) $397,957

cQ21

Question 21

As a scrum master, you are facilitating a sprint retrospective. In attendance is the development team of five, along with the product owner and the business analyst.

How many possible channels of communication exist?

- [ ] A) 10
- [ ] B) 21
- [ ] C) 28
- [ ] D) 56

Question 22

cQ22

Your customer is asking you for a preliminary estimate. Your numbers show that the project will most likely cost DKK 100,000.

What number will you give to your customer?

- [ ] A) DKK 100,000
- [ ] B) DKK 75,000 – 150,000
- [ ] C) DKK 85,000 – 150,000
- [ ] D) DKK 95,000 – 110,000

Question 23

cQ23

Your company owns an asset with an original value of $1,000. This asset will be depreciated using the double declining balance method over the period of five years.

What is the dollar value of the annual depreciation in Year 2?

- [ ] A) $400
- [ ] B) $144
- [ ] C) $240
- [ ] D) $86.40

Question 24

cQ24

The activity "Pack Container" in your network diagram has an early start of Day 12, a late start of Day 15, a duration of three, and a late finish of Day 17.

What is the total float of this activity?

- [ ] A) 1 day
- [ ] B) 2 days
- [ ] C) 3 days
- [ ] D) 4 days

cQ25

Question 25

A scrum master needs to inform project stakeholders of the team's velocity thus far. The team completed 21 story points during the first sprint, 23 in the second sprint, and 22 in the third sprint. For the upcoming fourth sprint, the team has committed to completing 26 story points.

What velocity should the scrum master report?

- ☐ A) 22
- ☐ B) 23
- ☐ C) 66
- ☐ D) 92

cQ26

Question 26

Your Company owns an asset with an original value of $1,000. This asset will be depreciated using the double declining balance method over the period of five years.

What is the percentage of the annual depreciation in Year 2?

- ☐ A) 20%
- ☐ B) $240
- ☐ C) 40%
- ☐ D) $140

cQ27

Question 27

Your eight-person team is getting support from two external consultants.

How many communication channels are added by hiring these consultants?

- ☐ A) 2
- ☐ B) 8
- ☐ C) 16
- ☐ D) 17

cQ28

Question 28

Your friend David is planning to retire 15 years from today.

How much should he invest today in a long-term investment, offering an annual interest rate of 3.5%, so that he ends up with $500,000.

- ☐ A) $201,509
- ☐ B) $231,627
- ☐ C) $279,597
- ☐ D) $298,445

Question 29

cQ29

The plan for the first iteration was to complete 100 story points. However, the team was only able to complete 80. Each story point earns $1,000 for the project. The actual cost of the iteration was $90,000. As the iteration retrospective approaches, the scrum master requests that the team prepares all the data required to calculate the various earned value metrics.

At the retrospective, the team determines that the project is _______________ schedule.

(On the real PMP exam you may be asked to provide your answer by filling in the blank with the letter representing the correct answer. But here in the book, we are asking you to select the answer below.)

- ☐ A) On
- ☐ B) Behind
- ☐ C) Ahead of
- ☐ D) Cannot be determined

Question 30

cQ30

Your designer has submitted his resignation. This means that you will be losing him, and your team size (including yourself) will go down from 12 to 11 people.

How many fewer communication channels will you personally have on your project after the designer leaves the company?

- ☐ A) 1
- ☐ B) 10
- ☐ C) 11
- ☐ D) 12

Question 31

cQ31

Your customer is asking for a rough order of magnitude estimate.

What numbers do you give him, assuming that your bottom up estimate gave you a project cost of approximately CHF 200,000?

- ☐ A) CHF 170,000 to CHF 300,000
- ☐ B) CHF 140,000 to CHF 340,000
- ☐ C) CHF 190,000 to CHF 220,000
- ☐ D) CHF 180,000 to CHF 250,000

cQ32

Question 32

A Kanban board is used to manage the workflow of a software development project. The project team has established a cycle time of five business days per user story. The lead time is 10 business days per story. There are 20 user stories remaining in the backlog.

What should the team report as an estimate to complete the backlog?

- [ ] A) 100 business days
- [ ] B) 200 business days
- [ ] C) 300 business days
- [ ] D) Cannot be determined without knowing the iteration length

cQ33

Question 33

Assuming a 3% interest rate, which of the following projects would you select?

- [ ] A) Project Gold with a total of 213,000 profit at the end of Year 4
- [ ] B) Project Silver with a total of 97,000 profit at the end of Year 1
- [ ] C) Project Bronze with a total of 128,000 profit at the end of Year 2
- [ ] D) Project Leather with a total of 168,000 profit at the end of Year 3

cQ34

Question 34

You have just been assigned to a new project that is very similar to the previous one. One particular task on the previous project took 146 days to finish. You are doing a top down estimate of the new project and you estimate that the same task on the new project will take at least 138 and at maximum 157 days.

What is the variance of this estimate?

- [ ] A) 3.16 days
- [ ] B) 146.5 days
- [ ] C) 64.8 days
- [ ] D) 10.03 days

cQ35

Question 35

You have received the following estimates from vendors:
Vendor 1: €75,000; Vendor 2: €65,000; Vendor 3: €93,500; Vendor 4: €82,000; Vendor 5: €94,000.

What is the median estimate that you have received?

- [ ] A) £81,900
- [ ] B) 5
- [ ] C) £94,000
- [ ] D) £82,000

Question 36

cQ36

Due to resource constraints, your company can not undertake all projects that are proposed. There are two new projects that have been proposed. Project Gold will take 1.5 years and will bring a profit of around €290,000 at the end of Year 2. Project Silver will take one year and reduce internal cost by €270,000 by the end of Year 4.

Assuming a 3% interest rate, which of the following is true?

- [ ] A) These projects are exactly equal in benefits.
- [ ] B) Project Gold has a PV that is about €33,000 higher than Project Silver
- [ ] C) Project Silver is more attractive than Project Gold and should be undertaken
- [ ] D) Project Silver has a PV that is about €25,000 higher than Project Gold

Question 37

cQ37

What is the early finish (EF) of Task One?

ES: 1	EF:
Name: One	**Duration: 6 days**
LS: 6	LF: 11
	5 days

- [ ] A) 5
- [ ] B) 6
- [ ] C) 7
- [ ] D) 8

Question 38

cQ38

AC = 105, EV = 100, PV = 97, CV = -5.

How much is the schedule variance (SV)?

- [ ] A) 1.03
- [ ] B) -3
- [ ] C) 3
- [ ] D) 8

cQ39

Question 39

Your quality assurance team is doing a review of a process. They find that the process used the following cycle times: 45sec, 49sec, 48sec, 50sec, 52sec, 49sec, 48sec, 50sec, 46sec.

How do you calculate the mean?

- ☐ A) Mean = n * (n – 1) /2
- ☐ B) Mean = (Pessimistic – Optimistic) / 6
- ☐ C) Mean = (45 + 49 + 48 + 50 + 52 + 49 + 48 + 50 + 46) / 9
- ☐ D) Mean = √sum (45 + 49 + 48 + 50 + 52 + 49 + 48 + 50 + 46) / 9

cQ40

Question 40

A company is considering the purchase of a robot that costs $50,000 upon delivery in 12 weeks and will generate $10,000 per year of net cash flow. The company is also considering contracting with a software development vendor for deliverables that will cost $36,000 payable after six two-week sprints and save $12,000 per year.

If the company only has sufficient funds to invest in one of these projects, which should they select?

- ☐ A) Purchase the robot because it has a payback period of five years
- ☐ B) Invest in the software because it has a payback period of three years
- ☐ C) Neither, because the NPV is negative for both projects
- ☐ D) Acquire the robot because it has a lower IRR

cQ41

Question 41

The following is a small section taken from a large network diagram for a construction project.

Which of the following statements is true?

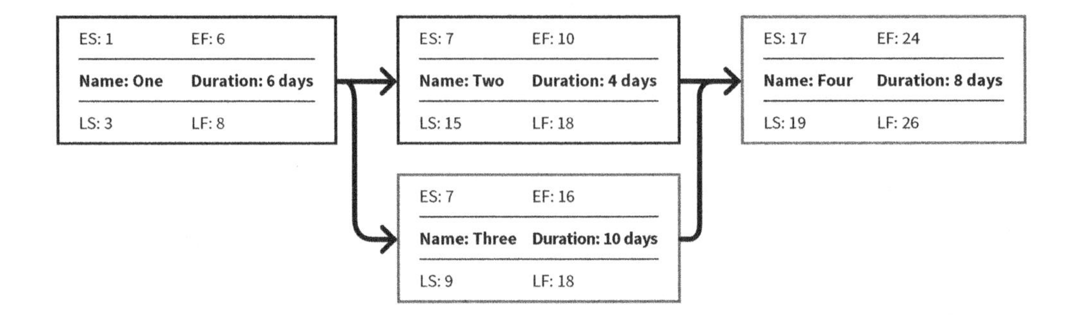

- [ ] A) Task 1 has a free float of two days
- [ ] B) Task 2 has a free float of six days
- [ ] C) Task 3 has a free float of nine days
- [ ] D) Task 4 has a free float of five days

Question 42

cQ42

Which of the following values correctly calculates the estimate to complete (ETC)?

- [ ] A) ETC = 30,000, when EAC = 100,000 and AC = 70,000
- [ ] B) ETC = 120,000, when BAC = 100,000 and EV = 20,000
- [ ] C) ETC = 110,000, when BAC = 125,000 and EV = 25,000 and CPI = 1.1
- [ ] D) ETC = 70,000, when BAC = 100,000 and AC = 30,000

Question 43

cQ43

You estimate that a task will take anywhere from 60-70 days to complete.

Assuming that you estimated towards 3 sigma, how certain are you about this duration?

- [ ] A) 68.27%
- [ ] B) 95.45%
- [ ] C) 99.73%
- [ ] D) 99.99%

Question 44

cQ44

Your earned value analysis shows the following values: EV = 90,000; ETC = 100,000; EAC = 190,000; PV = 110,000; AC = 90,000.

Which of the following is true?

- [ ] A) The project is ahead of schedule and on budget
- [ ] B) The project is on schedule and below budget
- [ ] C) The EAC is incorrect
- [ ] D) The project is behind schedule and on budget

Question 45

cQ45

The plan for the first iteration was to complete 100 story points. However, the team was only able to complete 80. Each story point earns $1,000 for the project. The actual cost of the iteration was $90,000. As the iteration retrospective approaches, the scrum master requests that the team prepares all the data required to calculate the various earned value metrics.

At the retrospective, the team determines that the cost performance index (CPI) of the iteration was ______________.

(On the real PMP exam you may be asked to provide your answer by filling in the blank with the letter representing the correct answer. But here in the book, we are asking you to select the answer below.)

- [ ] A) 1.25
- [ ] B) 0.80
- [ ] C) 1.11
- [ ] D) 0.89

Question 46

What is the expected monetary value (EMV) of the following event?

Probability	Impact in $
0.5	-8,000
0.2	-7,000
0.2	-4,500
0.1	2000

- [ ] A) 2,000
- [ ] B) -8,000
- [ ] C) -6,100
- [ ] D) -4,500

Question 47

You have received several bids for your project. You are now using a weighting system to determine which of the bids meets your needs best. The weighting system contains weights for price, quality, vendor experience, duration, risk management, and distance.

Which of the following bids would you select?

Maximum Score	25	18	18	15	13	11
Vendor	**Price**	**Quality**	**Experience**	**Duration**	**Risk Mgmt.**	**Distance**
PM Experts	21	12	13	9	11	8
The PM Shop	20	14	17	10	10	7
Gold Platers	18	13	16	9	12	9
ScopeCreep PM	17	15	16	11	12	9

- ☐ A) PM Experts
- ☐ B) The PM Shop
- ☐ C) Gold Platers
- ☐ D) ScopeCreep PM

Question 48

cQ48

An organization has just completed a needs analysis for a potential project. The project will require five two-week sprints to complete after which time the organization will receive $50,000 in incremental revenue. The cost has been estimated at $25,000.

What is the best course of action?

- ☐ A) Decline the project as costs are double the benefits
- ☐ B) Approve the project but only if the NPV < 0
- ☐ C) Reject the project because the BCR > 1
- ☐ D) Approve the project based on a BCR of 2

Question 49

cQ49

What is the ES of Task Six?

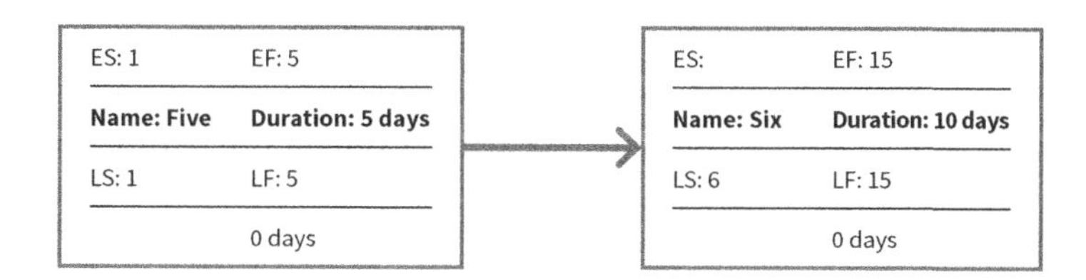

- ☐ A) 4
- ☐ B) 5
- ☐ C) 6
- ☐ D) 7

cQ50

Question 50

What is the critical path of the project that contains the following four tasks?

- Task A starts at the beginning of the project and has a duration of two days
- Task B starts after the completion of Task A and has a duration of three days
- Task C starts after the completion of Task A and has a duration of seven days
- Task D starts after the completion of both Tasks B and C and has a duration of four days

☐ A) 7 days
☐ B) 10 days
☐ C) 13 days
☐ D) 16 days

cQ51

Question 51

Your project is four weeks behind schedule, and you have been asked to crash the project in order to make up for the lost time. The tasks listed in the table below are all on the critical path.

Which of the tasks below would you crash?

Task	Original Duration	Crashed Duration	Time Savings	Original Cost	Crash Cost	Cost after Crashing
A	14	10	4	22,000	6,500	28,500
B	8	6	2	17,000	2,000	19,000
C	15	12	3	23,000	2,000	25,000
D	12	10	2	16,000	3,500	19,500
E	4	3	1	12,000	3,000	15,000
F	8	7	1	22,000	4,000	26,000

☐ A) Task A
☐ B) Tasks C & E
☐ C) Tasks B & D
☐ D) Tasks D & E & F

Question 52

cQ52

Your project is currently proceeding exactly on schedule and budget. The project team has finished four of eight sprints and completed 150 of the planned 300 story points. Each story point is budgeted at $100.

What is the estimate at completion (EAC) for the project?

- ☐ A) $0.00
- ☐ B) 1.0
- ☐ C) $15,000
- ☐ D) $30,000

Question 53

cQ53

You recently installed a new PMIS tool that also allows you to perform earned value analysis. The tool gives you the following data: EV = 231,000; PV = 261,000; AC = 256,000.

Which of the following do you expect to see in your PMIS tool?

- ☐ A) CV = -25,000; SV = +30,000
- ☐ B) CV = -25,000; SV = -30,000
- ☐ C) CV = +25,000; SV = +30,000
- ☐ D) CV = +25,000; SV = -30,000

Question 54

cQ54

Your company is constructing a new just-in-time (JIT) manufacturing facility in Puerto Rico. This facility will be producing 3,000 bicycles every day. The raw materials are delivered to the facility on standard pallets, each taking up 1m² (one square meter) of space. Every day approximately 500 pallets will be delivered to the facility. You have asked four local companies to submit their offers for constructing this new manufacturing facility.

If you had to pick a vendor based on just the following information, which one would you choose?

- ☐ A) Company A: 8,000m² of production space and 500m² of pallet storage
- ☐ B) Company B: 8,000m² of production space and 250m² of pallet storage
- ☐ C) Company C: 8,000m² of production space and 150m² of pallet storage
- ☐ D) Company D: 8,000m² of production space and 0m² of pallet storage

cQ55

Question 55

The plan for the first iteration was to complete 100 story points. However, the team was only able to complete 80. Each story point earns $1,000 for the project. The actual cost of the iteration was $90,000. As the iteration retrospective approaches, the scrum master requests that the team prepares all the data required to calculate the various earned value metrics.

At the retrospective, the team determines that the schedule performance index (SPI) of the iteration was _______________.

(On the real PMP exam you may be asked to provide your answer by filling in the blank with the letter representing the correct answer. But here in the book, we are asking you to select the answer below.)

- ☐ A) 1.25
- ☐ B) 0.80
- ☐ C) 1.11
- ☐ D) 0.89

cQ56

Question 56

EV = 105 and SPI = 0.9375.

How much is the schedule variance (SV)?

- ☐ A) Cannot be calculated based on these numbers
- ☐ B) -7
- ☐ C) -6
- ☐ D) 7

cQ57

Question 57

You work in the PMO of a mid-sized company. Your PPM tool shows that there are currently three new projects waiting for selection. They are Project Stone with an NPV of ¥15,000,000, Project Paper with an NPV of ¥17,000,000 and Project Scissors with an NPV of ¥13,000,000. You present these three projects at the monthly project selection board meeting. After initial discussion it was immediately decided that Project Scissors will not be pursued at all. At this point a lengthy discussion begins about the benefits of both Project Stone and Project Paper. After 45 minutes the CEO asks you: "What is the opportunity cost of selecting Project Stone instead of Project Paper?"

What is your answer?

- [ ] A) ¥17,000,000
- [ ] B) ¥15,000,000
- [ ] C) -¥2,000,000
- [ ] D) ¥2,000,000

Question 58

cQ58

You are three months into a nine-month project. The project is progressing as planned and you expect no major problems in the foreseeable future. Your PMIS is reporting the following values: BAC = 500,000; SPI = 1.1; CPI = 1.05; EV = 173,000; AC = 164,761.

How much is the EAC?

- [ ] A) 491,761
- [ ] B) 454,545
- [ ] C) 189,761
- [ ] D) 476,190

Question 59

cQ59

Your project team has 25 members. You have a monthly "All hands" meeting. In the past three months you have had the following attendance: January 21 attendees, February 16 attendees, March 23 attendees.

What is the mean attendance?

- [ ] A) 16
- [ ] B) 20
- [ ] C) 23
- [ ] D) 60

Question 60

cQ60

What is the Late Finish of Task One?

1	6
Name: One	**Duration: 6 days**
5	10

- [ ] A) LF = 1
- [ ] B) LF = 5
- [ ] C) LF = 6
- [ ] D) LF = 10

cQ61

Question 61

Your project consists of the following three sequential tasks. How long will the project take?

Task Number	Duration Estimates (Beta Distribution)		
	Optimistic	Most Likely	Pessimistic
1	10	12	15
2	9	14	21
3	17	23	32

- ☐ A) 36 days
- ☐ B) 49 days
- ☐ C) 50 days
- ☐ D) 68 days

cQ62

Question 62

How much is the cost performance index (CPI)?

- ☐ A) CPI = 50, when EV = 100 and AC = 50
- ☐ B) CPI = 1.0, when SPI = 0.1
- ☐ C) CPI = 0.9, when EV = 100 and PV = 110
- ☐ D) CPI = 0.9, when EV = 100 and AC = 110

cQ63

Question 63

Which of the following projects will you select?

- ☐ A) Project Gold: profit is 200,000, EV is 450,000, ROI is 8%
- ☐ B) Project Bear: investment is 350,000, ROI is 8.1%, payback period is four years
- ☐ C) Project Stellar: lowered expenses are 45,000, profit is -8,000, ROI is 7.5%
- ☐ D) Project HHGTTG: PV is 50,000

Question 64

cQ64

What is the late finish (LF) of Activity Six?

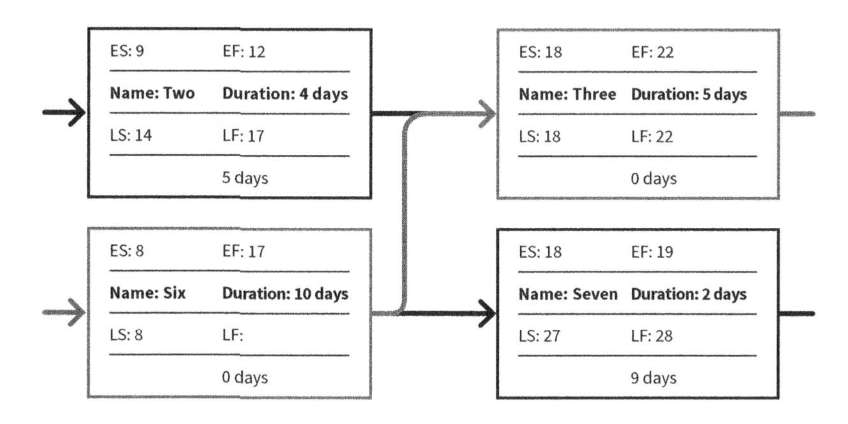

- [ ] A) 26
- [ ] B) 18
- [ ] C) 28
- [ ] D) 17

Question 65

cQ65

Your project is exactly half finished. You consult your earned value system and you receive the following numbers: BAC = 500,000; CPI = 1.1; SPI = 1.2; CV = -15,000; SV = -19,000.

How much is your EV?

- [ ] A) 416,666
- [ ] B) 500,000
- [ ] C) 250,000
- [ ] D) 227,272

Question 66

cQ66

Two hours after a successful project status presentation you get a call from your senior engineer. He asks to see you immediately for an urgent discussion. Three minutes later he is in your office, door closed, and he looks downcast. He tells you that your presentation earlier in the day had made him think. He had suddenly realized that he had missed several key project components. Because of that he realized that his original cost estimations were completely wrong. At the end of the meeting he promised to give you a new estimate tomorrow. The new estimate arrives less than 24 hours later, and your numbers now look as follows: BAC: 1,600,000. AC = 170,000; CPI = 1.03; SPI = 1.05; EV = 175,100.

How much do you now estimate that the project will cost, if the new estimate to complete that you received from your engineer is 1,570,000?

- ☐ A) 1,553,398
- ☐ B) 1,740,000
- ☐ C) 1,595,000
- ☐ D) 1,470,458

cQ67

Question 67

Your project consists of the following three tasks. What is the standard deviation of Task 2?

Task Number	Duration Estimates		
	Optimistic	Most Likely	Pessimistic
1	10	12	15
2	9	14	21
3	17	23	32

- ☐ A) 14.33 days
- ☐ B) 2 days
- ☐ C) 6.77 days
- ☐ D) 4 days

cQ68

Question 68

You are using the straight-line depreciation method for a company car that has a projected life of five years. You purchased this car for £17,000 and you expect that you will be able to sell the car at the end of the five years for £2,000.

How much is the depreciation of this car in the third year?

- ☐ A) £3,600
- ☐ B) £3,400
- ☐ C) £2,800
- ☐ D) £3,000

Question 69

cQ69

A project manager has to select between the following four vendors. Price has a 60% weight and duration a 40% weight.

Which of the vendors should the project manager select?

Vendor	Price	Schedule
PM Experts	20	10
The PM Shop	19	12
Gold Platers	16	11
ScopeCreep PM	15	13

- ☐ A) PM Experts
- ☐ B) The PM Shop
- ☐ C) Gold Platers
- ☐ D) ScopeCreep PM

Question 70

cQ70

Two months ago, your customer formally submitted several changes to the project. These changes were reviewed and approved by the change board. Today you are reviewing the first project numbers affected by these approved changes: EV = 240,000; AC = 253,700; PV = 250,000; SPI = 0.96; BAC = 700,000.

How much is your new ETC?

- ☐ A) 486,300
- ☐ B) 466,700
- ☐ C) ETC cannot be calculated and a new bottom up estimate is required
- ☐ D) 479,166

Question 71

cQ71

You are managing an ERP implementation project that is planned to complete in 12 months. After six months into the schedule, the project is already one month behind schedule.

What is the project's earned schedule (ES) at this stage?

- ☐ A) 7 months
- ☐ B) 6 months
- ☐ C) 5 months
- ☐ D) The ES cannot be determined

cQ72

Question 72

Your project consists of the following three sequential tasks.

How long will the project take to complete if you assume an accuracy of 1 standard deviation?

Task Number	Duration Estimates			Duration	Standard Deviation	Variance
	Optimistic	Most Likely	Pessimistic			
1	9	12	18	12.5	1.5	2.25
2	9	14	22	14.5	2.16	4.69
3	17	23	32	23.5	2.5	6.25

- [ ] A) 50.5 days
- [ ] B) 50.5 days ± 2.05
- [ ] C) 50.5 days ± 3.63
- [ ] D) 50.5 days ± 4.39

cQ73

Question 73

AC = 100, CPI = 0.9, SPI = 1.1.

How much is the cost variance?

- [ ] A) -8.18
- [ ] B) 10
- [ ] C) -10
- [ ] D) 8.18

cQ74

Question 74

You have just finished a 10-month long project.

Assuming that you were the project manager, how much of this time have you spent communicating with others in total?

- [ ] A) 7 months
- [ ] B) 8 months
- [ ] C) 9 months
- [ ] D) 10 months

Question 75

cQ75

A project is 50% complete. BAC = 200,000; EV = 92,000; AC = 97,000.

What is the TCPI based on BAC?

- [ ] A) 103,000
- [ ] B) 0.04
- [ ] C) 0.96
- [ ] D) 1.05

Question 76

cQ76

The project board is presented with the following information about current project opportunities: Project A has a duration of four years and an NPV of $40,000, Project B has a duration of three years and an NPV of $45,000, Project C has a duration of six years and an NPV of $62,000, and Project D has a duration of eight years and an NPV of $56,000.

Which project will you select?

- [ ] A) Project A
- [ ] B) Project B
- [ ] C) Project C
- [ ] D) Project D

Question 77

cQ77

Your current earned value numbers look as follows: EV = 200,000; AC = 210,000; BAC = 375,000; SPI = 1.05.

How much is the EAC if your primary project constraint is meeting your schedule? (Round up/down to four decimal places.)

- [ ] A) 376,666
- [ ] B) 385,000
- [ ] C) 394,736
- [ ] D) 386,767

cQ78

Question 78

Your project consists of the following three tasks.

What is the standard deviation of the project?

Task Number	Duration Estimates		
	Optimistic	Most Likely	Pessimistic
1	10	12	15
2	9	14	21
3	17	23	32

- ☐ A) 3.31 days
- ☐ B) 4.30 days
- ☐ C) 5.33 days
- ☐ D) 2.30 days

Question 79

You have received the following values from your statistical sampling: 80, 83, 85, 90, 82, 88, 90, 91, 94, 79.

What is the mode of this number set?

- ☐ A) 10
- ☐ B) 86.5
- ☐ C) 90
- ☐ D) 86.2

Question 80

You are the project manager of the Speedy Software implementation project.

Based on the following information, which tasks are on the critical path?

- Task A starts at the beginning of the project and has a duration of one day
- Task B starts after the completion of Task A and has a duration of two days
- Task C starts after the completion of Task B and has a duration of four days
- Task D starts after the completion of both Tasks C and E and has a duration of four days

- Task E starts after the completion of Task F and has a duration of two days
- Task F starts after the completion of Task A and has a duration of seven days

☐ A) A, B, C, E, D
☐ B) A, F, E, D
☐ C) A, B, C, F
☐ D) A, F, B, C, D

Question 81

cQ81

What is the late start of activity Four?

ES: 23	EF: 30
Name: Four	**Duration: 8 days**
LS:	LF: 30
	0 days

☐ A) 24
☐ B) 23
☐ C) 30
☐ D) 22

Question 82

cQ82

A project that is 80% complete. BAC = 435,000; EAC = 478,000; EV = 410,000; AC – 452,000.

What is the project's TCPI, based on EAC?

☐ A) 1.04
☐ B) .04
☐ C) .96
☐ D) 25,000

Question 83

cQ83

The SPI on your project is currently at 0.95, resulting in a three-week delay. You assume that this trend will continue, and you estimate that you are going to have to make up five weeks in order to stay on track and reach your target delivery date. As such, you decide to crash your project. Below are the tasks that you consider crashing.

Which ones would you crash in order to gain five weeks?

Task	Original Duration	Crashed Duration	Time Savings	On Critical Path?	Original Cost	Cost after Crashing
A	13	10	5	No	12,000	15,000
B	8	7	1	Yes	16,000	19,500
C	16	12	4	Yes	22,000	29,500
D	12	9	3	No	17,000	19,000
E	4	3	1	Yes	22,000	26,000
F	16	13	3	Yes	23,000	26,500
G	14	14	2	No	21,000	22,000
H	8	7	1	Yes	19,000	22,000

- ☐ A) Task A
- ☐ B) Tasks C & E
- ☐ C) Tasks D & G
- ☐ D) Tasks B & F & H

cQ84

Question 84

Following are some current measures on your project: actual time (AT) = three months; actual cost (AC) = $3,000; budget at completion (BAC) = $10,000; earned schedule (ES) = two months?

What is the project's SPI?

- ☐ A) 1.33
- ☐ B) 0.67
- ☐ C) 1.50
- ☐ D) 5.00

Question 85

An inspection has revealed the following weights of screws that are produced in your plant: 3.65g, 3.66g, 3.58g, 3.62g, 3.61g, 3.67g.

What is the median weight of the screws in this data set?

- ☐ A) 6
- ☐ B) 3.63167
- ☐ C) 3.58
- ☐ D) 3.635

Question 86

cQ86

What is the average of the following values: (100), 50, 75, (20), 99, (70), 40, 14?

- [ ] A) 63.6
- [ ] B) 11
- [ ] C) 58.5
- [ ] D) 14

Question 87

cQ87

On your last project, the task of "Develop Training Plan" took 12 days. On the current project the trainer estimates that it will take anywhere from 22 to 40 days, but she says that "It will probably take me 28 days". You want to be about 95% certain that the duration in your schedule is correct.

What duration will you assume?

- [ ] A) 26 to 32 days
- [ ] B) 29 days
- [ ] C) 20 to 38 days
- [ ] D) 23 to 35 days

Question 88

cQ88

Which of the following is true?

- [ ] A) SPI = -1, when EV = 100 and PV = 101
- [ ] B) SPI = 0.9, when EV = 100 and PV = 110
- [ ] C) SPI = 1.0, when CPI = 1.0
- [ ] D) SPI = 0.9, when EV = 100 and AC = 110

Question 89

cQ89

You return from a long overdue vacation on the beach and you find that your earned value numbers look as follows: EV = 100,000; CPI = 0.85; SPI = 0.77; AC = 117,000; PV = 130,000; ETC = 315,000; BAC = 420,000. You discuss these numbers with your team. In particular, you point out to them that based on the CPI and the SPI the project is both over budget and behind schedule. The team leader informs you that this does not come as too much of a surprise. You learn that during your absence, the team had faced unexpected technical issues, which must have caused these variances. The team lead promises that this was unusual, that the issues have been resolved, and that the project will now return to normal again.

Based on this information, what is your new EAC?

- [ ] A) 437,000
- [ ] B) 432,000
- [ ] C) 494,117
- [ ] D) 493,470

cQ90

Question 90

Your sponsor would like to know how long it takes to build the prototype on your project. He tells you that a similar project last year produced a prototype in 28 days. Your engineer tells you that the design of the prototype will take anywhere from 25 to 45 days and based on the design changes he thinks it will probably be close to about 32 days.

What is the simple average of the numbers that you have received?

- [ ] A) 31 days
- [ ] B) 32 days
- [ ] C) 33 days
- [ ] D) 34 days

Answers to the Computational Questions

cA1

Question 1: Answer

A scrum master is leading a project with a total budget of $335,000. Up until now, out of 335 story points planned for the entire project, the team has completed 12 user stories worth 74 story points. The team has begun to work on a user story, which is worth six story points.

What is the current earned value for the project?

A) $12,000
Incorrect. $12,000 could have resulted from multiplying the number of the completed user stories (which is 12 according to the scenario) by $1,000. However, the earned value should be based on the story points that have been completed rather than the number of user stories that have been completed.

☑ **B) $74,000**
Correct. The team has completed 74 story points. The value of each story point can be obtained from the project budget, which is $335,000, and the total number of story points, which is 335. Therefore, the value of each story point is $1,000. Hence, the current earned value of the project is $74,000.

C) $80,000
Incorrect. This answer could have been a result of 74 completed story points and 6 story points of the user story that is currently in development. In agile projects, partially completed work does not provide value to the customer. Therefore, no credit is given for partially completed work. Thus, the 6 story points currently in development would not be used to determine the earned value.

D) $335,000
Incorrect. $335,000 represents that total project budget. The team will only realize this amount as the earned value once all user stories have been developed, completed, and accepted. The question asks about the 'current' earned value rather than the total earned value at the end of the project.

Explanation:
This scenario requires the calculation of earned value in an agile environment. Earned value is the value of the work completed based on the budgeted value for that work. In this case, the project budget is $335,000 and the total number of story points is 335. Thus, the value for each story point can be calculated as $335,000 / 335 which is $1,000 per story point. The project team has successfully completed 74 story points. Therefore, the budgeted value of the completed work is $74,000, which represents the earned value for the project.

Note: with projects carried out using the agile project management approach, as in the scenario provided, partially completed work does not represent any value for the customer and, therefore, is not counted towards the calculation of the earned value. Therefore, the six story points of the user story that is currently in development should not be taken into account.

Reference:
A Guide to the Project Management Body of Knowledge, (PMBOK® Guide) – Sixth Edition, Project Management Institute Inc., 2017, Page(s) 261

Agile Practice Guide – First Edition, Project Management Institute Inc., 2017, Page(s) 69

Question 2: Answer

cA2

Your sponsor would like to know how long it takes to build the prototype on your project. He tells you that a similar project last year produced a prototype in 28 days. Your engineer tells you that the design of the prototype will take anywhere from 25 to 45 days and based on the design changes he thinks it will probably be close to about 32 days.

What is the three-point estimate (Beta distribution) of the activity duration?

A) 31 days
B) 32 days
☑ **C) 33 days**
D) 34 days

Explanation:
The formula for the PERT beta three-point estimate or weighted average is **[Pessimistic + (4 * Most Likely) + Optimistic] / 6.** The numbers to use are only those from your engineer. The sponsor's value of 28 days is irrelevant. Therefore, you calculate **[45 + (4 * 32) + 25] / 6 = 33 days**

Question 3: Answer

The activity "Ship Container" in your network diagram has an early start of Day 17, a late start of day 22 and a late finish of day 37.

What is the activity duration?

A) 15 days
☑ **B) 16 days**
C) 59 days
D) 14 days

Explanation:
The formula to calculate activity duration is **Late Finish – Late Start + 1**
Therefore, you calculate **37 – 22 + 1 = 16**

Question 4: Answer

After the last project meeting your sponsor has asked you to give her a new estimate of the cost at the end of the project. This is because during the meeting it was found that so much has gone wrong until now, that the numbers are probably off. It is expected that from now on things will progress normally. You gather all the necessary numbers from your PMIS.

Which formula will you use to create the expected total cost of the project?

A) EAC = BAC / CPI
B) EAC = AC + ETC
☑ **C) EAC = AC + BAC – EV**
D) ETC = EAC – AC

Explanation:
The sponsor has asked you to calculate the estimate at completion (EAC). Based on the information in the scenario we learn that the past variances

are not typical because things should be normal going forward from here. Hence, we will use the EAC formula, which is used when it is assumed that past variances will not happen again. We will calculate the actual cost to date plus original budget for the remaining work. (BAC - EV) is the original budget for the remaining work.

Question 5: Answer

cA5

You are managing a project using Kanban as the development framework. The project has consumed $9,000 of the $30,000 budgeted for the planned work. Based on the Kanban board below and assuming that each user story is of the same size and value, what can be said of the project's current status?

To Do (WIP Limit = 8)	Development (WIP Limit = 4)	Unit Testing (WIP Limit = 2)	Integration Testing (WIP Limit = 3)	Final Approval (WIP Limit = 3)	Deployed to Production
User story 21	User story 19	User story 17	User story 14	User story 11	User story 1
User story 22	User story 20	User story 18	User story 15	User story 12	User story 2
User story 23			User story 16	User story 13	User story 3
User story 24					User story 4
User story 25					User story 5
User story 26					User story 6
User story 27					User story 7
User story 28					User story 8
User story 29					User story 9
User story 30					User story 10

☑ **A) The project is running under budget**
Correct. To determine project performance related to budget, a cost performance index (CPI) should be calculated. The CPI is the earned value (EV) divided by actual cost (AC). The earned value is represented by the 10 completed user stories with a total value of $10,000. The actual cost is stated as $9,000. Therefore, the CPI = $10,000 / $9,000 = 1.1. A CPI greater than 1.0 means the project is running under budget.

B) The CPI is less than 1.0
Incorrect. The cost performance index (CPI) can be calculated as earned value (EV) divided by actual cost (AC). The earned value is represented by the 10 completed user stories with a total value of $10,000. The actual cost is stated as $9,000. Therefore, the CPI = $10,000 / $9,000 = 1.1, which is greater, no less than 1.0.

C) The project needs to be re-baselined
Incorrect. Re-baselining a project is an option that can be considered when the project budget or schedule is no longer viable. However, there is not enough information in the scenario to suggest that there is an issue with the project baselines. Therefore, re-baselining the project is unwarranted and premature.

D) The CV is a negative value
Incorrect. The cost variance (CV) can be calculated as the earned value (EV) minus the actual cost (AC). In this case, the earned value is represented by the 10 completed user stories with a total value of \$10,000, and the actual cost is provided in the scenario as \$9,000. Therefore, the CV = \$10,000 – \$9,000 = \$1,000, which is a positive value.

Explanation:
In order to answer this question correctly, one must calculate either the cost performance index (CPI) or the cost variance (CV). The formulas for each are **CPI = EV / AC** and **CV = EV – AC,** where EV is the earned value and AC is the actual cost. The actual cost of the project to date is stated in the question as \$9,000. Earned value is the value of the work completed based on the budgeted value for that work. With 30 total user stories and a budget of \$30,000, each user story can be calculated as \$30,000 / 30 which is \$1,000 per user story (note that the question stipulates that each user story is of the same size and value). The earned value is represented by the 10 user stories that have been deployed to production as seen in the far-right column of the Kanban board. With 10 stories completed at a value of \$1,000 each, the earned value is \$10,000. Applying the formulas, the CPI = \$10,000 / \$9,000, which is 1.1, and the CV = \$10,000 – \$9,000, which is \$1,000. Therefore, the project is running under budget.

Reference:
A Guide to the Project Management Body of Knowledge, (PMBOK® Guide) – Sixth Edition, Project Management Institute Inc., 2017, Page(s) 261-263, 267

Agile Practice Guide – First Edition, Project Management Institute Inc., 2017, Page(s) 65-66, 69

cA6

Question 6: Answer

Your project is budgeted at £500,000 with schedule duration of eight months. You are currently at the end of Month 4 and you know that you are £20,000 ahead of schedule. Your estimated earned value is £350,000.

How much of the project budget is complete?

☑ **A) 70%**
B) 42%
C) 5%
D) 50%

Explanation:
The formula for calculating percent complete of a project budget is
(EV / BAC) * 100%. Therefore, you calculate **(350,000 / 500,000) * 100% = 70%.**

Note that the 20,000 schedule variance is irrelevant to this calculation.

Question 7: Answer

cA7

PV = 100, EV = 105, BAC = 400, AC = 102, CV = 3, EAC = 390.

How much is the VAC?

A) VAC = 205
☑ **B) VAC = 10**
C) VAC = 3
D) VAC = -10

Explanation:
The formula for calculating the variance at completion (VAC) is
VAC = BAC – EAC. Therefore, you calculate **400 – 390 = 10.**

Question 8: Answer

cA8

PV = 100, EV = 105, BAC = 400, AC = 102, CV = 3, ETC = 300.

How much is the EAC if the variances from the BAC are expected to continue at the same rate?

☑ **A) 388**
B) 402
C) 397
D) 400

Explanation:
When variances are expected to continue at the current rate, the formula for calculating the estimate at completion (EAC) is: **EAC=BAC / CPI.** However, the question does not provide the CPI.

So, you first have to calculate the CPI:

CPI = EV / AC = 105 / 102 = 1.0294

Now you can calculate the EAC:

EAC = BAC / CPI = 400 / 1.0294 = 388.57

Question 9: Answer

Your development team just completed the first sprint. Based on the burndown chart below, what can be said about the project's schedule performance?

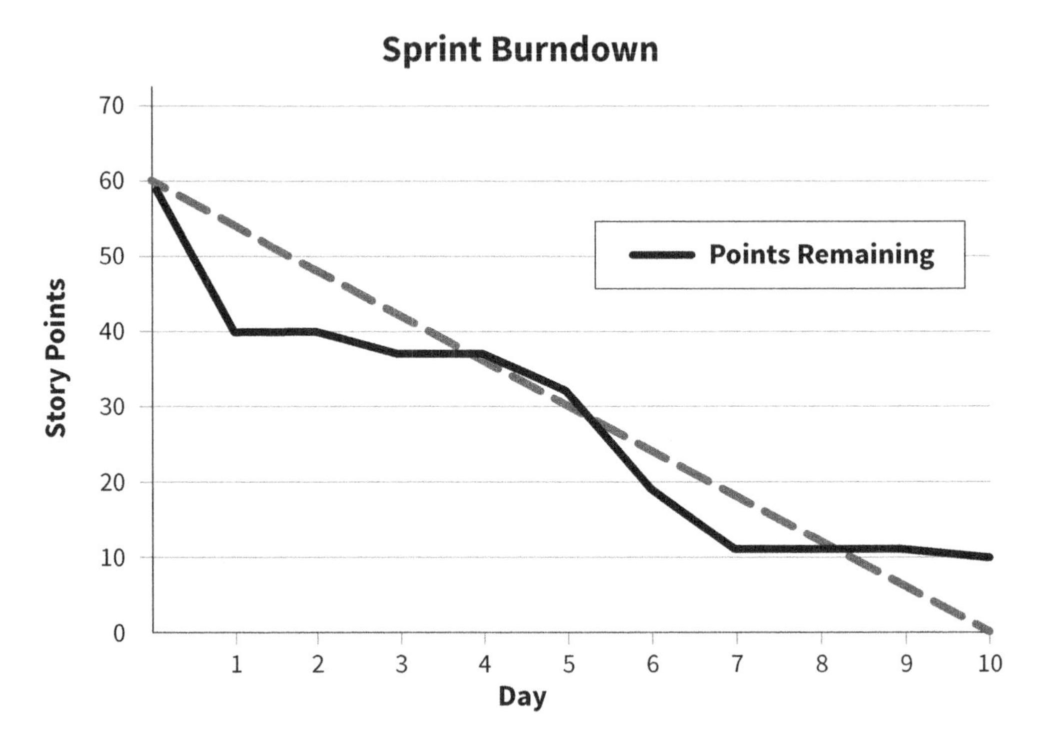

☑ **A) The SPI is 0.83 and the team failed to meet the sprint goal**
Correct. The formula for calculating the schedule performance index (SPI) is the earned value (EV) divided by the planned value (PV). The team completed 50 story points (earned value), while the sprint goal was 60 story points (planned value). Thus, the SPI = 50 / 60 = 0.83. According to the burndown chart, the sprint ended with 10 story points remaining, which means the team failed to meet the sprint goal.

B) The SPI is 1.0 and the team members met their commitment for the sprint
Incorrect. The burndown chart indicates that the team completed 50 story points of 60 planned for the sprint. Therefore, the team failed to meet the sprint goal, making this choice an incorrect answer without the need to calculate the SPI.

C) The SPI is 1.17 and the team is ahead of schedule
Incorrect. This answer choice results from the incorrect use of the SPI formula where the earned value (EV) and the planned value (PV) are transposed. The correct formula for the SPI is EV / PV. The sprint goal

(PV) was 60 story points, while the team only completed 50 story points (EV). Thus, the SPI = 50 / 60 = 0.83. Using the incorrect formula would result in an incorrect SPI of 1.17.

D) The SPI is 0.83 and the team completed the sprint backlog before the end of the sprint
Incorrect. While the value of the SPI has been correctly calculated in this answer choice (50 / 60 = 0.83), the burndown chart indicates that the team still had 10 story points remaining at the end of the sprint. Therefore, the team failed to complete the planned 60 story points by the end of the sprint, making this choice an incorrect answer.

Explanation:
Traditional earned value metrics, like the schedule performance index (SPI), can be applied to agile projects. In this case, the sprint goal was 60 story points (the first data point on the burndown chart). The sprint ended with 10 story points remained (the last data point on the burndown chart). Thus, the team completed 50 of the 60 planned story points and failed to achieve the sprint goal. The SPI can be calculated as earned value (EV) divided by the planned value (PV). In the burndown chart provided in the scenario, the earned value is 50 story points, and the planned value is 60 story points. Therefore, the SPI can be calculated as follows:

SPI = EV / PV = 50 / 60 = 0.83

An SPI value less than 1.0 means the project is behind schedule or, in other words, the team failed to meet the sprint goal.

Reference:
A Guide to the Project Management Body of Knowledge, (PMBOK® Guide) – Sixth Edition, Project Management Institute Inc., 2017, Page(s) 263, 267

Agile Practice Guide – First Edition, Project Management Institute Inc., 2017, Page(s) 62, 69

Question 10: Answer

cA10

You are planning a networking event. The idea is to bring 50 top executives from local companies who don't know each other together into one room and give them three minutes to talk with each other and then move on to the next person in the room. At the end of the event each attendee will have spoken to each of the other attendees. The event begins at 5pm.

When will the event end?

A) About 61 hours later

B) At 7:27pm
C) At 7:30pm
D) About 40 hours later

Explanation:
This is an interesting variation of the communications channels formula designed to test your logical thinking. In fact, the goal of the question is *not* to use the communication channels formula at all. If you use the formula you will get the wrong answer. Why? Because the question isn't asking you to calculate the communication channels. Instead the question asks the following:

We have 50 executives. Each of them will speak to the 49 others for 3 minutes. How long will it take?

The mistake you could make is to calculate the communication channels (50 * 49 / 2 = 1,225) multiply that by 3 minutes (= 3,675 minutes) making end-time 61.25 hours later. No executive would stay this long. Yes, you have correctly calculated the communications channels, but you have to remember that during the event you always have 25 *simultaneous* conversations going on in the room. I speak to you and the other 48 executives speak to each other as well.

The actual calculation you have to do is much simpler: If I am one of the 50 executives, then I have to speak to 49 others. If you are one of these executives, then you also have to speak to 49 others. In fact, each of the attending 50 executives has to speak to 49 others. Therefore, you calculate **49 * 3 minutes = 147 minutes = 2 hours 27 minutes.** This gives you an end time of 7:27pm.

Question 11: Answer

A project will be carried out using one-week sprints. The steering committee wants an estimate of how long the project will take. The project backlog has been estimated at 500 story points. The team estimates the velocity per sprint in the worst-case scenario as 10 story points, the best-case scenario with 25 story points, and the most likely scenario as 20 points.

Using a triangular distribution, how long will the project take?

A) 25 weeks
Incorrect. 25 weeks is the estimate calculated using the velocity provided by the team for the most likely scenario. However, the question is asking to find an estimate using a triangular distribution. Triangular distribution takes the average of the three estimates rather than just the estimate of the most likely scenario.

☑ **B) 32 weeks**
Correct. The worst-case duration can be calculated as 500 / 10 which is 50 sprints. The most likely case can be calculated as 500 / 20 which is

25 sprints. The best case can be calculated as 500 / 25 which is 20 sprints. Taking the average number of sprints would be (50 + 25 + 20) / 3 which is 31.67. Thus, the estimate would be 32. Since each sprint is one week in length, the duration estimate would be 32 weeks.

C) 50 weeks
Incorrect. 50 weeks is the estimate calculated using the velocity provided by the team for the worst-case scenario. However, the question is asking to find an estimate using a triangular distribution. Triangular distribution takes the average of the three estimates rather than just the estimate of the worst-case scenario

D) 64 weeks
Incorrect. Although two-week sprints are typical, the question stipulates that the sprint length will be one week for the project. If two-week sprints are used in the calculation, then one might have arrived at 64 weeks instead of 32 weeks.

Explanation:
In this scenario, we are asked to provide a duration estimate for the project using a triangular distribution. The formula for expected duration using a triangular distribution would be **(pessimistic + most likely + Optimistic) / 3.** The pessimistic duration can be calculated as 500 / 10 which is 50 sprints. The most likely case can be calculated as 500 / 20 which is 25 sprints. The optimistic duration can be calculated as 500 / 25 which is 20 sprints. Taking the average number of sprints would be (50 + 25 + 20) / 3, which is 31.67 or, rounding up to the next integer number, 32 sprints. Since each sprint is one week in length, the duration estimate would be 32 weeks.

Reference:
A Guide to the Project Management Body of Knowledge, (PMBOK® Guide) – Sixth Edition, Project Management Institute Inc., 2017, Page(s) 201, 244-245

Agile Practice Guide – First Edition, Project Management Institute Inc., 2017, Page(s) 61

Question 12: Answer

cA12

PV = 100, EV = 105, BAC = 400, AC = 102 and CV = 3?

What is the Estimate to Complete (ETC) if work will continue at the planned rate?

A) 298
B) 300
C) 305
☑ **D) 295**

Explanation:
The formula for calculating the ETC is: **ETC = EAC – AC**

First, since estimate at completion does not exist, you must calculate it using the formula: **EAC = AC + (BAC – EV) = 102 + (400 – 105) = 397**

Once you have the EAC, you plug the values into the formula: **ETC = EAC – AC** giving you **ETC = 397 – 102 = 295**

cA13

Question 13: Answer

The plan for the first iteration was to complete 100 story points. However, the team was only able to complete 80. Each story point earns $1,000 for the project. The actual cost of the iteration was $90,000. As the iteration retrospective approaches, the scrum master requests that the team prepares all the data required to calculate the various earned value metrics.

At the retrospective, the team determines that the project is ________________ budget.

(On the real PMP exam you may be asked to provide your answer by filling in the blank with the letter representing the correct answer. But here in the book, we are asking you to select the answer below.)

A) On
Incorrect. To understand project performance related to budget, the CPI should be calculated first, and then its result interpreted. With the details provided in the scenario: CPI = $80,000 / $90,000 = 0.89. A CPI of less than 1.0 means that the project is over budget. The project would have been on budget if its CPI was equal to 1.0.

B) Under
Incorrect. To determine how well the project is doing in terms of budget, the CPI should be calculated first, and then its result interpreted. The scenario provides 80 completed story points and the actual cost of $90,000. This means that: CPI = $80,000 / $90,000 = 0.89. Since the CPI is less than 1.0, the project is considered over, not under budget.

☑ **C) Over**
Correct. To answer whether the project is on, under, or over budget, the CPI should be calculated and its value interpreted. Based on the information provided in the scenario, the CPI = $80,000 / $90,000 = 0.89, which is less than 1.0, meaning that the project is over budget, making this choice the best answer to the question asked.

D) Cannot be determined
   Incorrect. There is sufficient information in the scenario to determine whether the project is on, under, or over budget. This determination can be made by calculating the CPI and interpreting its value. With the details provided in the scenario: CPI = $80,000 / $90,000 = 0.89, meaning the project is over budget, making this choice an incorrect answer.

Explanation:

Earned value management (EVM) is typically associated with the predictive (traditional) project management approaches. However, applying EVM metrics to projects carried out using agile methods can be done similarly and serve as an effective tool to measure team performance. For example, the schedule performance index (SPI) is the number of story points (features) completed divided by the number of the story points (features) planned. The cost performance index (CPI) is the earned value (EV, which is the value of the completed story points or features) divided by the actual costs incurred during the period under measurement.

The interpretation of the SPI and CPI values in agile projects are made similarly to the interpretation of those values in traditional projects. For example, an SPI less than 1.0 means the project (or iteration) is behind schedule, or, in other words, the team is working at a rate lower than planned. An SPI greater than 1.0 means the project (iteration) is ahead of schedule, i.e., the team is working at a rate higher than planned. A CPI less than 1.0 means the project (iteration) is over budget, or, in other words, the team earns less than a dollar compared to each dollar spent. A CPI greater than 1.0 indicates the project (iteration) is under budget, i.e., the team earns more than a dollar compared to each dollar spent.

The question asks to determine how well the project is doing regarding its adherence to the planned budget. To make this determination, one should calculate the CPI and interpret its value. Based on the explanation above, the CPI = $80,000 / $90,000 = 0.89. In other words, the team produced only 89 cents on the dollar compared to the plan (assuming the prediction is still correct), which means the project is over budget.

Note: the scenario is talking about an iteration while the question is asking about the project. However, according to the scenario, this was the first iteration. Therefore, the determination of whether the project is on, under, or over budget is essentially the same as for the iteration.

Reference:
Agile Practice Guide – First Edition, Project Management Institute Inc., 2017, Page(s) 69

cA14

Question 14: Answer

PV = 100, EV = 105, BAC = 400, AC = 102, CV = 3, ETC = 300, EAC = 407.

How much is the Actual Cost?

- A) 100
- ☑ **B) 102**
- C) 7
- D) 2

Explanation:
The answer to this question can be found right in the question. It states that "AC = 102", therefore actual cost is 102. This question is trying to throw you off by giving you way too much information.

cA15

Question 15: Answer

You are the project manager of the Gutenberg project. One major activity in this project is the purchase of a printing press at a cost of CHF 2,500,000. The printing press has an expected life of 25 years, but it will only be used for the project for five years.

Using straight line depreciation, what is the book value of the printing press at the end of its usage for the project?

- A) CHF 500,000
- B) CHF 1,500,000
- ☑ **C) CHF 2,000,000**
- D) CHF 2,500,000

Explanation:
In the straight-line depreciation method, the same value is depreciated from the investment every year. The cost of the press is 2.5 million with a lifespan of 25 years. This means that we depreciate 2,500,000 / 25 = 100,000 every year. After 5 years of depreciation the remaining book value is
2,500,000 – (5 * 100,000) = 2,000,000.

Question 16: Answer

You have received the following values from your statistical sampling: 80, 83, 85, 90, 82, 88, 90, 91, 94, 79.

What is the mean of this number set?

- A) 10
- B) 86.5
- C) 90
- ☑ **D) 86.2**

Explanation:
"Mean" is another term for "average". To calculate the mean (or average) you take the sum of all the members of the list divided by the number of items in the list: **(80 + 83 + 85 + 90 + 82 + 88 + 90 + 91 + 94 + 79) / 10 = 86.2**

Question 17: Answer

cA17

Your company is holding their annual employee get together. This year 123 employees have attended. Let's assume that each employee had a brief conversation with each of the other employees.

How many conversations took place?

A) 15,006
B) 123
☑ **C) 7,503**
D) 15,129

Explanation:
The formula to calculate communication channels (or in this case "conversations") is **n * (n – 1) / 2.** Therefore, you calculate **123 * (123 – 1) / 2 = 7,503**

Question 18: Answer

cA18

A scrum master needs to provide a duration estimate for a project that is about to start its first two-week sprint. The team provides a pessimistic estimate of 50 sprints, a most likely estimate of 25 sprints, and an optimistic estimate of 20 sprints. The scrum master uses a beta distribution to calculate the estimated project duration.

How many weeks will it take for the team to complete the project based on the scrum master's calculation?

☑ **A) 58 weeks**
Correct. The beta distribution formula can be stated as Estimate = [Pessimistic + (4 * Most Likely) + Optimistic] / 6. Applying the values from the scenario, the estimate can be calculated as: Estimate = [50 + (4 x 25) + 20] / 6 = 170 / 6 = 28.33. Rounding the number up to the next integer results in 29 sprints, or 58 weeks.

B) 29 weeks
Incorrect. According to the scenario, the project will be carried out in a cadence of two-week sprints. If one forgot to multiply the number of sprints by 2, the result might have been 29. However, the question

specifically asks for the project duration (i.e., the number of weeks) rather than the number of sprints.

C) 64 weeks
Incorrect. The triangular distribution method bases the estimate on the average of the three estimates. If one used the triangular distribution, the result would have been 32 sprints or 64 weeks. However, the question stipulates the use of the beta distribution method rather than the triangular distribution method.

D) 56 weeks
Incorrect. Applying the beta distribution formula will result in: Estimate = [Pessimistic + (4 * Most Likely) + Optimistic] / 6 = 28.33 sprints. If one rounds 28.33 down instead of up, the result would be 28 sprints or 56 weeks. However, since a project is not considered complete, even if a small amount of work remains, the result must always be rounded up.

Explanation:
There are various tools and techniques that can be used to calculate project duration. The question asks to use beta distribution. The formula to calculate estimate using beta distribution can be stated as:

Estimate = [Pessimistic + (4 * Most Likely) + Optimistic] / 6

Plugging the values from the scenario into the formula for the estimate, the result would be as follows:

Estimate = [50 + (4 x 25) + 20] / 6
Estimate = [50 + 100 + 20] / 6
Estimate = 170 / 6 = 28.33

Whenever a fraction of a sprint remains, it must be rounded up to the next whole number. Otherwise, if not rounded up, work would remain. Therefore, rounding 28.33 up to the next integer number would result in 29 sprints.

The question is asking about the project duration. According to the scenario, each sprint is two weeks in duration. Therefore, to answer the question correctly, the number of sprints should be multiplied by 2, resulting in 58 weeks.

Reference:
A Guide to the Project Management Body of Knowledge, (PMBOK® Guide) – Sixth Edition, Project Management Institute Inc., 2017, Page(s) 244-245, 241

Agile Practice Guide – First Edition, Project Management Institute Inc., 2017, Page(s) 61

Question 19: Answer

cA19

You have received the following values from your statistical sampling: 80, 83, 85, 90, 82, 88, 90, 91, 94, 79.

What is the median of this number set?

A) 10
☑ **B) 86.5**
C) 90
D) 86.2

Explanation:
The median is the middle value that separates the higher half from the lower half of the data set. To find it, arrange the numbers in ascending order, and then select the one in the middle: 79, 80, 82, 83, **<u>85, 88,</u>** 90, 90, 91, 94.

In this question, we have 10 values, and because of this there isn't a single number in the exact middle. Therefore, we have to take the two middle values and calculate their mean (average).

This is done by calculating **(85 + 88) / 2 = 86.5**

Question 20: Answer

cA20

Your friend Joe is planning to retire 20 years from today. He is investing $200,000 in a long-term investment at 3.5%.

How much will this money be worth in 20 years?

A) $399,757
B) $401,627
C) $379,597
☑ **D) $397,957**

Explanation:
You are asked to calculate the future value (FV) of a 200,000 investment at 3.5% for 20 years. The formula for future value is **FV = PV * (1 + r)^n.** Therefore, you calculate **200,000 * (1 + 0.035)^20 = 397,957.**

Question 21: Answer

As a scrum master, you are facilitating a sprint retrospective. In attendance is the development team of five, along with the product owner and the business analyst.

How many possible channels of communication exist?

A) 10
Incorrect. If one only included the five developers in the formula, one might have arrived at a total of 10 communication channels: 5 x (5 – 1) / 2 = 10. However, the scrum master, product owner, and business analyst should also be included in the calculation.

B) 21
Incorrect. This answer choice describes the number of communication channels if only 7 people are accounted for in the formula. For example, if one fails to include the scrum master, the result would be: 7 x (7 – 1) / 2 = 21. Carefully reading the scenario would have helped avoid this mistake.

☑ **C) 28**
Correct. The formula for calculating the number of communication channels is N * (N – 1) / 2. According to the scenario, the total number of people attending the sprint retrospective is 8. Therefore, applying this formula results in the following calculation: 8 x (8 – 1) / 2 = 28. Therefore, the total number of possible communication channels is 28.

D) 56
Incorrect. This answer could result from an incorrect application of the formula used to calculate the number of communication channels. For example, if one forgets to include the division by two in the formula, the result might have been as follows: 8 x (8 – 1) = 56. The correct formula, however, is: N * (N – 1) / 2.

Explanation:
The first step in calculating the number of communication channels is to determine the total number of participants in the communication. In this case, we have five developers, a scrum master, a product owner, and a business analyst, which is a total of 8 people. The formula for calculating the number of communication channels is **N * (N – 1) / 2,** where N is the number of people. Applying this formula results in:

8 x (8 – 1) / 2 = 28

Therefore, there are 28 possible channels of communication at the sprint retrospective described in the scenario.

The topic of this question is not covered in the *PMBOK® Guide*. However, the Project Management Professional (PMP)® Examination Content Outline (ECO) indicates that while there are some commonalities between the *PMBOK® Guide* and the ECO, the exam is not bound by the *PMBOK® Guide*. The list of enablers specified in the tasks of the ECO domains is not exhaustive either. The ECO assumes that prospective PMP aspirants are familiar with other sources of information/preparation, including but not limited to PMI Code of Ethics and Professional Conduct, PMI's Practice Standards (e.g., Scheduling, Earned Value Management, etc.); organizational behavior theories such as Tuckman's Ladder, Theory X and Theory Y, Maslow's hierarchy of needs; commonly frowned upon project management practices, such as gold plating; and others. We intentionally have these questions in our simulator so that you would be better prepared for the real exam. PMP aspirants are encouraged to explore additional sources of information and/or to be familiar with them from their project management experience.

Reference:
A Guide to the Project Management Body of Knowledge, (PMBOK® Guide) – Sixth Edition, Project Management Institute Inc., 2017, Page(s) 370

https://www.project-management-prepcast.com/131-pmp-exam-tips/333-what-is-the-communications-channels-formula-for-communications-management

https://www.pmi.org/learning/library/overcoming-communications-complexity-ambiguity-projects-6631

Question 22: Answer

cA22

Your customer is asking you for a preliminary estimate. Your numbers show that the project will most likely cost DKK 100,000.

What number will you give to your customer?

A) DKK 100,000
B) DKK 75,000 – 150,000
☑ **C) DKK 85,000 – 150,000**
D) DKK 95,000 – 110,000

Explanation:
The percentages for the various estimates that you need to know for the exam are as follows: rough order of magnitude estimate, ROM = -25% to +75%; preliminary estimate = -15% to +50%; budget estimate = -10% to +25%; definitive estimate = -5% to +10%; final estimate = 0%. You have been asked to provide a preliminary estimate. Therefore, your range has to be -15% to +50% from the 100,000 starting point.

Question 23: Answer

Your company owns an asset with an original value of $1,000. This asset will be depreciated using the double declining balance method over the period of five years.

What is the dollar value of the annual depreciation in Year 2?

A) $400
B) $144
☑ **C) $240**
D) $86.40

Explanation:
To calculate the annual depreciation % for the double-declining-balance method, you have to first calculate the straight-line depreciation rate. Since the asset has a 5-year life, the straight-line depreciation rate is 100% / 5 years = 20% per year. With double-declining-balance method, as the name suggests, the double of that rate (40%) is used. The following table illustrates how this percentage is then used in the double-declining balance method:

Book Value Beginning of Year	Depreciation Rate	Depreciation Expense	Accumulated Depreciation	Book Value End of Year
$1,000	40%	$400	$400	$600
$600	40%	**$240**	$640	$360
$360	40%	$144	$784	$216
$216	40%	$86.40	$870.40	$129.60
$129.60	100%	$129.60	$1,000	$0

Question 24: Answer

The activity "Pack Container" in your network diagram has an early start of Day 12, a late start of day 15, a duration of three, and a late finish of day 17.

What is the total float of this activity?

A) 1 day
B) 2 days
☑ **C) 3 days**
D) 4 days

Explanation:
The total float of an activity determines how many days you can delay an activity without delaying the project. There are two formulas both will give the same result:

Total Float = LS – ES
Total Float = LF – EF

In our question, we have the following values:

ES = 12
LS = 15
LF = 17

Therefore, we calculate **Total Float = LS – ES = 15 – 12 = 3 days.**

Question 25: Answer

cA25

A scrum master needs to inform project stakeholders of the team's velocity thus far. The team completed 21 story points during the first sprint, 23 in the second sprint, and 22 in the third sprint. For the upcoming fourth sprint, the team has committed to completing 26 story points.

What velocity should the scrum master report?

☑ **A) 22**

Correct. Unless a specific calculation method is requested by the question, the formula for calculating velocity is a simple average of the velocities for the completed sprints divided by the number of sprints. In the scenario provided, velocity is calculated as follows: (21 + 23 + 22) / 3 = 22 story points.

B) 23

Incorrect. If the team successfully completes the 26 story points planned for the fourth sprint, then the project would have a velocity of 23, i.e.: (21 + 23 + 22 + 26) / 4 = 23. However, at this point, it's unknown if the team will actually meet its commitment for the next sprint. Therefore, the planned velocity should not be included in the formula.

C) 66

Incorrect. This answer choice represents the total number of story points completed by the team in the first three sprints. However, the question is asking to provide velocity thus far. Velocity is the average number of story points completed per sprint rather than the total number of story points completed.

D) 92

Incorrect. 92 story points would be the sum of the number of story points already completed by the team in the first three sprints plus the 26 story points planned to be completed in the fourth sprint. However, this figure does not represent velocity, which is the average of the story points completed so far.

Explanation:
To provide the project stakeholders with the team's velocity thus far, one should calculate the average of the velocities for the completed sprints. The formula for calculating velocity is a simple average: the total number of story points completed divided by the number of sprints. With the values provided in the scenario, the calculation is as follows:

(21 + 23 + 22) / 3 = 22 story points

The planned story points for the fourth sprint should not be included in the calculation as it is not known whether or not the team will actually deliver all of the story points planned for the sprint.

Reference:
Agile Practice Guide – First Edition, Project Management Institute Inc., 2017, Page(s) 61
https://www.pmi.org/learning/library/estimates-project-pitfalls-4300

Question 26: Answer

Your Company owns an asset with an original value of $1,000. This asset will be depreciated using the double declining balance method over the period of five years.

What is the percentage of the annual depreciation in Year 2?

A) 20%
B) $240
☑ **C) 40%**
D) $140

Explanation:
For the detailed explanation please refer to question #22 above. Also, please note that the question asks, "What is the percentage" and not "What is the dollar value".

Question 27: Answer

Your eight-person team is getting support from two external consultants.

How many communication channels are added by hiring these consultants?

A) 2
B) 8
C) 16
☑ **D) 17**

Explanation:
To find the answer you have to subtract the communication channels of an eight-person team from those of a 10-person team.

An eight-person team: **n * (n – 1) / 2 = 8 * (8 – 1) / 2 = 8 * 7 / 2 = 28 channels**

A 10-person team: **n * (n – 1) / 2 = 10 * (10 – 1) / 2 = 10 * 9 / 2 = 45 channels**

And the difference is: **45 – 28 = 17**

Question 28: Answer

cA28

Your friend David is planning to retire 15 years from today.

How much should he invest today in a long-term investment, offering an annual interest rate of 3.5%, so that he ends up with $500,000.

A) $201,509
B) $231,627
C) $279,597
☑ **D) $298,445**

Explanation:
You are asked to calculate the present value (PV) of $500,000 at 3.5% for 15 years. The formula for present value is: **PV = FV / (1 + r)^n.** Therefore, you calculate **500,000 / (1 + 0.035)^15 = 298,445**

Question 29: Answer

The plan for the first iteration was to complete 100 story points. However, the team was only able to complete 80. Each story point earns $1,000 for the project. The actual cost of the iteration was $90,000. As the iteration retrospective approaches, the scrum master requests that the team prepares all the data required to calculate the various earned value metrics.

At the retrospective, the team determines that the project is _______ schedule.

(On the real PMP exam you may be asked to provide your answer by filling in the blank with the letter representing the correct answer. But here in the book, we are asking you to select the answer below.)

A) On
Incorrect. To understand project performance related to schedule, the SPI should be calculated first, and then its result interpreted. With the details provided in the scenario: SPI = 80 / 100 = 0.8. An SPI less than 1.0 means that the project is behind schedule. The project would have been on schedule if its SPI was equal to 1.0.

☑ **B) Behind**
Correct. To determine whether the project is on, ahead, or behind schedule, one should calculate the SPI and interpret its value. Based on the information provided in the scenario, the SPI = 80 / 100 = 0.8. An SPI less than 1.0 means that the project is behind schedule, making this choice the best answer to the question asked.

C) Ahead of
Incorrect. The determination as to how well the project is doing in terms of schedule, the SPI should be calculated first, and then its result interpreted. The scenario provides 100 planned story points and 80 completed. This means that: SPI = 80 / 100 = 0.8. An SPI which is less than 1.0 means that the project is behind, not ahead of schedule.

D) Cannot be determined
Incorrect. There is sufficient information in the scenario to determine whether the project is on, ahead, or behind schedule. This determination can be made by calculating the SPI and interpreting its value. With the details provided in the scenario: SPI = 80 / 100 = 0.8, meaning the project is behind schedule.

Explanation:
Earned value management (EVM) is typically associated with the predictive (traditional) project management approaches. However, applying EVM metrics to projects carried out using agile methods can be done similarly and serve as an effective tool to measure team performance. For example, the schedule performance index (SPI) is the number of story points (features) completed divided by the number of the story points (features) planned. The cost performance index (CPI) is the earned value (EV, which is the value of the completed story points or features) divided by the actual costs incurred during the period under measurement.

The interpretation of the SPI and CPI values in agile projects are made similarly to the interpretation of those values in traditional projects. For example, an SPI less than 1.0 means the project (or iteration) is behind schedule, or, in other words, the team is working at a rate lower than planned. An SPI greater than 1.0 means the project (iteration) is ahead of schedule, i.e., the team is working at a rate higher than planned. A CPI less than 1.0 means the project (iteration) is over budget, or, in other words, the team earns less than a dollar compared to each dollar planned. A CPI greater than 1.0 indicates the project (iteration) is under budget, i.e., the team earns more than a dollar compared to each dollar planned.

The question asks to determine how well the project is doing in terms of its adherence to the planned schedule. To make this determination, one should calculate the SPI and interpret its value. Based on the explanation above, the SPI = 80 / 100 = 0.8. In other words, the team worked at only 75% of the rate planned, which means the project is behind schedule.

Note: the scenario is talking about an iteration while the question is asking about the project. However, according to the scenario, this was the first iteration. Therefore, the determination of whether the project is on, behind, or ahead of schedule is essentially the same as for the iteration.

Reference:
Agile Practice Guide – First Edition, Project Management Institute Inc., 2017, Page(s) 69

Question 30: Answer

cA30

Your designer has submitted his resignation. This means that you will be losing him, and your team size (including yourself) will go down from 12 to 11 people.

How many fewer communication channels will you personally have on your project after the designer leaves the company?

☑ **A) 1**
B) 10
C) 11
D) 12

Explanation:

This question doesn't require you to use the communication channel formula. Let's first look at the question: it does **not** ask, "How many fewer communication channels *will be there on the project* after the designer leaves the company?" Instead, the question asks: "How many fewer communication channels *will you personally have* on your project after the designer leaves the company?" So, to find the correct answer, we have to concentrate on your own channels and not on those of the team. Let's do that.

We know that the team has 12 team members, including you. This means that there are 11 other team members on the project and you communicate with them. Since there are 11 other team members, that means that you personally have 11 communication channels – one with each of the other team members.

One of these 11 team members has resigned and will leave the company. This means that there are now only 10 other team members on the team, leaving you with only 10 communication channels. So, the difference for you is:
11 – 10 = 1.

In other words:

Team of 12 = you personally communicate with 11 others = 11 channels
Team of 11 = you personally communicate with 10 others = 10 channels
The difference is 1

cA31

Question 31: Answer

Your customer is asking for a rough order of magnitude estimate.

What numbers do you give him, assuming that your bottom up estimate gave you a project cost of approximately CHF 200,000?

A) CHF 170,000 to CHF 300,000
☑ **B) CHF 140,000 to CHF 340,000**
C) CHF 190,000 to CHF 220,000
D) CHF 180,000 to CHF 250,000

Explanation:
A rough order of magnitude (ROM) estimate is from -25% to +75%. Answer B is the best because it is the closest to this range. Answer A would be a preliminary estimate, C would be a definite estimate, and D would be a budget estimate.

Question 32: Answer

A Kanban board is used to manage the workflow of a software development project. The project team has established a cycle time of five business days per user story. The lead time is 10 business days per story. There are 20 user stories remaining in the backlog.

What should the team report as an estimate to complete the backlog?

☑ **A) 100 business days**
Correct. The formula for determining the time to completion can be expressed as a cycle time per user story multiplied by the number of user stories remaining in the backlog. In the scenario provided, the time to completion is 5 days * 20 user stories = 100 business days.

B) 200 business days
Incorrect. If the lead time of 10 business days is multiplied by the stories remaining, the result would be 200 business days. However, lead time includes the time the story spends in the backlog before the team actually begins working on the story. Therefore, it's the cycle time, not the lead time, that should be used to calculate the time to completion.

C) 300 business days
Incorrect. This answer choice represents an incorrect calculation that sums up the cycle time with the lead time and then multiplies the result by the number of the remaining user stories. However, lead time and cycle time overlap and should not be added together to determine the time to completion, making this choice an incorrect answer.

D) Cannot be determined without knowing the iteration length
Incorrect. Although the use of iterations might be incorporated into a Kanban framework, iterations are not an inherent component of Kanban. An estimate for the time to completion can be calculated with the cycle time per user story and the number of stories remaining in the backlog, typically listed in the "To Do" column of the Kanban board.

Explanation:
To correctly answer this question, one should understand the difference between cycle time and lead time. Cycle time is the time the passes from the moment the team starts working on a task (user story) until the moment the team completes it. Lead time, on the other hand, is the total time that starts ticking from the moment a work item (user story) is put on the board until the item is delivered to the customer. This means that lead time "encompasses" cycle time. In other words, there are typically two "waiting" periods: first, between the moment a user story is put on the board until the moment the team starts working on it and, second, from the moment the team completes the user story until the moment it's delivered to the customer. Since the question is asking about the estimate to complete the backlog (rather than deliver to the customer), one should only take the cycle time into consideration and ignore the lead time, which is superfluous information that is not needed to answer the question correctly.

The formula for determining the time to completion can be expressed as follows: **Cycle time * Stories remaining.** With the numbers provided in the scenario:

Time to completion = 5 business days * 20 stories
= 100 business days

Reference:
Agile Practice Guide – First Edition, Project Management Institute Inc., 2017, Page(s) 61, 65
https://www.projectmanagement.com/articles/295009/Go-Deeper-on-Metrics

Question 33: Answer

Assuming a 3% interest rate, which of the following projects would you select?

☑ **A) Project Gold with a total of 213,000 profit at the end of Year 4**
B) Project Silver with a total of 97,000 profit at the end of Year 1
C) Project Bronze with a total of 128,000 profit at the end of Year 2
D) Project Leather with a total of 168,000 profit at the end of Year 3

Explanation:
The "profit at the end of year x" represents a future value (FV). To determine which of these projects to select you must calculate the present value (PV) for each of the 4 projects and select the project with the highest PV. PV is calculated by using the formula **PV = FV / (1 + r)^n.** Here are the results shown as a table:

Project	FV	1 + r	n	PV
Gold	213,000	1.03	4	**189,248**
Silver	97,000	1.03	1	94,175
Bronze	128,000	1.03	2	120,652
Leather	168,000	1.03	3	153,744

Question 34: Answer

You have just been assigned to a new project that is very similar to the previous one. One particular task on the previous project took 146 days to finish. You are doing a top down estimate of the new project and you estimate that the same task on the new project will take at least 138 and at maximum 157 days.

What is the variance of this estimate?

A) 3.16 days
B) 146.5 days
C) 64.8 days
☑ **D) 10.03 days**

Explanation:
The formula to calculate the variance of a task is as follows: **Variance = [(Pessimistic – Optimistic) / 6]^2.** Therefore, you would calculate:

[(157 – 138) / 6]^2 = (19 / 6)^2 = 3.1666^2 = 10.03 days

Question 35: Answer

cA35

You have received the following estimates from vendors: Vendor 1: €75,000; Vendor 2: €65,000; Vendor 3: €93,500; Vendor 4: €82,000; Vendor 5: €94,000.

What is the median estimate that you have received?

A) £81,900
B) 5
C) £94,000
☑ **D) £82,000**

Explanation:
The median is the middle value that separates the higher half from the lower half. In our example, you have to first order the numbers ascending:

€65,000; €75,000; **€82,000**; €93,500; €94,000

Now it is easy to see, that the median value is €82,000. It is exactly in the middle.

Question 36: Answer

Due to resource constraints, your company can not undertake all projects that are proposed. There are two new projects that have been proposed. Project Gold will take 1.5 years and will bring a profit of around €290,000 at the end of year 2. Project Silver will take one year and reduce internal cost by €270,000 by the end of Year 4.

Assuming a 3% interest rate, which of the following is true?

A) These projects are exactly equal in benefits.
☑ **B) Project Gold has a PV that is about €33,000 higher than Project Silver**
C) Project Silver is more attractive than Project Gold and should be undertaken
D) Project Silver has a PV that is about €25,000 higher than Project Gold

Explanation:
Project Gold has a PV of €273,352 and project Silver has a PV of €239,891. This is a difference of €33,461, making answer B the best one. Here are the calculations:

Project	Future Value	Interest Rate	Years	Formula	Present Value
Gold	290,000	3% (1.03)	2	**290000 / 1.03^2**	273,352
Silver	270,000	3% (1.03)	4	**270000 / 1.03^4**	239,891

cA37

Question 37: Answer

What is the early finish (EF) of Task One?

ES: 1	EF:
Name: One	**Duration: 6 days**
LS: 6	LF: 11
	5 days

A) 5
☑ **B) 6**
C) 7
D) 8

Explanation:
The formula to calculate the early finish (EF) of a task is

EF = ES + duration – 1 = 1 + 6 – 1 = 6

cA38

Question 38: Answer

AC = 105, EV = 100, PV = 97, CV = -5.

How much is the schedule variance (SV)?

A) 1.03
B) -3
☑ **C) 3**
D) 8

Explanation:
The formula for calculating the SV is as follows:

SV = EV – PV = 100 – 97 = 3

cA39

Question 39: Answer

Your quality assurance team is doing a review of a process. They find that the process used the following cycle times: 45sec, 49sec, 48sec, 50sec, 52sec, 49sec, 48sec, 50sec, 46sec.

How do you calculate the mean?

A) Mean = n * (n – 1) /2
B) Mean = (Pessimistic – Optimistic) / 6
☑ **C) Mean = (45 + 49 + 48 + 50 + 52 + 49 + 48 + 50 + 46) / 9**
D) Mean = √sum (45 + 49 + 48 + 50 + 52 + 49 + 48 + 50 + 46) / 9

Explanation:
In mathematics, an average refers to a measure of the "middle" of a data set. The most common method is the arithmetic mean. That is why the "average" is sometimes also and simply called the "mean". As such, the question asks you to calculate the average of the times given. This is calculated as follows: the sum of all the members of the list divided by the number of items in the list, which is what described in the answer choice C.

Question 40: Answer

cA40

A company is considering the purchase of a robot that costs $50,000 upon delivery in 12 weeks and will generate $10,000 per year of net cash flow. The company is also considering contracting with a software development vendor for deliverables that will cost $36,000 payable after six two-week sprints and save $12,000 per year.

If the company only has sufficient funds to invest in one of these projects, which should they select?

A) Purchase the robot because it has a payback period of five years
Incorrect. The payback period for purchasing the robot can be determined by dividing the investment by the net cash flow. For the robot, the payback period can be calculated as $50,000 divided by $10,000 per year, which would be 5 years. Since this choice has a higher payback period than the other option, it should be rejected.

☑ **B) Invest in the software because it has a payback period of three years**
Correct. In order to calculate the payback period, one must divide the investment by the net cash flow. With the details provided in the scenario, the payback period would be as follows: $36,000 / $12,000 = 3 years. Since the payback period for the software development project is shorter, this would be the project to select.

C) Neither, because the NPV is negative for both projects
Incorrect. Net present value (NPV) is a method for the financial evaluation of projects. It is the difference between the present value of inflows of capital and the present value of outflows of capital over a period of time. Without knowing the discount rate, there is no way to determine the NPV of these projects, making this choice an incorrect answer.

D) Acquire the robot because it has a lower IRR
Incorrect. The internal rate of return (IRR) is the interest rate at which the present value of all future cash flows equals the initial investment.

All other things being equal, the project with the higher IRR should be selected over a project with a lower IRR. However, there is no sufficient information in the scenario to determine the IRR of either project.

Explanation:
One method of selecting a project is to determine the payback period for each of the options. All other things being equal, the project with the shortest payback period would be the best choice. The payback period can be determined by dividing the investment by the net cash flow. Applying the formula results in the following payback periods:

The payback period for the option of purchasing the robot = $50,000 / $10,000 = 5 years

The payback period for the software development project = $36,000 / $12,000 = 3 years

Therefore, based on the shorter payback period method, the software development project is the preferable option.

Note that both projects have a lead time of 12 weeks, after which the investment would be made. Since the lead times are the same, this information is not relevant to answering the question correctly.

Reference:
A Guide to the Project Management Body of Knowledge, (PMBOK® Guide) – Sixth Edition, Project Management Institute Inc., 2017, Page(s) 34, 473

Question 41: Answer

The following is a small section taken from a large network diagram for a construction project.

Which of the following statements is true?

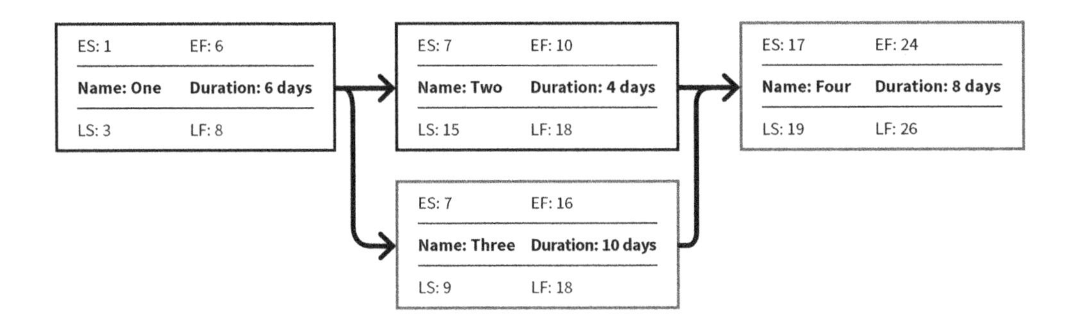

A) Task 1 has a free float of two days

✓ **B) Task 2 has a free float of six days**

C) Task 3 has a free float of nine days

D) Task 4 has a free float of five days

Explanation:

The fact that this network diagram is for a construction project is of no consequence for finding the correct answer. All you have to do is apply the formula **Free Float = Earliest ES of successor activity – EF of current activity – 1** to each of the four tasks as follows:

- Task One: ES successor – EF current 7 – 6 – 1 = 0
- Task Two: ES successor – EF current 17 – 10 – 1 = 6
- Task Three: ES successor – EF current 17 – 16 – 1 = 0
- Task Four: ES successor – EF current ?? – 24 – 1 = unknown

By the way... by "*Earliest* ES of Following Activity" we mean this:

- Task A is followed by Task B and Task C.
- Task B has an ES of 10
- Task C has an ES of 8
- Therefore, the *Earliest* ES of these two would be Task C with 8.

Question 42: Answer

cA42

Which of the following values correctly calculates the estimate to complete (ETC)?

✓ **A) ETC = 30,000, when EAC = 100,000 and AC = 70,000**

B) ETC = 120,000, when BAC = 100,000 and EV = 20,000

C) ETC = 110,000, when BAC = 125,000 and EV = 25,000 and CPI = 1.1

D) ETC = 70,000, when BAC = 100,000 and AC = 30,000

Explanation:

There are two ways to calculate the Estimate to Complete (ETC) and two orphaned formulas* used in earlier editions.

- ETC = EAC – AC
- ETC = new estimate
- *ETC = BAC – EV
- *ETC = (BAC – EV) / CPI

Answers A, B and C all contain the numbers to calculate each of the formulas listed above, but only answer A has the correct result of 30,000. The results shown for answer B and answer C are immaterial since the PMI® no longer recognizes the use of these formulas* for calculating ETC.

Answer D is completely impossible, because you cannot calculate the ETC by using BAC and AC in any combination.

* Orphaned formulas are formulas that do not appear in *PMBOK® Guide*. However, as the *PMBOK® Guide* is not the only reference source used by the PMI® to design their PMP exam questions, we have decided to keep the questions that use these formulas.

cA43

Question 43: Answer

You estimate that a task will take anywhere from 60-70 days to complete.

Assuming that you estimated towards 3 sigma, how certain are you about this duration?

A) 68.27%
B) 95.45%
☑ **C) 99.73%**
D) 99.99%

Explanation:
The values for sigma are as follows: 1 sigma = 68.27%; 2 sigma = 95.45%; 3 sigma = 99.73%; 6 sigma = 99.99%. Therefore, if you are "certain by 3 sigmas" then you are 99.73% certain.

Question 44: Answer

Your earned value analysis shows the following values: EV = 90,000; ETC = 100,000; EAC = 190,000; PV = 110,000; AC = 90,000.

Which of the following is true?

A) The project is ahead of schedule and on budget
B) The project is on schedule and below budget
C) The EAC is incorrect

☑ **D) The project is behind schedule and on budget**

Explanation:
The project is behind schedule because the earned value is only 90,000 while the planned value at this time in the project should have been 110,000. Therefore, the project is 20,000 behind schedule. The project is on budget because both actual cost and earned value are 90,000.

Question 45: Answer

cA45

The plan for the first iteration was to complete 100 story points. However, the team was only able to complete 80. Each story point earns $1,000 for the project. The actual cost of the iteration was $90,000. As the iteration retrospective approaches, the scrum master requests that the team prepares all the data required to calculate the various earned value metrics.

At the retrospective, the team determines that the cost performance index (CPI) of the iteration was ________________.

(On the real PMP exam you may be asked to provide your answer by filling in the blank with the letter representing the correct answer. But here in the book, we are asking you to select the answer below.)

A) 1.25
Incorrect. This value, 1.25, could have resulted from the following calculation: 100 / 80 = 1.25. However, to calculate the SPI, one should divide the number of completed story points by the number of planned. In the scenario, the team planned 100 story points but only completed 80. Therefore, SPI = 80 /100 = 0.80.

B) 0.80
Incorrect. In agile, the schedule performance index (SPI) can be calculated using the following formula: SPI = [number of completed story points] / [number of planned story points]. Based on the values provided in the scenario, SPI = 80 / 100 = 0.80.

C) 1.11
Incorrect. This value, 1.11, could have resulted from the following calculation: $100,000 / $90,000 = 1.11, where $100,000 is the planned value (PV) and $90,000 is the actual cost (AC). However, the SPI is calculated differently: SPI = 80 /100 = 0.80, where 80 is the number of the completed story points and 100 is the number of those that were planned.

☑ **D) 0.89**
Correct. The cost performance indicator (CPI) is the earned value (EV, the value of completed story points or features) divided by the actual cost (AC). The EV is 80 story points multiplied by $1,000, resulting in $80,000. The AC is given in the scenario: $90,000. Therefore, CPI = $80,000 / $90,000 = 0.89, making this choice the correct answer.

Explanation:

Earned value management (EVM) is typically associated with the predictive (traditional) project management approaches. However, applying EVM metrics to projects carried out using agile methods can be done similarly and serve as an effective tool to measure team performance. For example, the schedule performance index (SPI) is the number of story points (features) completed divided by the number of the story points (features) planned. The cost performance index (CPI) is the earned value (EV, which is the value of the completed story points or features) divided by the actual costs incurred during the period under measurement.

The interpretation of the SPI and CPI values in agile projects are made similarly to the interpretation of those values in traditional projects. For example, an SPI less than 1.0 means the project (or iteration) is behind schedule, or, in other words, the team is working at a rate lower than planned. An SPI greater than 1.0 means the project (iteration) is ahead of schedule, i.e., the team is working at a rate higher than planned. A CPI less than 1.0 means the project (iteration) is over budget, or, in other words, the team earns less than a dollar compared to each dollar planned. A CPI greater than 1.0 indicates the project (iteration) is under budget, i.e., the team earns more than a dollar compared to each dollar planned.

The question asks to determine the CPI. Based on the explanation above, the **CPI = $80,000 / $90,000 = 0.89.** In other words, the team produced only 89 cents on the dollar compared to the plan (assuming the prediction is still correct).

Reference:
Agile Practice Guide – First Edition, Project Management Institute Inc., 2017, Page(s) 69

Question 46: Answer

What is the expected monetary value (EMV) of the following event?

Probability	Impact in $
0.5	-8,000
0.2	-7,000
0.2	-4,500
0.1	2000

A) 2,000
B) -8,000
☑ **C) -6,100**
D) -4,500

Explanation:
The expected monetary value (EMV) is calculated by multiplying the probability with the impact and then adding up the total.

Probability	Impact in $	Probability * Impact
0.5	-8,000	-4,000
0.2	-7,000	-1,400
0.2	-4,500	-900
0.1	2000	200
		-6,100

Question 47: Answer

cA47

You have received several bids for your project. You are now using a weighting system to determine which of the bids meets your needs best. The weighting system contains weights for price, quality, vendor experience, duration, risk management, and distance.

Which of the following bids would you select?

Maximum Score	**25**	**18**	**18**	**15**	**13**	**11**
Vendor	**Price**	**Quality**	**Experience**	**Duration**	**Risk Mgmt.**	**Distance**
PM Experts	21	12	13	9	11	8
The PM Shop	20	14	17	10	10	7
Gold Platers	18	13	16	9	12	9
ScopeCreep PM	17	15	16	11	12	9

A) PM Experts
B) The PM Shop
C) Gold Platers
☑ **D) ScopeCreep PM**

Explanation:
In order to answer this question, you will have to add up all individual scores for the four vendors. ScopeCreep PM has the highest score.

Maximum Score	25	18	18	15	13	11	100
Vendor	**Price**	**Quality**	**Exp.**	**Duration**	**Risk Mgmt.**	**Dist.**	**Total**
PM Experts	21	12	13	9	11	8	74
The PM Shop	20	14	17	10	10	7	78
Gold Platers	18	13	16	9	12	9	77
ScopeCreep PM	17	15	16	11	12	9	80

Question 48: Answer

An organization has just completed a needs analysis for a potential project. The project will require five two-week sprints to complete after which time the organization will receive $50,000 in incremental revenue. The cost has been estimated at $25,000.

What is the best course of action?

A) Decline the project as costs are double the benefits
Incorrect. According to the scenario, the organization will receive $50,000 in incremental revenue. This incremental revenue is considered the benefit. The costs, on the other hand, are given as $25,000. With these numbers, the benefit is double the cost and not vice versa, making his choice an incorrect answer.

B) Approve the project but only if the NPV < 0
Incorrect. NPV stands for net present value. NPV is a method for the financial evaluation of projects. Typically, a project is selected if its NPV is deemed to be positive. Unless there are other considerations (which cannot be determined from the scenario provided), investing in a project with a negative NPV makes no sense.

C) Reject the project because the BCR > 1
Incorrect. BCR stands for benefit-to-cost ratio. A BCR is one of the project selection methods. With the numbers provided in the scenario, the project indeed has a BCR > 1 ($50,000 / $25,000 = 2). However, having a BCR of greater than 1.0 would be a reason to approve the project rather than reject it.

☑ **D) Approve the project based on a BCR of 2**
Correct. The benefits cost ratio (BCR) can be calculated as the benefits the project is estimated to generate divided by the costs the project is estimated to incur. In the scenario provided, the BCR would be

$50,000 / $25,000 = 2. A BCR of greater than 1 would be a reason to approve the project, making this choice the best answer to the question asked.

Explanation:
The information provided in the question allows one to calculate the benefits cost ratio (BCR). The BCR is one of the project selection methods. The BCR can be calculated as the benefits divided by the costs. When a BCR is greater than 1.0, the benefits outweigh the costs and, therefore, a project is considered profitable. Consequently, a project with a BCR of less than 1.0 means the costs are greater than the benefits, thus making the project unworthy of the investment.

In the scenario provided, the benefits would be the incremental revenue of $50,000 and the cost has been provided as $25,000. Applying the formula, the result would be as follows:

BCR = $50,000 / $25,000 = 2

A BCR of greater than 1.0 would be a reason to approve the project absent any other considerations.

Note that the time requirement of 5 two-week sprints is superfluous information that is not needed to answer this question correctly.

Reference:
A Guide to the Project Management Body of Knowledge, (PMBOK® Guide) – Sixth Edition, Project Management Institute Inc., 2017, Page(s) 34

https://www.projectmanagement.com/blog-post/4081/What-is-BCR-

Question 49: Answer

cA49

What is the ES of Task Six?

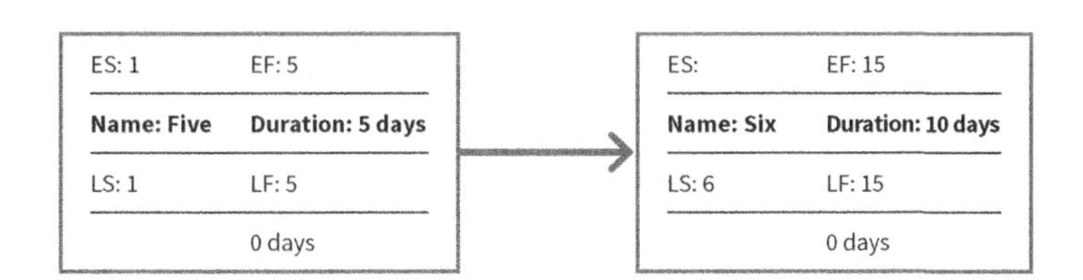

A) 4
B) 5

C) 6
D) 7

Explanation:

The formula to calculate the early start (ES) is:

ES = EF of predecessor + 1 = 5 + 1 = 6

Question 50: Answer

What is the critical path of the project that contains the following four tasks?

- Task A starts at the beginning of the project and has a duration of 2 days
- Task B starts after the completion of task A and has a duration of 3 days
- Task C starts after the completion of task A and has a duration of 7 days
- Task D starts after the completion of both tasks B and C and has a duration of four days

A) 7 days
B) 10 days
☑ **C) 13 days**
D) 16 days

Explanation:
To properly calculate the critical path on your project you have to draw a network diagram and then do a backward pass / forward pass. This will give you the following diagram:

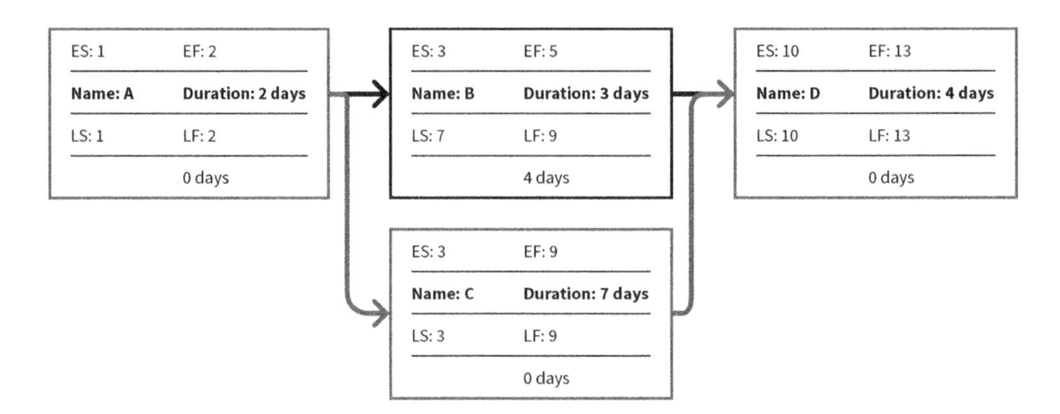

However, drawing this diagram can take you up to 5 minutes, which is too long on the exam. The shortcut we recommend applying during the exam is to draw the boxes for each task approximately to scale of their duration and line them up like this:

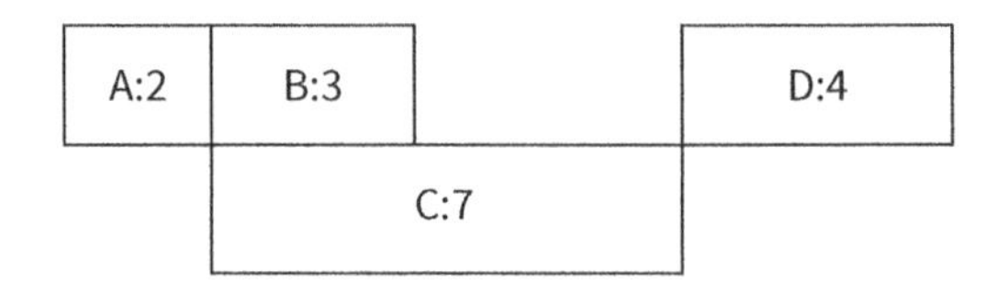

On a simple network diagram this takes a lot less time and shows you the result easily.

Question 51: Answer

cA51

Your project is four weeks behind schedule and you have been asked to crash the project in order to make up for the lost time. The tasks listed in the table below are all on the critical path.

Which of the tasks below would you crash?

Task	Original Duration	Crashed Duration	Time Savings	Original Cost	Crash Cost	Cost after Crashing
A	14	10	4	22,000	6,500	28,500
B	8	6	2	17,000	2,000	19,000
C	15	12	3	23,000	2,000	25,000
D	12	10	2	16,000	3,500	19,500
E	4	3	1	12,000	3,000	15,000
F	8	7	1	22,000	4,000	26,000

A) Task A
☑ **B) Tasks C & E**
C) Tasks B & D
D) Tasks D & E & F

Explanation:
When crashing a project, you will always crash those tasks that have the smallest crash cost. While all the 4 answers will give you a 4-week reduction in duration, answer B is the cheapest:

A) Task A	= 6,500	
B) Tasks C & E	**= 2,000 + 3,000**	**= 5,000**
C) Tasks B & D	= 2,000 + 3,500	= 5,500
D) Tasks D & E & F	= 3,500 + 3,000 + 4,000	= 10,500

By the way... The quickest way to find the answer to this question is to take the combinations provided in the answer choices A, B, C, and D and add up the crash cost for each. If you try to figure out in the table, which combinations of tasks give you a reduction of 4, you will loose too much time. Therefore, this is a question where you work your way from the answers back to the solution.

Question 52: Answer

Your project is currently proceeding exactly on schedule and budget. The project team has finished four of eight sprints and completed 150 of the planned 300 story points. Each story point is budgeted at $100.

What is the estimate at completion (EAC) for the project?

A) $0.00
Incorrect. This answer choice represents the cost variance (CV), which is the earned value (EV) less actual costs (AC): CV = EV – AC. Since, according to the scenario, the project is proceeding on budget, EV is equal to AC and, therefore, the CV would be $0.00. However, the question is asking for the EAC rather than the CV.

B) 1.0
Incorrect. This answer represents the cost performance index (CPI) and schedule performance index (SPI) for this project. Since the project is proceeding on schedule and budget, CPI and SPI would both be 1.0. However, the question asks for the estimate at completion (EAC) rather than the CPI or SPI.

C) $15,000
Incorrect. $15,000 represents the estimate to complete (ETC), not estimate at completion (EAC) as asked by the question. The budget at completion (BAC) is $30,000 (300 story points multiplied by $100). With four of eight sprints complete, and the project on budget, the project would have expended half of the project budget, or $15,000. Thus, the ETC = $30,000 – $15,000 = $15,000.

☑ **D) $30,000**
Correct. The estimate at completion (EAC) can be calculated as budget at completion (BAC) divided by the cost performance Index (CPI). Since the project is on budget, its CPI is equal to 1.0. Therefore, EAC = $30,000 / 1.0 = $30,000, making this choice the best answer to the question asked.

Explanation:
One of the formulas for the estimate at completion (EAC) is budget at completion (BAC) divided by cost performance index (CPI):

EAC = BAC / CPI

The question states that the project is on budget, thus the CPI must be 1.0. The BAC is the sum of the budgeted project work. According to the scenario, the project has a total of 300 story points, and each story point has a budgeted value of $100. Therefore, the BAC is:

BAC = 300 x $100 = $30,000

Hence, applying the formula for the EAC would yield the following result:

EAC = BAC / CPI = $30,000 / 1.0 = $30,000

In summary, when a project is proceeding exactly on budget, the BAC and the EAC are the same.

Reference:
A Guide to the Project Management Body of Knowledge, (PMBOK® Guide) – Sixth Edition, Project Management Institute Inc., 2017, Page(s) 267

Agile Practice Guide – First Edition, Project Management Institute Inc., 2017, Page(s) 69

Question 53: Answer

cA53

You recently installed a new PMIS tool that also allows you to perform Earned Value Analysis. The tool gives you the following EV data: EV = 231,000; PV = 261,000; AC = 256,000.

Which of the following do you expect to see in your PMIS tool?

A) CV = -25,000, SV = +30,000
☑ **B) CV = -25,000, SV = -30,000**
C) CV = +25,000, SV = +30,000
D) CV = +25,000, SV = -30,000

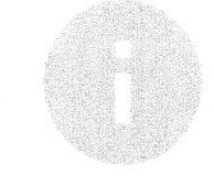

Explanation:
You have to apply the formulas for CV and SV as follows:

CV = EV – AC = 231,000 – 256,000 = -25,000
SV = EV – PV = 231,000 – 261,000 = -30,000

Question 54: Answer

Your company is constructing a new just-in-time (JIT) manufacturing facility in Puerto Rico. This facility will be producing 3,000 bicycles every day. The raw materials are delivered to the facility on standard pallets, each taking up 1m² (one square meter) of space. Every day approximately 500 pallets will be delivered to the facility. You have asked four local companies to submit their offers for constructing this new manufacturing facility.

If you had to pick a vendor based on just the following information, which one would you choose?

A) Company A: 8,000m² of production space and 500m² of pallet storage
B) Company B: 8,000m² of production space and 350m² of pallet storage
C) Company C: 8,000m² of production space and 250m² of pallet storage
☑ **D) Company D: 8,000m² of production space and 0m² of pallet storage**

Explanation:
This is an example of a question with a large amount of unnecessary information. The answer to the question can be found in the first sentence: "Your company is constructing a new **just-in-time** manufacturing facility in Puerto Rico." Per definition, the amount of inventory in a just in time environment is 0% or very close to 0%. This means that the new facility doesn't require any special pallet storage space. Of course, in the real world a thousand other factors would need to be considered to make a decision, but for this question, answer D is the best one.

Question 55: Answer

The plan for the first iteration was to complete 100 story points. However, the team was only able to complete 80. Each story point earns $1,000 for the project. The actual cost of the iteration was $90,000. As the iteration retrospective approaches, the scrum master requests that the team prepares all the data required to calculate the various earned value metrics.

At the retrospective, the team determines that the schedule performance index (SPI) of the iteration was ____________________.

(On the real PMP exam you may be asked to provide your answer by filling in the blank with the letter representing the correct answer. But here in the book, we are asking you to select the answer below.)

A) 1.25
Incorrect. This value, 1.25, could have resulted from the following calculation: 100 / 80 = 1.25. However, to calculate the SPI, one should divide the number of completed story points by the number of planned. In the scenario, the team planned 100 story points but only completed 80. Therefore, SPI = 80 /100 = 0.80.

☑ **B) 0.80**
Correct. In agile, the schedule performance index (SPI) can be calculated using the following formula: SPI = [number of completed story points] / [number of planned story points]. Based on the values provided in the scenario, SPI = 80 / 100 = 0.80.

C) 1.11
Incorrect. This value, 1.11, could have resulted from the following calculation: $100,000 / $90,000 = 1.11, where $100,000 is the planned value (PV) and $90,000 is the actual cost (AC). However, the SPI is calculated differently: SPI = 80 /100 = 0.80, where 80 is the number of the completed story points and 100 is the number of those that were planned.

D) 0.89
Incorrect. This answer choice represents the cost performance indicator (CPI), which is the earned value (EV, the value of completed story points or features) divided by the actual costs (AC). The EV is 80 story points multiplied by $1,000, resulting in $80,000. The AC is given in the scenario: $90,000. Therefore, CPI = $80,000 / $90,000 = 0.89.

Explanation:

Earned value management (EVM) is typically associated with the predictive (traditional) project management approaches. However, applying EVM metrics to projects carried out using agile methods can be done similarly and serve as an effective tool to measure team performance. For example, the schedule performance index (SPI) is the number of story points (features) completed divided by the number of the story points (features) planned. The cost performance index (CPI) is the earned value (EV, which is the value of the completed story points or features) divided by the actual costs incurred during the period under measurement.

The interpretation of the SPI and CPI values in agile projects are made similarly to the interpretation of those values in traditional projects. For example, an SPI less than 1.0 means the project (or iteration) is behind schedule, or, in other words, the team is working at a rate lower than planned. An SPI greater than 1.0 means the project (iteration) is ahead of schedule, i.e., the team is working at a rate higher than planned. A CPI less than 1.0 means the project (iteration) is over budget, or, in other words, the team earns less than a dollar compared to each dollar planned. A CPI greater than 1.0 indicates the project (iteration) is under budget, i.e., the team earns more than a dollar compared to each dollar planned.

The question asks to determine the SPI. Based on the explanation above, the SPI = 80 /100 = 0.80. In other words, the team worked at only 80% of the rate planned.

Reference:
Agile Practice Guide – First Edition, Project Management Institute Inc., 2017, Page(s) 69

Question 56: Answer

EV = 105 and SPI = 0.9375.

How much is the schedule variance (SV)?

A) Cannot be calculated based on these numbers
☑ **B) -7**
C) -6
D) 7

Explanation:
The formula to calculate the schedule variance is as follows: SV = EV – PV. However, in this question the planned value isn't given. Yet, the available two values (EV = 105 and SPI = 0.9375) enable us to calculate the PV. The complete process is as follows:

- The formula for the SPI is: **SPI = EV / PV**
  - We invert this formula in order to calculate the PV:
    PV = EV / SPI = 105 / 0.9375 = 112
- Now we apply the normal formula for SV:
  SV = EV – PV = 105 – 112 = -7

Question 57: Answer

You work in the PMO of a mid-sized company. Your PPM tool shows that there are currently three new projects waiting for selection. They are Project Stone with an NPV of ¥15,000,000, Project Paper with an NPV of ¥17,000,000 and Project Scissors with an NPV of ¥13,000,000. You present these three projects at the monthly project selection board meeting. After initial discussion it was immediately decided that Project Scissors will not be pursued at all. At this point a lengthy discussion begins about the benefits of both Project Stone and Project Paper. After 45 minutes the CEO asks you: "What is the opportunity cost of selecting Project Stone instead of Project Paper?"

What is your answer?

☑ **A) ¥17,000,000**
B) ¥15,000,000
C) -¥2,000,000
D) ¥2,000,000

Explanation:
This is an extremely simple question, presented to you as if it were a complex problem. The opportunity cost when selecting between two projects is simply the value of the project that is not selected. Or in numbers:

- Project Paper has a value of ¥17,000,000.
- If you don't do this project, then your lost opportunity is ¥17,000,000.
- The value of the project that was actually selected is irrelevant.
- You do not have to do any calculation whatsoever

Here is another way of explaining this: let us assume that you had enough resources in your company to tackle both projects. In this case you would make the profit of ¥15,000,000 from project Stone plus the profit of ¥17,000,000 from project Paper, giving you a total profit of ¥32,000,000. But because you only have capacity for project Stone, you are unable to realize the profit from project Paper. Therefore, your lost opportunity is the profit from the project that you did not do.

Note also, that project Scissors was never part of this equation. The CEO only asked what the opportunity cost was when selecting between the other two projects.

Question 58: Answer

cA58

You are three months into a nine-month project. The project is progressing as planned and you expect no major problems in the foreseeable future. Your PMIS is reporting the following values: BAC = 500,000; SPI = 1.1; CPI = 1.05; EV = 173,000; AC = 164,761.

How much is the EAC?

A) 491,761
B) 454,545
C) 189,761
☑ **D) 476,190**

Explanation:
There are many ways to calculate the estimate at completion (EAC) depending on how the project has been progressing. Therefore, questions about the EAC will always contain some information about the current "health" (or progression) of the project. There are certain *keywords* that you can look for. This information is important in order for you to pick the correct variation of the formula. Don't ignore it! Sometimes the question doesn't use the exact *keywords,* but a variation. So, your interpretation is needed. You will come across the following scenarios (*keywords* are underlined):

- No variances from the BAC have occurred, or variances are expected to continue at the same rate of spending (variances will probably remain the same through the end of the project):
  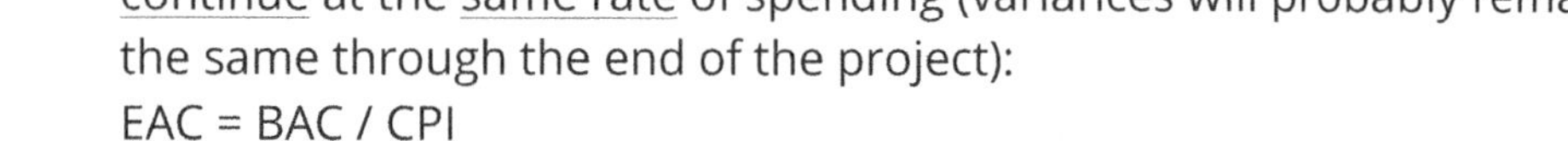
  EAC = BAC / CPI

- Original estimate was fundamentally flawed, or conditions have changed and invalidated original estimating assumptions:
  EAC = AC + ETC
- Current variances are thought to be one-time events that will probably **not** happen again for the remainder of the project:
  EAC = AC + BAC – EV
- The project is over budget but has to meet a schedule deadline:
  EAC = AC + [(BAC – EV) / (CPI * SPI)]

For instance, in our question, here the information is: "The project is progressing as planned and you expect no major problems in the foreseeable future." This indicates that there were no variances and that you expect it to continue at the same rate. Hence you need to use the first formula:

EAC = BAC / CPI = 500,000 / 1.05 = 476,190

cA59

Question 59: Answer

Your project team has 25 members. You have a monthly "All hands" meeting. In the past three months you have had the following attendance: January 21 attendees, February 16 attendees, March 23 attendees.

What is the mean attendance?

A) 16
☑ **B) 20**
C) 23
D) 60

Explanation:
In mathematics, an average refers to a measure of the "middle" of a data set. The most common method is the arithmetic mean. That is why the "average" is sometimes also and simply called the "mean". It is calculated by taking the sum of all the members of the list divided by the number of items in the list. In this question, the mean is calculated as follows: **21 + 16 + 23 / 3 = 20.**

Question 60: Answer

What is the Late Finish of Task One?

1	6
Name: One	**Duration: 6 days**
5	10

A) LF = 1
B) LF = 5
C) LF = 6
☑ **D) LF = 10**

Explanation:
In network diagrams, start and finish days are usually displayed in the same location of the boxes, irrespective whether you have a label or not:

ES = Early Start = top left
EF = Early Finish = top right
LS = Late Start = bottom left
LF = Late Finish = bottom right

You can also remember it as follows: start is on the left, finish is on the right, early is at the top, late is at the bottom.

Question 61: Answer

cA61

Your project consists of the following three sequential tasks.

How long will the project take?

Task Number	Duration Estimates (Beta Distribution)		
	Optimistic	Most Likely	Pessimistic
1	10	12	15
2	9	14	21
3	17	23	32

A) 36 days
B) 49 days
☑ **C) 50 days**
D) 68 days

Explanation:

To find the correct, you have to calculate the three-point average (beta distribution) of the estimates for all tasks and add them up. The three-point average is calculated as follows:

[Pessimistic + (4 * Most Likely) +Optimistic] / 6

This means you will end up with the following results:

Task Number	Duration Estimates			PERT
	Optimistic	Most Likely	Pessimistic	
1	10	12	15	12.16
2	9	14	21	14.33
3	17	23	32	23.50
				50.00

Question 62: Answer

How much is the Cost Performance Index?

A) CPI = 50, when EV = 100 and AC = 50
B) CPI = 1.0 when SPI = 0.1
C) CPI = 0.9 when EV = 100 and PV = 110
☑ **D) CPI = 0.9 when EV = 100 and AC = 110**

Explanation:
The formula to calculate the CPI is as follows: **CPI = EV / AC.** Only answer D gives us all the correct figures.

Question 63: Answer

Which of the following projects will you select?

A) Project Gold: profit is 200,000, EV is 450,000, ROI is 8%
☑ **B) Project Bear: investment is 350,000, ROI is 8.1%, payback period is four years**
C) Project Stellar: lowered expenses are 45,000, profit is -8,000, ROI is 7.5%
D) Project HHGTTG: PV is 50,000

Explanation:
When selecting between several projects that offer multiple variables look for those values that give you a "definite" number. For instance: profit is not definite, because you don't know the investment or the duration of the project. Similarly, the payback period is not definite. The only definite value among all the various variables given in this question is the return on investment because it tells you at what percentage your investment will be "paid back" to you. And when selecting between several projects, you will always select the one with the highest ROI.

Other values that can be considered "definite" are: net present value (NPV) and internal rate of return (IRR).

Question 64: Answer

cA64

What is the late finish (LF) of Activity Six?

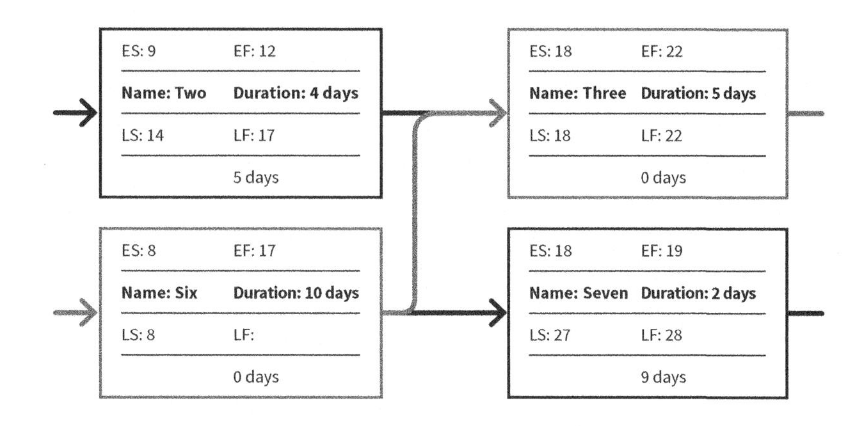

A) 26
B) 18
C) 28
☑ **D) 17**

Explanation:
The formula to calculate the late finish (LS) of an activity is as follows:
LF = LS of successor – 1 = 18 – 1 =17. If an activity has two successors as in this example, then we use the earlier of the two LS. Also note that Activity Six is on the critical path, hence, the late finish should be equal to the early finish.

Question 65: Answer

Your project is exactly half finished. You consult your earned value system and you receive the following numbers: BAC = 500,000; CPI = 1.1; SPI = 1.2; CV = -15,000; SV = -19,000.

How much is your EV?

A) 416,666
B) 500,000
☑ **C) 250,000**
D) 227,272

Explanation:
The project is "exactly half finished" means that the % complete = 50%.

Therefore, you calculate the EV as follows:

EV = % complete * BAC = 50% * 500,000 = 250,000

Question 66: Answer

Two hours after a successful project status presentation you get a call from your senior engineer. He asks to see you immediately for an urgent discussion. Three minutes later he is in your office, door closed, and he looks downcast. He tells you that your presentation earlier in the day had made him think. He had suddenly realized that he had missed several key project components. Because of that he realized that his original cost estimations were completely wrong. At the end of the meeting he promised to give you a new estimate tomorrow. The new estimate arrives less than 24 hours later, and your numbers now look as follows: BAC: 1,600,000. AC = 170,000; CPI = 1.03; SPI = 1.05; EV = 175,100.

How much do you now estimate that the project will cost, if the new estimate to complete that you received from your engineer is 1,570,000?

A) 1,553,398
☑ **B) 1,740,000**
C) 1,595,000
D) 1,470,458

Explanation:
There are many ways to calculate the EAC depending on how the project has been progressing. Therefore, questions about the EAC will always contain some information about the current "health" (or progression) of the project. There are certain *keywords* that you can look for. This information is important in order for you to pick the correct variation of the formula. Don't ignore it! Sometimes the question doesn't use the exact *keywords,* but a variation. So, your interpretation is needed. You will come across the following scenarios (*keywords* are underlined):

- No variances from the BAC have occurred, or variances are expected to continue at the same rate of spending (variance will remain):
  EAC = BAC / CPI
- Original estimate was fundamentally flawed, or conditions have changed and invalidated original estimating assumptions:
  EAC = AC + ETC
- Current variances are thought to be a single event that will not happen in the future:
  EAC = AC + BAC – EV

- The project is over budget but has to meet a schedule deadline:
  EAC = AC + [(BAC – EV) / (CPI * SPI)]

For instance, this question states, "Because of that he realized that his original cost estimations were completely wrong." This indicates that there was a fundamental flaw in the estimate. Hence, you need to use the second formula:

EAC = AC + ETC = 170,000 + 1,570,000 = 1,740,000

Question 67: Answer

cA67

Your project consists of the following three tasks.

What is the standard deviation of Task 2?

Task Number	Duration Estimates		
	Optimistic	**Most Likely**	**Pessimistic**
1	10	12	15
2	9	14	21
3	17	23	32

A) 14.33 days

B) 2 days

C) 6.77 days

D) 4 days

Explanation:
The standard deviation of a single task is calculated as follows:
(Pessimistic – Optimistic) / 6. Therefore, you would calculate: **(21 – 9) / 6 = 2.**

Question 68: Answer

cA68

You are using the straight-line depreciation method for a company car that has a projected life of 5 years. You purchased this car for £17,000 and you expect that you will be able to sell the car at the end of the 5 years for £2,000.

How much is the depreciation of this car in the third year?

A) £3,600

B) £3,400

C) £2,800

☑ **D) £3,000**

Explanation:
This question introduces the concept of the "scrap value" or "resale value". When depreciating an asset, the scrap value is first subtracted. Here is how:

Original Cost	£17,000
Minus Scrap Value	-£2,000
Total to depreciate	**£15,000**
Divided by life of asset	5 Years
Depreciation each year	£3,000

Book Value – Beginning of Year	Depreciation Expense	Accumulated Depreciation	Book Value – End of Year
£17,000 = Original Cost	£3,000	£3,000	£14,000
£14,000	£3,000	£6,000	£11,000
£11,000	£3,000	£9,000	£8,000
£8,000	£3,000	£12,000	£5,000
£5,000	£3,000	£15,000	**£2,000 = Scrap Value**

Question 69: Answer

A project manager has to select between the following four vendors. Price has a 60% weight and duration a 40% weight.

Which of the vendors should the project manager select?

Vendor	Price	Schedule
PM Experts	20	10
The PM Shop	19	12
Gold Platers	16	11
ScopeCreep PM	15	13

A) PM Experts
☑ **B) The PM Shop**
C) Gold Platers
D) ScopeCreep PM

Explanation:

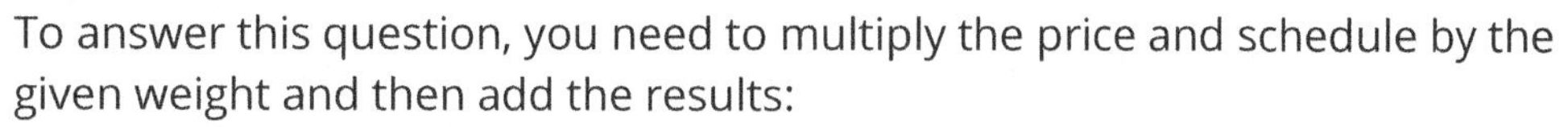

To answer this question, you need to multiply the price and schedule by the given weight and then add the results:

Vendor	Price	Schedule	Weighted Price 60%	Weighted Schedule 40%	Weighted Total 100%
PM Experts	20	10	12	4	16
The PM Shop	19	12	11.4	4.8	**16.2**
Gold Platers	16	11	9.6	4.4	14
ScopeCreep PM	15	13	9	5.2	14.2

Question 70: Answer

cA70

Two months ago, your customer formally submitted several changes to the project. These changes were reviewed and approved by the change board. Today you are reviewing the first project numbers affected by these approved changes: EV = 240,000; AC = 253,700; PV = 250,000; SPI = 0.96; BAC = 700,000.

How much is your new ETC?

☑ **A) 486,300**
B) 466,700
C) ETC cannot be calculated and a new bottom up estimate is required
D) 479,166

Explanation:

In this question, the customer has submitted changes. These changes were approved, implemented and then caused project variances. Because the variances are caused by **approved** changes, we can assume that the variances will continue in the future. As such, the variances are expected to remain.

To calculate ETC, the correct formula to use is: **ETC = EAC – AC.** The result is a monetary value that will tell us how much more the project will cost.

First, calculate EAC by using the formula that assumes the variances will remain. That formula is EAC = BAC / CPI. At this point you will realize that the CPI is not given in the question, therefore you have to calculate it:

CPI = EV / AC = 240,000 / 253,700 = 0.946

Next, calculate the EAC:

EAC = BAC / CPI = 700,000 / 0.946 = 740,000

Now, calculate the ETC:

ETC = EAC – AC = 740,000 – 253,700 = 486,300

Question 71: Answer

You are managing an ERP implementation project that is planned to complete in 12 months. After six months into the schedule, the project is already one month behind schedule.

What is the project's earned schedule (ES) at this stage?

A) 7 months
B) 6 months
☑ **C) 5 months**
D) The ES cannot be determined

Explanation:
We know that: Schedule Variance (SV) = Earned Schedule (ES) – Actual Time (AT). Rearranging the equation, we get: **ES = AT + SV = 6 + (-1) = 5 months**

cA72

Question 72: Answer

Your project consists of the following three sequential tasks.

How long will the project take to complete if you assume an accuracy of 1 standard deviation?

Task Number	Duration Estimates			Duration	Standard Deviation	Variance
	Optimistic	Most Likely	Pessimistic			
1	9	12	18	12.5	1.5	2.25
2	9	14	22	14.5	2.16	4.69
3	17	23	32	23.5	2.5	6.25

A) 50.5 days
B) 50.5 days ± 2.05
☑ **C) 50.5 days ± 3.63**
D) 50.5 days ± 4.39

Explanation:
One standard deviation of a series of activities is calculated by adding up the variances of all the activities and then taking the square root. In our scenario, this would be: **$\sqrt{(2.25 + 4.69 + 6.25)} = 3.63$.**

Note: It is unlikely that on your PMP exam you will come across questions that require you to calculate the variance of multiple activities such as this one. Focus on understanding how to calculate the standard deviations of a single activity. However, it is good to know how to solve questions like this one because the PMI is constantly revising the PMP exam and removing old questions and adding new ones.

Question 73: Answer

cA73

AC = 100, CPI = 0.9, SPI = 1.1.

How much is the cost variance?

A) -8.18
B) 10
☑ **C) -10**
D) 8.18

Explanation:
The formula to calculate the cost variance is as follows: CV = EV – AC. However, in this question, the earned value (EV) is not given. Yet, two of the three available values (AC = 100 and CPI = 0.9) enable us to calculate the EV. The complete process is as follows:

- The formula for the CPI is: **CPI = EV / AC.**
  - We invert this formula in order to calculate the EV:
    EV = AC * CPI = 100 * 0.9 = 90
- Now we apply the normal formula for CV:
  CV = EV – AC = 90 – 100 = -10

The SPI given in the question is extraneous information and not needed for the calculation.

Question 74: Answer

cA74

You have just finished a 10-month long project.

Assuming that you were the project manager, how much of this time have you spent communicating with others in total?

A) 7 months
B) 8 months
☑ **C) 9 months**
D) 10 months

Explanation:
According to Harold Kerzner, a project manager spends 90% of their time communicating. Therefore, out of a 10-month project you have spent 90% (or 9 months) communicating. Some of us talk even more... ☺

Question 75: Answer

A project is 50% complete. BAC = 200,000; EV = 92,000; AC = 97,000.

What is the TCPI based on BAC?

A) 103,000
B) .04
C) .96
☑ **D) 1.05**

Explanation:
The calculated project of cost performance that must be achieved on the remaining work to meet a specific management goal (e.g., BAC or EAC). It is the work remaining divided by the funds remaining.

TCPI (based on BAC) = (BAC – EV) / (BAC – AC)
TCPI = (200,000 – 92,000) / (200,000 – 97,000)
TCPI = 108,000 / 103,000
TCPI = 1.0485

Question 76: Answer

The project board is presented with the following information about current project opportunities: Project A has a duration of four years and an NPV of $40,000, Project B has a duration of three years and an NPV of $45,000, Project C has a duration of six years and an NPV of $62,000, and Project D has a duration of eight years and an NPV of $56,000.

Which project will you select?

A) Project A
B) Project B
☑ **C) Project C**
D) Project D

Explanation:
When calculating the NPV of a project, the duration (number of years) is already factored in to the result. Therefore, when presented with a selection of several projects and their NPV, you can simply select the one with the highest NPV. Project C has the highest NPV of the 4 projects presented and is, therefore, should be selected.

Question 77: Answer

cA77

Your current Earned Value numbers look as follows: EV = 200,000; AC = 210,000; BAC = 375,000; SPI = 1.05.

How much is the EAC if your primary project constraint is meeting your schedule? (Round up/down to four decimal places.)

A) 376,666
☑ **B) 385,000**
C) 394,736
D) 386,767

Explanation:
There are many ways to calculate the EAC depending on how the project has been progressing. Therefore, questions about the EAC will always contain some information about the current "health" (or progression) of the project. There are certain *keywords* that you can look for. This information is important in order for you to pick the correct variation of the formula. Don't ignore it! Sometimes the question doesn't use the exact *keywords,* but a variation. So, your interpretation is needed. You will come across the following scenarios (*keywords* are underlined):

- No variances from the BAC have occurred or are expected to continue at the same rate of spending (variance will probably remain the same through the end of the project):
  EAC = BAC / CPI
- Original estimate was fundamentally flawed, or conditions have changed and invalidated original estimating assumptions:
  EAC = AC + ETC
- Current variances are thought to be a single occurrence and will probably **not** occur again to the end of the project:
  EAC = AC + BAC – EV
- You are over budget but need to meet a schedule deadline:
  EAC = AC + [(BAC – EV) / (CPI * SPI)]

For instance, in our question here the information is: "...if your primary project constraint is meeting your schedule?" This means we must meet a schedule deadline and therefore need to use the 4th formula:

EAC = AC + [(BAC – EV) / (CPI * SPI)]
EAC = 210,000 + [(375,000 – 200,000) / (????? * 1.05)]

At this point, you will realize that the CPI is not given in the question. Therefore, we first have to calculate the CPI. Here are the complete steps of calculating the result:

Step 1: Calculate the CPI:

CPI = EV / AC
CPI = 200,000 / 210,000 = 0.9523809 (This means we are over budget)
CPI = 0.9524 (rounded "up" to 4 decimal places)

Step 2: Calculate the EAC:

EAC = AC + [(BAC – EV) / (CPI * SPI)]
EAC = 210,000 + [(375,000 – 200,000) / (0.9524 * 1.05)]
EAC = 210,000 + (175,000 / 1.0000)
EAC = 210,000 + 175,000
EAC = 385,000

Note: If you rounded to 2 decimal places then CPI = 0.95 and CPI * SPI = 0.99. With these numbers answer D would be correct. So, make sure that you follow the rounding instructions given in the scenario.

Question 78: Answer

Your project consists of the following three tasks.

What is the standard deviation of the project?

Task Number	Duration Estimates		
	Optimistic	Most Likely	Pessimistic
1	10	12	15
2	9	14	21
3	17	23	32

☑ **A) 3.31 days**
B) 4.30 days
C) 5.33 days
D) 2.30 days

Explanation:
The formula for calculating the standard deviation of a series of activities is **√sum[(Pessimistic – Optimistic) / 6]^2.** This translates to: Add up the variances of all the activities and then take the square root. Here is how this is done:

- Calculate the standard deviation of each task (2nd to last column)
- Calculate the variance by multiplying the standard deviation by itself (last column)
- Add up the variance. The result is: 10.94
- Take the square root from the variance total. The result is: √10.94 = 3.31

Task Number	Duration Estimates			Standard Deviation	Variance
	Optimistic	Most Likely	Pessimistic		
1	10	12	15	0.83	0.69
2	9	14	21	2.00	4.00
3	17	23	32	2.50	6.25
					10.94

Note: It is unlikely that on your PMP exam you will come across questions that require you to calculate the variance of multiple activities such as this one. Focus on understanding how to calculate the standard deviations of single activities. However, it is good to know how to solve questions like this one because the PMI is constantly revising the PMP exam and removing old questions and adding new ones.

Question 79: Answer

cA79

You have received the following values from your statistical sampling: 80, 83, 85, 90, 82, 88, 90, 91, 94, 79.

What is the mode of this number set?

A) 10
B) 86.5
☑ **C) 90**
D) 86.2

Explanation:
The mode is the most frequent value in a data set. The easiest way to determine the mode is to list the numbers is ascending order and then count which number occurs most often in the series: 79, 80, 82, 83, 85, 88, **90, 90,** 91, 94

Question 80: Answer

You are the project manager of the Speedy Software implementation project.

Based on the following information, which tasks are on the critical path?

- Task A starts at the beginning of the project and has a duration of one day
- Task B starts after the completion of Task A and has a duration of two days
- Task C starts after the completion of Task B and has a duration of four days
- Task D starts after the completion of both Tasks C and E and has a duration of four days
- Task E starts after the completion of Task F and has a duration of two days
- Task F starts after the completion of Task A and has a duration of seven days

A) A, B, C, E, D
☑ **B) A, F, E, D**
C) A, B, C, F
D) A, F, B, C, D

Explanation:
To properly calculate the critical path on your project, you have to draw a network diagram and then do a backward pass / forward pass. This will give you the following drawing:

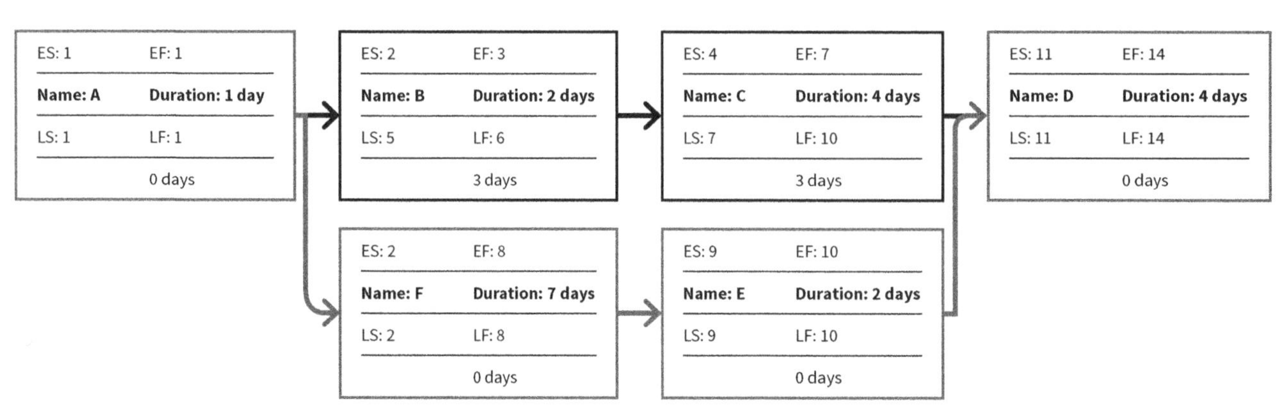

However, the approach of "doing it right" will take too long on the exam. The shortcut (during the exam) is to draw the boxes for each task approximately to scale of their duration and line them up like this:

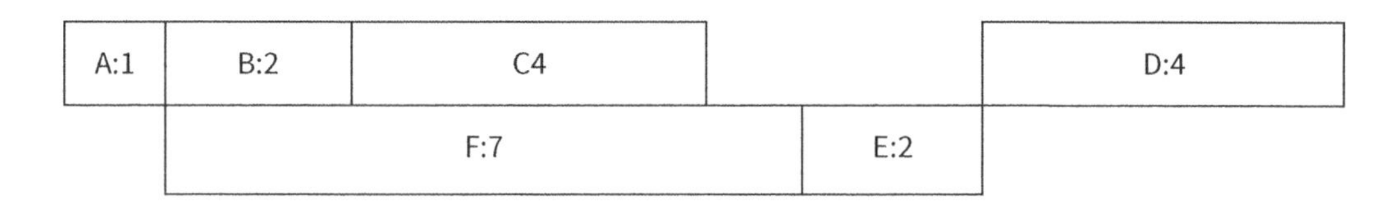

This takes a lot less time and shows you the result easily. Remember: it doesn't have to be pretty... it just has to be right.

Question 81: Answer

cA81

What is the late start of Activity Four?

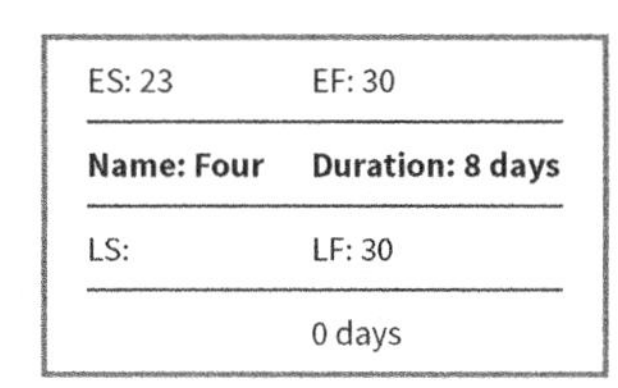

A) 24
☑ **B) 23**
C) 30
D) 22

Explanation:
The formula for calculating the LS of an activity is as follows:

LS = LF – duration + 1 = 30 – 8 + 1 = 23

By the way... did you notice that both the EF and LF of this task are the same? Consequentially the ES and LS are also the same.

Question 82: Answer

A project that is 80% complete. BAC = 435,000; EAC = 478,000; EV = 410,000; AC = 452,000.

What is the project's TCPI, based on EAC?

A) 1.04
B) 0.04
☑ **C) 0.96**
D) 25,000

Explanation:
To-complete performance index (TCPI) is a measure of the cost performance that is required to be achieved with the remaining resources in order to meet a specified management goal (e.g., BAC or EAC), expressed as the ratio of the cost to finish the outstanding work to the remaining budget. It is the work remaining divided by the funds remaining. If the BAC is no longer viable, then a new EAC should be prepared, and the project should be managed toward this new value.

TCPI (based on EAC) = (BAC – EV) / (EAC – AC)
TCPI = (435,000 – 410000) / (478000 – 452000)
TCPI = 25,000 / 26,000
TCPI = 0.96

Question 83: Answer

The SPI on your project is currently at 0.95, resulting in a three-week delay. You assume that this trend will continue, and you estimate that you are going to have to make up five weeks in order to stay on track and reach your target delivery date. As such, you decide to crash your project. Below are the tasks that you consider crashing.

Which ones would you crash in order to gain five weeks?

Task	Original Duration	Crashed Duration	Time Savings	On Critical Path?	Original Cost	Cost after Crashing
A	13	10	5	No	12,000	15,000
B	8	7	1	Yes	16,000	19,500
C	16	12	4	Yes	22,000	29,500
D	12	9	3	No	17,000	19,000
E	4	3	1	Yes	22,000	26,000
F	16	13	3	Yes	23,000	26,500
G	14	14	2	No	21,000	22,000
H	8	7	1	Yes	19,000	22,000

A) Task A
B) Tasks C & E
C) Tasks D & G
☑ **D) Tasks B & F & H**

Explanation:
To answer this question correctly you have to do two things: 1) Realize that all tasks that are not on the critical path can be ignored. Only tasks on the critical path can be crashed. 2) Calculate the Crash Cost for those tasks on the critical path and figure out, which of the given answers is the cheapest:

Task	Original Duration	Crashed Duration	Time Savings	On Critical Path?	Original Cost	Cost after Crashing	Crash Cost
A	13	10	5	No	12,000	15,000	—
B	8	7	1	Yes	16,000	19,500	3,500
C	16	12	4	Yes	22,000	29,500	7,500
D	12	9	3	No	17,000	19,000	—
E	4	3	1	Yes	22,000	26,000	4,000
F	16	13	3	Yes	23,000	26,500	3,500
G	14	14	2	No	21,000	22,000	—
H	8	7	1	Yes	19,000	22,000	3,000

A) Task A = Not on the critical path
B) Tasks C & E = 7,500 + 4,000 = 11,500
C) Tasks D & G = Not on the critical path
☑ **D) Tasks B & F & H = 3,500 + 3,500 + 3,000 = 10,000**

Question 84: Answer

cA84

Following are some current measures on your project: actual time (AT) = three months; actual cost (AC) = $3,000; budget at completion (BAC) = $10,000; earned schedule (ES) = two months?

What is the project's SPI?

A) 1.33
☑ **B) 0.67**
C) 1.50
D) 5.00

Explanation:
There are two formulas for schedule performance index (SPI):

SPI = EV / AC
Or **SPI = ES / AT**

In this scenario, we can only apply the second equation, i.e.,
SPI = ES / AT = 2/3 = 0.67

cA85

Question 85: Answer

An inspection has revealed the following weights of screws that are produced in your plant: 3.65g, 3.66g, 3.58g, 3.62g, 3.61g, 3.67g.

What is the median weight of the screws in this data set?

A) 6
B) 3.63167
C) 3.58
☑ **D) 3.635**

Explanation:
The median is the middle value that separates the higher half from the lower half of the data set. To find it, arrange the numbers in ascending order, and then select the one in the middle: 3.58, 3.61, **3.62, 3.65,** 3.66, 3.67. In this question, we have 6 values, and because of this there isn't a single number in the exact middle. Therefore, we have to take the two middle values and calculate their mean (average). This is done by calculating **(3.62 + 3.65) / 2 = 3.635**

Question 86: Answer

What is the average of the following values: (100), 50, 75, (20), 99, (70), 40, 14?

A) 63.6
☑ **B) 11**
C) 58.5
D) 14

Explanation:
In the USA a number in brackets like (100) is the same as -100 or "minus 100". Since the PMI is the USA-based organization, you should be familiar with this denomination. Therefore, you will first have to add up these numbers as follows:

-100 + 50 + 75 + -20 + 99 + -70 + 40 + 14 = 88

The average can then be calculated as follows: **88 / 8 = 11**

Question 87: Answer

cA87

On your last project, the task of "Develop Training Plan" took 12 days. On the current project the trainer estimates that it will take anywhere from 22 to 40 days, but she says that "It will probably take me 28 days". You want to be about 95% certain that the duration in your schedule is correct.

What duration will you assume?

A) 26 to 32 days
B) 29 days
C) 20 to 38 days
☑ **D) 23 to 35 days**

Explanation:

To calculate a duration at about 95% certainty for this question you will have to perform the following steps:

- First, calculate the PERT duration (three-point beta distribution):
  [Pessimistic + (4 * Most Likely) + Optimistic] / 6
  [40 + (4 * 28) + 22] / 6 = 29 days

- Second, calculate the standard deviation:
  σ = (Pessimistic – Optimistic) / 6
  σ = (40 – 22) / 6 = 3 days

- At this point you know that the PERT three-point estimate duration of the task is 29 days and that one standard deviation is 3 days.

- The question requires you to give a certainty of about 95%
  - 1 standard deviation = 68.27% certainty
  - 2 standard deviations = 95.45% certainty

- Therefore, you have to include a spread of 2 standard deviations from your duration:
  29 days ± 2 standard deviations
  29 days ± 6 days = 23 to 35 days

Question 88: Answer

Which of the following is true?

A) SPI = -1, when EV = 100 and PV = 101

☑ **B) SPI = 0.9 when EV = 100 and PV = 110**
C) SPI = 1.0 when CPI = 1.0
D) SPI = 0.9 when EV = 100 and AC = 110

Explanation:
The formula to calculate the schedule performance index (SPI) is as follows:

SPI = EV / PV = 100 – 110 = 0.9

Question 89: Answer

You return from a long overdue vacation on the beach and you find that your earned value numbers look as follows: EV = 100,000; CPI = 0.85; SPI = 0.77; AC = 117,000; PV = 130,000; ETC = 315,000; BAC = 420,000. You discuss these numbers with your team. In particular, you point out to them that based on the CPI and the SPI the project is both over budget and behind schedule. The team leader informs you that this does not come as too much of a surprise. You learn that during your absence, the team had faced unexpected technical issues, which must have caused these variances. The team lead promises that this was unusual, that the issues have been resolved, and that the project will now return to normal again.

Based on this information, what is your new EAC?

☑ **A) 437,000**
B) 432,000
C) 494,117
D) 493,470

Explanation:
There are many ways to calculate the EAC depending on how the project has been progressing. Therefore, questions about the EAC will always contain some information about the current "health" (or progression) of the project. There are certain *keywords* that you can look for. This information is important in order for you to pick the correct variation of the formula. Don't ignore it! Sometimes the question doesn't use the exact *keywords,* but a variation. So, your interpretation is needed. You will come across the following scenarios (*keywords* are underlined):

- No variances from the BAC have occurred or are expected to continue at the same rate of spending (variance will probably remain the same through the end of the project):
  EAC = BAC / CPI

- Original estimate was fundamentally flawed, or conditions have changed and invalidated original estimating assumptions:
  EAC = AC + ETC

- Current variances are thought to be a single event that will probably **not** occur again through the end of the project:
  EAC = AC + BAC – EV
- You are over budget but need to meet a schedule deadline:
  EAC = AC + [(BAC – EV) / (CPI * SPI)]

For instance, in our question here the information is: "The team lead promises that this was **unusual**, that the issues have been resolved and that the project will now return to normal again." This means that the variances are not typical, will not happen again, and that we need to use the 3rd formula:

EAC = AC + BAC – EV
EAC = 117,000 + 420,000 – 100,000
EAC = 437,000

Question 90: Answer

Your sponsor would like to know how long it takes to build the prototype on your project. He tells you that a similar project last year produced a prototype in 28 days. Your engineer tells you that the design of the prototype will take anywhere from 25 to 45 days and based on the design changes he thinks it will probably be close to about 32 days.

What is the simple average of the numbers that you have received?

A) 31 days
B) 32 days
C) 33 days
☑ **D) 34 days**

Explanation:
The formula for the PERT triangular three-point estimate or simple average is **(Pessimistic + Most Likely + Optimistic) / 3.** The numbers to use were provided by the engineer. The sponsor's value of 28 days from the previous project is irrelevant. Therefore, you calculate **(45 + 32 + 25) / 3 = 34 days.**

Did you notice that the scenario in this question was exactly the same as for question number 1? The only difference was that for question number 1 you were asked to use beta distribution, and for this question we asked to use the triangular distribution. Let's review these two:

Concept	Formula	Words to look for
PERT Beta Distribution	**[Pessimistic + (4 * Most Likely) + Optimistic] / 6**	Beta or weighted average
PERT Triangular Distribution	**(Pessimistic + Most Likely + Optimistic) / 3**	Triangular or simple average

For the PMP Exam, PERT Beta is the preferred formula, but in this question, a "simple" average has been required to be used.

PART FOUR

Formula Pocket Guide & Reference Articles

Two Approaches for Calculating ES, EF, LS and LF

There are two approaches for calculating ES, E, LS and LF:

- First approach: calculate the network diagram starting on day 0
- Second approach: calculate the network diagram starting on day 1

In the *PMP® Exam Formula Study Guide,* we use the second approach, because when your sponsor tells you that your project starts on the first day of September, then that is September 1, not September 0. This is also the way that all modern scheduling tools seem to work. You schedule your project based on **a calendar start date and not "on day 0".**

That is why there is a slight difference between the calculations: you have to add/subtract 1 from the results in the **second** approach.

Of course, this often leads to confusion among PMP students who want to know which formula they should use on the exam.

We have discussed this with several of our PMP trainer colleagues, and they agree that the Project Management Institute (PMI)® **does not** "support" a specific method of calculating a network diagram. (Remember that next to the two options shown above you could also calculate a network path starting on a specific calendar date in hours instead of days, making the calculations even more complex).

The Formula Pocket Guide

Earned Value

CV = EV – AC
CPI = EV / AC
SV = EV – PV
SV = ES – AT
SPI = EV / PV
SPI = ES / AT
EAC *'cost performance is not expected to change'* = BAC / CPI
EAC *'original budget fundamentally flawed'* = AC + Bottom-up ETC
EAC *'cost variance will **not** happen again'* = AC + BAC – EV
EAC *'if both CPI and SPI influencing'* = AC + [(BAC – EV) / (CPI * SPI)]
ETC = EAC – AC
ETC *'original budget flawed'* = new estimate
ETC *'unearned budget'* = BAC – EV
ETC *'if both CPI and SPI influencing'* = ETC = (BAC – EV) / (CPI * SPI)
ETC *'cost performance is not expected to change'* = (BAC / CPI) – AC
Percent Complete = EV / BAC * 100
VAC = BAC – EAC
EV = Sum of PV of completed work
EV = % complete * BAC
TCPI *'based on BAC'* = (BAC – EV) / (BAC – AC)
TCPI *'based on EAC'* = (BAC – EV) / (EAC – AC)

Three-Point Estimating (PERT)

Three-point Beta = (Pessimistic + (4 * Most Likely) + Optimistic) / 6
Three-point Triangular = (Pessimistic + Most Likely + Optimistic) / 3
σ = (Pessimistic – Optimistic) / 6
Activity Variance = [(Pessimistic – Optimistic) / 6]^2

Communications

Communication Channels = n * (n – 1) / 2

Probability

EMV = Probability * Impact in currency

Network Diagram

Activity Duration = EF – ES + 1 or Activity Duration = LF – LS + 1
Total Float = LS – ES or Total Float = LF – EF
Free Float = ES of Following – EF of Present – 1
EF = ES + duration – 1
ES = EF of predecessor + 1
LF = LS of successor – 1
LS = LF – duration + 1

Project Selection

PV = FV / (1 + r)^n
FV = PV * (1 + r)^n
NPV = Select biggest number. (Formula not required for the exam)
ROI = Select the biggest number. (Formula not required for the exam)
IRR = Select the biggest number. (Formula not required for the exam)
Payback Period = Add up the projected cash inflow minus expenses until the result of the calculation is equal to the initial investment
BCR = Benefit / Cost
CBR = Cost / Benefit
Opportunity Cost = The profit of the project not chosen

Depreciation

Straight-line Depreciation:
Depreciation Expense = (Asset Cost – Scrap Value) / Useful Life
Depreciation Rate = 100% / Useful Life

Double Declining Balance Method:
Depreciation Rate = 2 * (100% / Useful Life)
Depreciation Expense = Depr. Rate * Book Value at Beginning of Year
Book Value = Book Value at beginning of year – Depreciation Expense

Mathematical Basics

Average (Mean) = Sum of all members divided by the number of items
Median = Arrange values from lowest value to highest
Pick the middle one. If there is an even number of values, calculate the mean of the two middle values.
Mode = Find the value in a data set that occurs most often

Values

1 sigma = 68.27% (68.2689492...)
2 sigma = 95.45% (95.4499736...)
3 sigma = 99.73% (99.7300204...)
6 sigma = 99.99% (99.9999998027...)
Control Limits = ± Three sigma from mean
Control Specifications = Defined by customer; looser than the control limits
Rough Order of Magnitude estimate = -25% to +75% *(PMBOK®)*
Preliminary estimate = -15% to +50%
Budget estimate = -10% to +25%
Definitive estimate = -5% to +10%
Final estimate = 0%
Float on the critical path = 0 days
Pareto's Law = 80/20
Time a PM spends communicating = 90%
Crashing a project = Crash tasks with least expensive crash cost on critical path first
JIT inventory = 0% (or very close to 0%)
Minus 100 = (100) or -100

Acronyms

AC	Actual Cost
AT	Actual Time
BAC	Budget at Completion
BCR	Benefit Cost Ratio
CBR	Cost Benefit Ratio
CPI	Cost Performance Index
CV	Cost Variance
DUR	Duration
EAC	Estimate at Completion
EF	Early Finish
EMV	Expected Monetary Value
ES	Early Start
ES	Earned Schedule
ETC	Estimate to Complete
EV	Earned Value
FV	Future Value
IRR	Internal Rate of Return

JIT	Just-in-Time
LF	Late Finish
LS	Late Start
NPV	Net Present Value
PERT	Program Evaluation and Review Technique
PV	Planned Value
PV	Present Value
ROI	Return on Investment
SPI	Schedule Performance Index
SV	Schedule Variance
TCPI	To Complete Performance Index
VAC	Variance at Completion
σ	Sigma / Standard Deviation
^	"To the power of" (2^3 = 2*2*2 = 8)

Download this Formula Pocket Guide from https://www.project-management-formulas.com/pocket

Both of these calculations will lead to the correct answer. However, in the exam, the big difference is that the first approach (starting on day 0) involves fewer calculations because you don't have to "+1 or -1" each time. So, in order to reduce your "risk" of doing a calculation wrong and saving time during the exam, you might want to initiate the network diagram with day 0. **However,** in "real life" starting with day 1 is more appropriate.

Since PMI is aware of these varying methods, you **should not** see a question on the exam where only the application of one or the other leads to the correct answer.

Visit the following link to watch a 45 minute video on how to perform a forward pass and backward pass: **https://www.project-management-prepcast.com/network-diagram**.

PMP® Formulas and Calculations – The Complete Guide

When I speak to Project Management Professional (PMP)® students, there's often one thing on their mind: How are they going to learn all the PMP formulas? In particular the ones where you need to calculate a result?

There's no getting away from it. There are a lot of these formulas and calculations that you may need to know on the exam.

In this (almost) complete guide we'll go through the PMP formulas with examples. Stick with me and by the end you'll see that learning the PMI formulas isn't going to be that bad. Read on and you'll learn a lot about how to crack formula-based PMP questions to help pass your PMP exam.

What Formula Question Types are on the PMP Exam?

For the PMP exam, you must know how to correctly answer questions with formulas about earned value, communications, procurement, probability, network diagrams, project selection, depreciation, and some mathematical basics. You also have to know a lot of acronyms.

As we saw earlier in the guide, these are the types of questions you have to expect:

- **Apply a formula:** These are straightforward questions where you are given values and are expected to apply the correct formula.
- **Apply two formulas:** In these questions you get a set of values and are asked to calculate a result. At first these look as if you can simply apply one formula. But as you are applying this first formula you suddenly realize that one value is missing. This missing value must then first be calculated via a second formula.
- **Invert a formula:** These questions test your ability to take a basic formula and invert it. For instance instead of asking "4 + 6 = ?" the question would be "4 + ? = 10" and it is your job to invert the formula and calculate "10 – 4 = 6".
- **Result interpretation:** In these types of questions you are given a result and asked, "What does this result mean for the project?"
- **Find the correct formula:** For these types of questions you are given a scenario and various formulas as options. Your task is to select the formula which best applies to the given scenario.
- **Use a formula based on keywords:** There is more than one way to calculate earned value results. Which formula to use depends on the progression (or health) of your project. These are scenario-based questions that contain certain keywords. You must recognize these keywords and apply the correct formula.

So you can easily see that being "mathematically ready" for your PMP exam means more than simply knowing your earned value (EV) formulas. Yes, you'll definitely see at least one EV question on your exam but there's a lot more to the test than simply that.

The Earned Value Formulas

Many PMP aspirants find the concepts behind earned value management (EVM) hard to understand and the formula even harder, so that's where we are going to start.

First, let's define the term:

> **Earned Value (EV).** The measure of work completed expressed in terms of the budget authorized for that work. [1]

The thing that complicates it for many people is the question: "What on earth is value?" For the earned value calculations you just have to remember that value equals money. The total value of a project (in EVM terms) is equal to the budget of the project. As you work through the project, you spend the budget in order to achieve the project's objectives, which in turn deliver business value. You can assess how much value you have 'earned' (read: 'achieved') by knowing how far through the project you are and how much you have spent.

The earned value management formulas are simply the calculations that give you the data to work out the EV position on your project. There are 12 earned value calculations in total.

Still not clear? You'll see what I mean with an example.

The Earned Value Calculation

Let's say we're working on a project to design an app for a smartwatch. Overall we are trying to answer the following two questions:

- Are we over, on, or below budget?
- Are we ahead, on, or behind schedule?

The earned value management formulas give us the information we need to determine that, and we'll get further into how we can calculate cost and schedule performance a little later.

The formula: **EV = % complete * BAC**

What you get: A monetary value.

(BAC = Budget at Completion)

Let's assume the following situation: Our smartwatch app project is going to take six months and cost $60,000. We're two months into the project and we've spent $20,000. Our project sponsor wants to know if the project is doing "OK".

Generally, when sponsors ask a question like that, then they want to know if you are burning through the budget too quickly and if you are going to hit the end date which they have published to the Board. The EVM formulas can tell you exactly that.

Let's continue with the example and assume that that project was supposed to deliver 36 work packages, and that each package has the same planned value (PV) and takes the same amount of effort to complete. Now, let's say that the project team has completed 12 work packages so far during the first two months of the project. We can see that 12/36 shows that the team is a third of the way through the project. As a percentage, 33.33% of the work has been completed. That's the % complete figure in the simple formula.

The budget at completion (BAC) is the total amount budgeted for the project, in this case $60,000.

Plugging those figures into the formula we get: **33% * $60,000 = $20,000.** The earned value (EV) of the project is $20,000.

> The formula: **EV = Sum of PVs of all completed activities**
>
> **What you get:** Project's earned value. Why? If each work package requires a different level of effort to complete, we cannot use the number of completed work packages as an indicator of the project's percentage of completion. In such cases, we need to go one level deeper, for example, breaking the work packages into person-hours of effort. When determining a project's percentage of completion is difficult, grab the latest project schedule. Each project activity should have its own planned value (PV) assigned to it. Add the PVs for all the completed activities (the emphasis is on 'completed'), and this value will be your project's earned value.

Is There a Formula for Planned Value?

Earned value alone isn't that useful a figure. You need to have something to compare it to. Planned value (PV) is great for that.

> **Planned Value (PV).** The authorized budget assigned to scheduled work. [2]

There is no formula for PV. It's simply the approved budget for a task. You can use PV for the budget of a phase, stage or work package. It's normally measured over a particular time period.

How to Calculate Schedule Variance

Schedule variance tells us whether our smartwatch app project is ahead, on, or behind schedule.

> **Schedule Variance (SV).** A measure of schedule performance on the project, expressed as the difference between project's earned value and planned value. [3]

One argument that I often get from my students is something along the lines of "I don't see how SV is possible! I mean we are using numbers from the budget and you expect me to believe that they help predict how I'm doing on the schedule??" It's not an unreasonable argument. But it is indeed possible. For now, I'm going to ask you to take a leap of faith (I did when I originally came across SV) and I'll explain how it all works. Let us begin with the formula:

> The formula: **SV = EV – PV**
>
> **What you get:** A monetary amount. A negative number means you are behind schedule (that's bad). A positive number means you are ahead of schedule (generally that's good).

Although we generally see a negative SV as something bad and a positive SV as something good, contemporary project management considers all variances, positive or negative, as potentially harmful to the project and the performing organization. Variance tolerances are defined, such as ±5% or ±15%, and whenever the variances are found outside this range, an investigation is recommended. One may argue saying, "I don't get it, how can a positive 20% SV be bad for the project or the organization? A positive 20% SV means I am 20% ahead of schedule and I should be getting a bonus for that!" Well, we didn't say that a positive 20% SV is always bad. We said it is potentially harmful to the project and the organization. If the 20% faster progress happened due to the brilliance of the project team, they need to be rewarded. However, in most cases, it has been found that positive schedule variance is a result of conservative estimation during project planning. If a project is conservatively estimated or scheduled, it will consume organizational resources for a more extended period than it should have been, which is not good for the organization.

Earlier we showed you that the project team had completed 12 out of 36 planned work packages, meaning the project is 33.33% complete. The team has just finished the second month in the project, and with the total project duration of 6 months, the team has consumed 33.33% of the time planned.

It seems that we are on track!

But wait a minute, what if the project was front-loaded? A front-loaded project requires more resources and work to be completed at the beginning of the project in comparison to the end. Let us now assume that in this project we planned to complete 66.67% of the work in the first two months, and very few resources are involved in the last three months of the project. Therefore, now, looking again at 33.33% of the time consumed and 33.33% of work packages completed, we understand that these values are not good for the front-loaded project since according to the plan we should have completed 66.67% of the work.

The EV of our fantastic new app development project is $20,000, as we saw earlier. However, the Planned Value (PV) is $40,000 (66.67% of $60,000). In other words this means according to our plan we should have completed $40,000 worth of work. Using those numbers in the schedule variance formula we get **$20,000 – $40,000 = -$20,000**

These are really simplified figures to help you understand the math more easily and you can clearly see that this is bad news. Now, when we start to dig into the numbers, we can see that the project is running behind schedule.

One of the emerging trends in project management is the new approach to schedule variance. The development of the new SV formula was a result of criticism of the traditional SV formula that expresses schedule variance in monetary terms. The new SV formula expresses the schedule variance in time units. This formula uses two components: earned schedule (ES) and actual time (AT). However, the calculation of these components is relatively complicated. Therefore, it is unlikely that you will be required to make any calculations on the exam that involves ES and AT. Anyway, if you want to see the formula, here it is:

The formula:
SV = Earned Schedule (ES) – Actual Time (AT)

What you get: Time units. The interpretation of SV calculated by this formula is the same as the traditional SV formula, i.e., positive SV = project ahead of schedule; negative SV = project behind schedule.

The Cost Variance (CV) Formula

Schedule variance is one way to get a view on how your project is performing. Another way to look at it is to use the cost variance formula.

The CV formula is also used to work out if the project is over, on, or under budget.

The formula: **CV = EV – AC**

What you get: A monetary amount. A negative number means you are over budget (that's bad). A positive number means you are under budget (hurrah!). It's most useful to report CV alongside the project budget so that you can easily see the magnitude of any variance. As mentioned earlier, contemporary project management sees all project variances, positive or negative, as potentially harmful to the project and the performing organization. Similarly to schedule variance, the cost variance outside the defined threshold limit (e.g., ±15%) should be investigated, and a root cause identified. For example, positive cost variance could be a result of conservative estimation during project planning. If a project was conservatively estimated, extra funds allocated to it could have been spent elsewhere by the organization.

(AC = Actual Cost)

If we take the figures from our smartwatch project we can see what this means to the example. The EV is $20,000. Let's assume that the actual cost of the work done so far – the money we have spent already – is $20,000. Putting these in the formula gives us: **$20,000 – $20,000 = $0.**

Perfect! We are exactly on budget! (For the purposes of this example, anyway...)

So, what do we know about the project so far? It's neither over nor under budget, but it is running behind schedule. We thought we would have completed more activities as per the plan by now, but we did not. This is an early warning sign that the timescales for the project might slip.

It's important to consider the context behind the numbers. Our company has never delivered this kind of smartwatch app before, so we're learning as we go. Maybe that's why we aren't making the progress we expected. Maybe one of the big mobile platforms has taken longer than expected to get back to us about how to get our product in their store. There could be lots of reasons that explain the numbers, so when you're reporting the project's status to the sponsor, don't just rely on the numbers to tell the story.

How to Calculate the Cost Performance Index (CPI)

We report to the project sponsor. She understands the reasons for the numbers but wants to know if the situation can be recovered.

A useful piece of information to help paint the whole picture is the cost performance index (CPI) calculation. This is an alternative way of looking at the cost performance of a project and is often preferable to CV because the answer you get is a ratio. Ratios are self-explanatory and don't need further information to highlight how far off-track performance is.

CPI in project management measures the cost efficiency of a project.

The formula: **CPI = EV / AC**

What you get: A number. You're aiming for 1. That means that you are getting $1 of value for every $1 spent. You are using your project budget as planned. If it's more than 1, you are getting more than $1 for every $1 spent. This could mean that your initial budget was not put together in a robust way and your estimates were too conservative. If the number is less than 1 then that's bad news. You are getting less than $1 of value for the project for every $1 spent. This normally happens when you are spending your budget in ways you hadn't expected, such as dealing with unforeseen risks or your initial estimates were just too tight.

Using the figures from our app development project we get:

$20,000 / $20,000 = 1

That looks good. We're spending money in the right way and on the right things, but there's still more to uncover about how this project is performing.

Using Estimate at Completion (EAC)

Next, we look at the EAC formula. That's Estimate at Completion and it works out the expected final and total cost of the project, based on project performance.

The EAC formula PMPs need to know most often is:

The formula: **EAC = BAC / CPI**

What you get: A monetary value.

(BAC = budget at completion)
(CPI = cost performance index)

The formula above is the one that you will most likely use on the PMP exam. However, there is another EAC approach, and that is a thorough bottom-up re-estimate of remaining work. This is done when you think that the original project estimates are now thought to be invalid. And this is what we'll do now.

Therefore, for this project we decide to re-estimate the costs of the remaining works (ETC). We use bottom-up estimation and find out that we need further $50,000 to complete the rest of the project. Since we have already spent $20,000 on the project already, the new estimate at completion (EAC) becomes $70,000.

Cost-wise, it's still not that bad. Our project sponsor can now be confident that we're going to hit the new budget target, i.e., EAC, that we have determined for the project. However, remember SV? That didn't look so good. She asks us to dig into that a bit further.

The Schedule Performance Index (SPI) Formula

The SPI formula is used to work out if the project is:

- Ahead, on, or behind schedule.
- Going to finish when predicted.

The formula: **SPI = EV / PV**

What you get: A number. Again, as this one is a ratio too you are aiming for 1 as that means you are working through the project at the rate you had expected. If the number is greater than one, it means you are racing through your tasks faster than you had planned (but it doesn't comment on the quality of the work done – just something to think about!). If the number is less than 1 it means you are progressing more slowly than planned and the tasks are taking longer.

The SPI calculation, when applied to our app project, shows this:
$20,000 / $40,000 = 0.5

Ouch! We are working at half the speed that we planned. This is where the project is struggling! We had better stop doing project management formulas and start helping our team get the work done!

As we mentioned earlier, one of the emerging trends in project management is the new approach to schedule variance. Same goes to the schedule performance index (SPI) that uses earned schedule (ES) and actual time (AT). Since the calculation of these components is relatively complicated, we believe it is unlikely that you will be required to make any calculations on the exam that involves ES and AT. Anyway, if you want to see the formula, here it is:

The formula:
SPI = Earned Schedule (ES) / Actual Time (AT)

What you get: The interpretation of SPI calculated by this formula is the same as the traditional SPI formula, i.e., greater than 1 = the project is ahead of schedule; less than 1 = the project is behind schedule.

But before we leap into the To Do list, let's just check a couple of other formulas.

How to Use the Variance at Completion (VAC) Formula

Variance at completion (VAC) is another useful earned value management formula. It helps you look forward and anticipate the difference between your original BAC and the newly calculated EAC. In other words, it's the total cost we originally planned minus the total cost that we now expect.

> The formula: **VAC = BAC – EAC**
>
> **What you get:** A monetary value. This shows you how much over or under budget (the variance) we will be at the end of the project. A value of $0 means you'll hit budget. Less than zero means you'll be over budget so ideally you're looking for a number near $0.

For our project, right now we're looking at: **$60,000 – $70,000 = -$10,000**

That tells us there will be a negative variance of $10,000 by the time this smartwatch app is developed. Our sponsor is going to want to know about that too.

The Estimate to Complete Formula (ETC)

The Estimate to Complete (ETC) formula is essentially an inversion of the EAC calculations, so if you can do that one, you can work this one out easily.

There are several ways to calculate ETC in project management but this is the simplest and easiest to use in straightforward situations. It's also the one from *A Guide to the Project Management Body of Knowledge (PMBOK® Guide).*

> The formula: **ETC = EAC – AC**
>
> **What you get:** A monetary value that tells you how much more the project will cost.

Our app development project is pretty straightforward so the calculation looks like: **$70000 – $20,000 = $50,000**

In other words, we need another $50,000 to see the project through to the end.

What if your situation isn't straightforward? There are 4 other ways to define and calculate ETC. They are all covered in Part One of this guide.

Understanding the To Complete Performance Index (TCPI)

The last bit of PMP mathematics we are going to do is to work out the TCPI. It's worth a mention because it's one of the formulas that people find most difficult. TCPI is used to calculate the cost performance that must be achieved to hit your cost target (either BAC or EAC).

You can work out TCPI against your BAC or EAC. We know that the smartphone project has already had the budget re-estimated once so it's best to use the latest figures. We're going to use the EAC to work it out.

> The formula: **TCPI = (BAC – EV) / (EAC – AC)**
>
> **What you get:** A figure.

Let's do this in stages.

BAC – EV = $60,000 – $20,000 (remember? That's our EV) **= $40,000**
EAC – AC = $70,000 – $20,000 = $50,000
$40,000 / $50,000 = 0.8

TCPI on our development project is 0.8. In order to get the intuition behind TCPI, let's break the formula in two parts. The first part, BAC – EV, indicates how much project work is remaining, i.e., how much value remains that needs to be achieved. The second part, EAC – AC, indicates the money available to finish the project. Hence, the TCPI gives you the ratio of work that needs to be completed and the money available to complete the project.

The smartwatch app project started off looking quite good but we had to re-estimate the budget and we uncovered that we aren't getting through the tasks as quickly as we need to. In fact, the amount of work to do is unlikely to get done in time if we only apply the same amount of effort as we are now.

Thanks to the PMP cost management formulas we know a lot more about our project now.

The Formula for Standard Deviation

Ah, standard deviation! Doesn't this take you back to high school math. Standard deviation is simply a reflection of the uncertainty in the estimates. It just highlights the variability of an activity in statistical terms and you use it when an activity has different estimates: optimistic, most likely and pessimistic.

> The formula: **σ = (Pessimistic – Optimistic) / 6**
>
> **What you get:** A figure that represents the variation in the estimates, in the same units of measurement as your estimate.

The σ is the sign that represents standard deviation and is read as "sigma".

There's a task on the smartwatch app project to build the notification tools, so that when something new happens the user gets an alert. Given that we haven't done this task before we want a good understanding of the risk and we've used subject matter experts from an agency to help estimate the work.

The pessimistic estimate is 12 hours. The optimistic estimate, if we had an expert developer in-house, is 5 hours. Pop those into the formula and we get: **(12 – 5) / 6 = 1.16**

The larger the standard deviation, the greater the risk. The risk level on this task seems OK but we can always take it to our sponsor for a second opinion.

The Advantage of PERT Formula

You have another tool to help you estimate: PERT. The most likely PERT formula PMP aspirants are going to come across in the exam gives you a weighted average for your estimates. It's a three point estimate for the expected duration of a schedule activity using pessimistic, optimistic and most likely durations.

> The formula:
> **Beta = (Pessimistic + (4 * Most Likely) + Optimistic) / 6**
>
> **What you get:** The estimated duration of the activity as a weighted average.

Let's see what the weighted average is for the task to build the notification module of our smartwatch app. First, we need another piece of data: the most likely duration for the task, which our lead developer tells us is 8 hours. That gives us: **(12 + (4 * 8) + 5) / 6 = 8.2 hours**

Now there's a number our sponsor can understand.

How to Use the Communication Channels Formula

The sponsor isn't the only person on the project team who needs to know this information. The team is only 6 people but there are still multiple communication channels. How many exactly? Well, there's a communication channels formula to work that out!

> The formula: **n * (n – 1) / 2**
>
> **What you get:** The number of communication channels in the team.

In the formula, 'n' stands for the number of people. On our project, the communication channel math looks like this: **6 * (6 – 1) / 2 = 15**

That's 15 different routes for messages!

Recommendation: Practice. Practice. Practice!

There are nearly 50 formulas that you have to master for the PMP exam.

Mastering these formulas is more than simply knowing them! You have to know how to apply them to a given question scenario and you may even have to apply TWO formulas. You may have to invert a formula, you might be asked to interpret a formula (CPI = 0.8 means?),you may be asked to determine which formula is most appropriate in a given scenario based on certain keywords in the question, or you may have to select the best next steps for the project team based on the result of a formula.

Being able to do this takes time and practice. Don't expect miracles overnight. Here is my recommended approach:

- First of all, study the right formulas. There are unfortunately still some websites out there that list incorrect or outdated PMP exam formulas!
- Review the EVM formulas that are listed in the *PMBOK® Guide* every other day for two weeks. Pause for one week, then do it again. The more you repeat, the more they will sink in.
- Make sure that you know all the earned value formulas in and out. PMI loves earned value!
- Answer at least one formula-based question on every day that you are studying for the exam. Since most people take about 3 months for their preparation that means you will answer about 90 formula-based questions.

Knowing and understanding all the formulas and their variations, concepts, keywords, values and acronyms may seem daunting at first. But if you plan on taking just one small step forward every day and practice, practice, practice, then you'll soon find that the calculations start to come naturally.

Seven Tips for Preparing to Answer Formula-Based Questions

1. Study the correct PMP exam formulas

Over the years, PMI has updated the formulas required for the exam. Make sure the resources you are using reflect the most recent version of the *PMBOK® Guide and the Agile Practice Guide, so you are studying the correct information.*

2. Develop a learning plan

It might feel like you'll never get to a point where you know and understand every formula, as well as the variations, concepts, terminology, use, and value. But with a learning plan, you can take just one small step every day and practice, practice, practice. You'll soon find that the calculations start to come naturally. The best way to get confident with the math is to review the formulas regularly. Do sample calculations or questions every other day for two weeks. Take a week off as a break and then repeat for the following fortnight. As you get closer to your exam date, be sure to answer at least one formula-based question every day.

3. Create a formula sheet

One part of your learning plan should be to make a formula sheet. This is simply a list of all the relevant result interpretations as well as formulas. Write down the interpretations and calculations using pen and paper. Use this page as part of your regular studies. The important difference between this sheet and anything you can download from the internet is the fact that you created it yourself. You learn and retain more that way.

4. Make a cheat sheet

The next study resource you can create is a cheat sheet. This is more than simply a list of the formulas. A cheat sheet includes details about what the formula is for and what the outcomes represent (the interpretation). It's a more detailed set of notes about the calculations. You can use it for jogging your memory if you can't remember what formula to use in a scenario or how to interpret the results.

5. Put together your own flashcards

The third study resource we recommend is creating flashcards. You can buy them, but many students prefer to make their own as the process of making flashcards helps you to remember and recall the information on them. Use small notecards or cut some cardboard into a convenient size.

- To study interpretational concepts: Write a result on the front (i.e., CPI = 0.9) and write the interpretation of the result on the back.

- To study computational concepts: Write the formula on the front of the card and write your explanation and notes on the back.

Now ask your family to hold up a card and you will tell them about the interpretation or formula, and when it is used – or test yourself!

6. Know how to apply them

Exam success relies on more than simply being able to recall the formulas. You also have to know how to apply them in a given scenario-based question. That could include:

- Inverting the formula
- Applying two formulas: you might have to do this if the data you need is missing from the scenario, and you have to work it out as an interim step to the 'real' answer
- Interpreting the output of a formula and commenting on the result
- Knowing what the best next steps are based on your own interpretation of a result
- Choosing which formula is the most appropriate to use in the scenario: for example, there are multiple ways of calculating Estimate At Completion (EAC), so you have to spot keywords in the question to choose the right approach
- Choosing the relevant data to apply in the formula (and ignoring irrelevant data in the scenario)

Make sure that you know all the earned value management formulas backward, forward, inside, and out. PMI loves to ask earned value questions!

7. Practice using them at work

The formulas can seem very theoretical unless you have practiced using them in real life. Even if your job doesn't require it, why don't you work out the Planned Value, or use TCPI to calculate the cost performance? Put your new knowledge to use, and you'll soon see the benefit of the calculations. This can really help understand why you would choose to use one formula over another and help you select the correct data to use as inputs.

Got Questions?

If you are not sure about how exactly to use a formula then we have a forum where you can post your question:

https://www.project-management-prepcast.com/forum

Over a dozen community moderators, and hundreds of students just like you use this forum regularly to discuss PMP related topics. It's the friendliest and most helpful PMP community out there.

ABOUT THE AUTHOR

Cornelius Fichtner
PMP, CSM, PMI-OC Fellow
Founder and President

Cornelius is involved in all aspects of the company. As President and Founder, he defines the strategic direction and works with trainers and coaches to design and develop new products. You probably know him best from his podcasts: he records and narrates lessons for our students.

For Cornelius, no day is like the previous one. He answers student questions in our forums and on email, develops sample exam questions and even edits webpages if needed. During the development of our new products, websites and services he always demands and expects that what we create is beyond reproach. It simply has to be 100% correct but at the same time provide an 'edutainment' factor so that students and customers enjoy learning and using our products.

Cornelius came to project management by accident. He started out as a software developer but quickly realized that he preferred talking to people to writing code. He moved into what was then called "organizational planning" and even became certified in the field. It took him about 3-4 years to make the switch and completely leave software development all the while leading more and more complex and important projects.

Cornelius has been working as a Project Manager in his native Switzerland, in Germany and in the USA since 1990 and received his Project Management Professional (PMP)® credential in April 2004. He has led projects for a management consulting company, a national retailer, an internet startup company, and for one of the oldest financial service providers in the USA.

Cornelius says: "I think the main way I help customers pass their exams is by letting my enthusiasm for project management shine through in our training lessons. Students often comment how I'm able to make a dry subject like PM theory come alive. I'm able to motivate, excite and inspire them on this 'dry' subject, and so they keep going on the road to passing their exam. I'm able to put myself into the shoes of our students and see our products from their perspective. This enables me to create training material that has the customer at heart and will help them to not only prepare for and pass their exams but also helps them become better project managers. I'm the voice and face of pretty much all our training lessons. However, I definitely have a face for radio!"

Cornelius holds PMP and CSM credentials and lives in Tucson, Arizona, USA with his wife, their two cats, and four computers. He is a member of the American Wine Society Tucson Chapter. He enjoys juggling and says that he is excellent with three balls, OK with four, but can only keep five balls in the air for a couple of seconds.

REFERENCES

[1] Project Management Institute Inc., 2017, *A Guide to the Project Management Body of Knowledge, (PMBOK® Guide)* – Sixth Edition, Glossary

[2] Ibid

[3] Ibid

FURTHER RESOURCES

These additional resources will help you prepare for the exam.

PM Exam Simulator™

The PM Exam Simulator

Test yourself and access a realistic, online, computer-based exam environment to answer PMP exam sample questions before heading out for the exam room. Face the latest exam format with confidence and pass comfortably based on 2,100 sample questions in practice tests and quizzes. This simulator is also known as 'PrepCast Simulator' or simply 'PrepCast'.

Find out more: https://www.pm-exam-simulator.com/
Try it for free: https://free.pm-exam-simulator.com/

PM PrepCast™

The Project Management PrepCast: PMP Training

The PM PrepCast offers project management training to help you meet your education requirement and pass your PMI exam. Learn with certified instructors who bring their on-the-job experience to help you understand the concepts and prepare for the test. With a range of resources from on-demand learning to instructor-led training, we can help you achieve your certification and take the next step in your career.

Find out more: https://www.project-management-prepcast.com/

PM Formulas™

The Formula Pocket Guide

Earned Value

CV = EV – AC
CPI = EV / AC
SV = EV – PV
SV = ES – AT
SPI = EV / PV
SPI = ES / AT
EAC *'cost performance is not expected to change'* = BAC / CPI
EAC *'original budget fundamentally flawed'* = AC + Bottom-up ETC
EAC *'cost variance will **not** happen again'* = AC + BAC – EV
EAC *'if both CPI and SPI influencing'* = AC + [(BAC – EV) / (CPI * SPI)]
ETC = EAC – AC
ETC *'original budget flawed'* = new estimate
ETC *'unearned budget'* = BAC – EV
ETC *'if both CPI and SPI influencing'* = ETC = (BAC – EV) / (CPI * SPI)
ETC *'cost performance is not expected to change'* = (BAC / CPI) – AC
Percent Complete = EV / BAC * 100
VAC = BAC – EAC
EV = Sum of PV of completed work
EV = % complete * BAC
TCPI *'based on BAC'* = (BAC – EV) / (BAC – AC)
TCPI *'based on EAC'* = (BAC – EV) / (EAC – AC)

Three-Point Estimating (PERT)

Three-point Beta = (Pessimistic + (4 * Most Likely) + Optimistic) / 6
Three-point Triangular = (Pessimistic + Most Likely + Optimistic) / 3
σ = (Pessimistic – Optimistic) / 6
Activity Variance = [(Pessimistic – Optimistic) / 6]^2

Communications

Communication Channels = n * (n – 1) / 2

Probability

EMV = Probability * Impact in currency

Network Diagram

Activity Duration = EF – ES + 1 or Activity Duration = LF – LS + 1
Total Float = LS – ES or Total Float = LF – EF
Free Float = ES of Following – EF of Present – 1
EF = ES + duration – 1
ES = EF of predecessor + 1
LF = LS of successor – 1
LS = LF – duration + 1

Project Selection

PV = FV / (1 + r)^n
FV = PV * (1 + r)^n
NPV = Select biggest number. (Formula not required for the exam)
ROI = Select the biggest number. (Formula not required for the exam)
IRR = Select the biggest number. (Formula not required for the exam)
Payback Period = Add up the projected cash inflow minus expenses until the result of the calculation is equal to the initial investment
BCR = Benefit / Cost
CBR = Cost / Benefit
Opportunity Cost = The profit of the project not chosen

Depreciation

Straight-line Depreciation:
Depreciation Expense = (Asset Cost – Scrap Value) / Useful Life
Depreciation Rate = 100% / Useful Life

Double Declining Balance Method:
Depreciation Rate = 2 * (100% / Useful Life)
Depreciation Expense = Depr. Rate * Book Value at Beginning of Year
Book Value = Book Value at beginning of year – Depreciation Expense

Mathematical Basics

Average (Mean) = Sum of all members divided by the number of items
Median = Arrange values from lowest value to highest
Pick the middle one. If there is an even number of values, calculate the mean of the two middle values.
Mode = Find the value in a data set that occurs most often

Values

1 sigma = 68.27% (68.2689492…)
2 sigma = 95.45% (95.4499736…)
3 sigma = 99.73% (99.7300204…)
6 sigma = 99.99% (99.9999998027…)
Control Limits = ± Three sigma from mean
Control Specifications = Defined by customer; looser than the control limits
Rough Order of Magnitude estimate = -25% to +75% *(PMBOK®)*
Preliminary estimate = -15% to +50%
Budget estimate = -10% to +25%
Definitive estimate = -5% to +10%
Final estimate = 0%
Float on the critical path = 0 days
Pareto's Law = 80/20
Time a PM spends communicating = 90%
Crashing a project = Crash tasks with least expensive crash cost on critical path first
JIT inventory = 0% (or very close to 0%)
Minus 100 = (100) or -100

Acronyms

AC	Actual Cost
AT	Actual Time
BAC	Budget at Completion
BCR	Benefit Cost Ratio
CBR	Cost Benefit Ratio
CPI	Cost Performance Index
CV	Cost Variance
DUR	Duration
EAC	Estimate at Completion
EF	Early Finish
EMV	Expected Monetary Value
ES	Early Start
ES	Earned Schedule
ETC	Estimate to Complete
EV	Earned Value
FV	Future Value
IRR	Internal Rate of Return
JIT	Just-in-Time
LF	Late Finish
LS	Late Start
NPV	Net Present Value
PERT	Program Evaluation and Review Technique
PV	Planned Value
PV	Present Value
ROI	Return on Investment
SPI	Schedule Performance Index
SV	Schedule Variance
TCPI	To Complete Performance Index
VAC	Variance at Completion
σ	Sigma / Standard Deviation
^	"To the power of" (2^3 = 2*2*2 = 8)

Visit www.pm-prepcast.com for Exam Resources

Made in the USA
Monee, IL
25 February 2023